ROCK & ROLL STOCKBROKER

DON GOODMAN

Contents

Chapter 1	The Long and Winding Road	1
Chapter 2	Poetry, Rock Music and the Shaboo Inn	5
Chapter 3	Finding the Door	21
Chapter 4	The Odd Squad	36
Chapter 5	Giving Good Phone	51
Chapter 6	Dialing for Dollars	68
Chapter 7	Be My Eyes, Raymond	78
Chapter 8	Gurus, Granville, and Gann Angles	83
Chapter 9	A New Way of Living	94
Chapter 10	Option Expiration and the Emergency Room	105
Chapter 11	Worst Trade Ever	114
Chapter 12	Penny Stock God	120
Chapter 13	Bad Investors Kill Their loved Ones	127
Chapter 14	Plumber Gone Mad	138
Chapter 15	Mr. Dick and the Aliens	143
Chapter 16	Leaders of the Pack	150
Chapter 17	People Say the Dumbest Things	157
Chapter 18	Don't Make Me Come Back Again	166
Chapter 19	You're Not Johnny	174
Chapter 20	Gimme Shelter	183
Chapter 21	Oh, Mama, Could This Really Be The End?	194
Chapter 22	Here Comes the Sun	202

Chapter 23	The Wisdom of Q	211
Chapter 24	The Coming of Annie	223
Chapter 25	Taking Communion	233
Chapter 26	Heavy is the Head	243
Chapter 27	Bedbugs	256
Chapter 28	The Evil Within	265
Chapter 29	Goodbye Old Friend	275
Chapter 30	Call-In Centers and Schindler's List	286
Chapter 31	Escape From Merrill Lynch	291
Chapter 32	The Second Time Around	302
Chapter 33	Homeward Bound	308

CHAPTER 1

THE LONG AND WINDING ROAD

I discovered Wall Street through the windshield of a taxi cab.

From 1971 to 1976, I drove a taxi in Manhattan in order to eat and put myself through two degrees in writing poetry at Brooklyn College.

Of all of the possible college majors in the Western World, I'd decided to make a college career and profession out of writing poetry.

Possibly because of all the mind-altering substances in which I was indulging, it seemed like the right thing to do at the time.

Each day after classes, I either drove to work, if my car happened to be operational, or took a bus across Brooklyn to the Bensonhurst section, 86th Street and 18th Avenue to be exact, in order to pick up my taxi at the Tone Taxi garage. Then I drove until two or three in the morning.

Usually, after I picked up whatever taxi I'd be driving that shift, I'd head through the Brooklyn Battery Tunnel, paying the toll with my own money, emerging in the Wall Street area of Manhattan. That was always a good place to pick up a fare going uptown.

If I worked nights, I'd arrive in the Wall Street area right around rush hour, and take my fares up to Park Avenue or Fifth Avenue, or Central Park West, to the incredibly gorgeous huge buildings with doormen and canopies that stretched from the marble entrances to the curb at the end of the sidewalk, where a well-dressed doormen waited to open the taxi doors for my passengers.

When I had no classes, and I worked the morning/day taxi shift, it was a constant shuttle of people from uptown going downtown to Wall Street, and people from Wall Street going uptown to their fancy apartments and townhouses. The connection between Wall Street, money, and the finer things in life was clear to me.

I didn't know what this Wall Street stuff was about, but I knew I wanted some of it.

The problem was that as poetry major, I had never taken a single business course, and didn't even understand the types of courses that I would need to take to gain entrance into that world of high finance.

I didn't even know where to begin.

There were only two connections that I was able to make with Wall Street that gave me a glimpse at the door.

The first was when I sent away for the course catalog from the New York Institute of Finance. I looked at the offerings, and had no idea what they were talking about in the course descriptions. Then, I looked at the prices of the courses, and mentioned them to my wife Debbie, who immediately nixed the idea as a waste of money because she was sure that I'd never pass a single class.

The other connection was through conversations with my friend and next door neighbor in our apartment building on Ocean Avenue in Brooklyn, Howie Adelman.

Everyone called Howie "Big Bear" or "Tapes" because he was a huge Deadhead, and Grateful Dead tape collector.

Back then, all of the Grateful Dead live shows were only available as bootleg tapes which were traded between fans and collectors. "Big Bear" had hundreds of tapes, and spent most of his time listening to them, and entertaining friends, while routinely smoking copious amount of anything that was smokeable, snort-able, or otherwise ingestible.

Howie occasionally did clerical work for his uncle who worked on the Cocoa Exchange in the Wall Street area. I was fascinated.

How could they trade vast amounts of cocoa from all around the world? Where was the cocoa? I wondered. How could Howie's uncle, who was presumably from Brooklyn, know anything about cocoa?

Howie's job was just to carry order tickets from one part of the exchange floor over to a different spot where there were offices and people handling the orders. It all sounded so exotic. Imagine, trading cocoa in Manhattan.

Howie also told me that sugar and coffee were also traded at an exchange. I imagined the docks in Manhattan piled high with crates full of coffee and cocoa, and maybe sugar cane.

It seemed reasonable that with everyone using the end products of these commodities, there had to be a lot of the raw material floating around somewhere. I wanted to learn how it was all done.

But I never got the chance because in 1977, Debbie saw a job in *The New York Times* for an experienced social worker in a far away and unknown place called Hartford Hospital in Hartford, Connecticut.

With her Barnard-Columbia background and an already impressive resume, Debbie was offered the job, and we soon moved away from our homeland of Brooklyn, New York, to a cute little town in southern New England called Windsor, Connecticut.

With that move, I left behind any immediate possibility of finding my way into the corridors of Wall Street, and started focusing on making a decent living.

Hartford Connecticut was known as the "Insurance Capital of the World." Maybe one of the insurance companies could use someone who wrote poetry.

CHAPTER 2

Poetry, Rock Music and the Shaboo Inn

When I lived in Brooklyn, I was always active both writing and reading my poetry. On occasion, I was invited to read my works at the St. Marks Poetry Project in Manhattan. Many of the "up and coming', as well as the more" established" New York City poets gathered there weekly for the readings which were held in the meeting room of an old church.. The audiences ranged from dozens of people, to standing room only readings which would sometimes be broadcast on WBAI, the "alternative" radio station.

Back then, there were many venues to read poetry in New York City that ranged from college campuses to open readings which were held at numerous bars and restaurants all around the city. One of my favorite places to read was at Chumley's, a long-time hangout for literary types going back to the Prohibition Era in the West Village.

I studied poetry at Brooklyn College with John Ashbery, who, at the time, was already well known from his early poetry works, art criticisms, and association with Andy Warhol, and several of the "Beat Poets," including Alan Ginsberg."

John Ashbery's presence gave the Brooklyn College writing program a legitimacy that it might not have had otherwise.

John didn't seem to like my poetry at all. Maybe it was because I always came to class drunk or tripping, or in some other state which made me stand out, even among the small group of poets in his graduate class.

I liked John's poems, particularly the stuff in *Three Poems* and *Self Portrait in a Convex Mirror*. His rambling stream of consciousness prose-poetry style showed me how to extend my thoughts in more lengthy poetic compositions.

John's stature as a poet drew many of his friends to come and visit our classes. I might still have a photo somewhere of Alan Ginsberg walking into our classroom and giving John a big wet kiss on the lips.

John never hid the fact that he was gay, but then, so were half of the people in my graduate writing program.

There was a woman named Clare in the class who I thought was a breathtakingly talented poet. Her poetry was ultimately feminine sounding, sweet, melodic and enrapturing. Every time she read one of her poems, I wanted to jump into bed with her.

Unfortunately, Clare was a lesbian who never even knew that I either existed, or was even in the class with her.

I tried the sweet approach, the sensitive approach, the macho approach, the intellectual approach; I tried them all, but it was like being invisible.

One day, Clare's partner came to meet her in the class. Her partner was a huge black woman, maybe one of the largest women that I have ever seen, with long thick dreadlocks, in a powder blue dress. I tried to introduce myself, but it was like I wasn't even there.

John would have probably preferred that I wasn't there.

By the time I got to our classes, I was usually exhausted from working different jobs; stoned out on various drugs, drunk, or otherwise altered so that I probably didn't seem like I was very serious about my writing, and was showing up just to be self-indulgent and annoying.

One particularly embarrassing moment in class was when my overly tight jeans split open at the crotch area when I was not wearing any underwear. I was so stoned that I didn't even notice that I was hanging out until I saw John staring at me with his mouth open, speechless, until someone else pointed out to me that I was over exposed.

By the time Debbie and I left for Connecticut, I had published a number of poems, and given a number of readings, but had never made a dime for either.

I first met Debbie in high school, when we were both poor white kids from the same nasty neighborhood in Crown Heights Brooklyn. Sometimes, after we went on dates, we had to start off looking around as soon as we got off the bus to make sure we weren't being followed by any of the gangs or thugs that lurked on corners or in the darkness of doorways.

Debbie was very practical and organized. She went to Barnard College on a scholarship, and then followed it up with graduate school at Columbia where she earned a MSW in Social Work.

In contrast, by the time I graduated high school, the only thing I wanted to do was to write poetry, and maybe teach someday. From Debbie's standpoint, I'm sure that this was not a career choice that she thought would enable us to achieve our middle class dreams.

She would have preferred that I went on to become a lawyer or an accountant, or some type of business person.

Understandably, she was not very encouraging or enthusiastic when after undergraduate school I decided to go to Brooklyn College to get a MFA in writing poetry.

Debbie had reluctantly been reading my poetry all through college, and didn't think much of it… and given that so much of it complains about her, perhaps there's a reason. So when Brooklyn College started a new graduate writing program for poets, and indicated that they would only accept ten people into the program, Debbie told me not to bother applying because I would never be accepted.

I applied anyway, and was accepted on a full scholarship of sorts. The college would waive the class fees; I only had to pay the registration fees, which was always a struggle, and was always met with resistance by Debbie who clearly preferred that I spend my time driving a taxi. Debbie felt that driving a taxi was the best real job I'd ever have, and didn't want to waste money on me learning how to write more poetry,

She was right for a time, because I did get fired from every low level job that I found. I was even fired by a number of the taxi cab fleets.

I finally ended up driving for last refuge of failed taxi drivers, a bottom of the barrel taxi company located on 18th Avenue in the Bensonhurst section of Brooklyn, called Tone Taxi.

Tone Taxi had the kind of taxi cabs that a normal person would send away.

All of Tone's taxis were banged up with numerous dents, scrapes, missing parts and broken lights. The interiors were usually torn up, or sloppily repaired with cloth tape. Most of the cars had the lingering odors of urine, vomit, or just about anything else imaginable.

Since no one ever bothered to clean the back seat areas of the taxis after a shift, the passenger area sometimes became a collection of abandoned passenger garbage like empty coffee cups, crumpled cigarette packs or other similar trash. However, after one of the drivers found a five pound bag a marijuana in a package left in the back seat, I tried to make it a point to periodically check to see what was in the back of my taxi cab during my shifts.

Tone Taxi's cars were so bad that there were times that I picked up hookers and their Johns, and despite whatever they happened to be doing in the back seat, the car still smelled better when they left than before they got in. There were several pimps who got in the cab and then got out because they didn't want to mess up their nice clothes.

People in business clothes almost always rejected my taxi cab, saying that they would rather wait for another. On some days, I have to pick up five fares to keep three.

I seemed to pick up more than my share of drug dealers. They never cared about the condition of the taxi, and were just happy to get a driver who didn't mind making lots of stops, and then waiting a few minutes at each stop. The dealers usually tipped well, and would sometimes throw me a small piece of whatever their wares were.

One Sunday morning, I picked up a very nice, straight looking guy in Midtown who obviously had to make some deliveries. We made a few stops around Manhattan, and then headed over the 59th Street Bridge to make a few drop offs in Queens.

There was very little traffic around at that time of day, so the guy lit up a few joints of some really strong pot that tasted like it was mixed with opium laced hash. By the time we finished our run. I was feeling very Zen. I felt like I felt like was flying in my taxi, getting stoned.

The guy gave me a twenty dollar tip, which I stashed in my shirt. He also left me several small chunks of black hash which I put in the cellophane wrapping from my pack of cigarettes, and pushed way down deep into my pants pocket.

After dropping off my generous passenger, I headed north on Park Avenue, when I was hailed by the doorman in front of the Waldorf Astoria hotel. The doorman stood next to a couple who had several pieces of fancy looking leather luggage. I staggered out of the cab to open the trunk, which required a screwdriver to open it since the trunk's lock apparatus had been removed.

A heavy elderly man with white hair and a short white beard got into the cab with a middle aged woman who had badly bleached blonde hair, and a fur shawl draped around her shoulders. They both had heavy European accents which I presumed to be Swedish when they said in broken English that they wanted to go to Lufthansa Airlines at Kennedy Airport.

The taxi must have smelled really bad, between the pot, hash, urine and whatever else was going on back there scent wise. The couple seemed to be squirming and moving from side to side on the back seat during the ride out to the airport. I don't remember much of the ride, other than constantly seeing them shuffle around in my rear view mirror, muttering to each other.

Suddenly, we were already at Kennedy Airport, and the man started yelling "Lufthansa! Lufthansa!" but it was too late, I had just passed the terminal.

I gave a half turn towards the back seat and apologized profusely, making a circular motion with my hand indicating that I would circle the airport to get back to the Lufthansa terminal.

I was trying to pay close attention, but I was feeling really stoned out. Everything started to look like a big carousel of revolving grey terminal doors.

There was some moderate traffic at the airport, and I was getting a little disoriented. I wanted to be careful and pay attention, when I heard both the man and his wife again start yelling "Lufthansa! Stop! Lufthansa, Lufthansa!"

But it was too late; I had passed the Lufthansa terminal again.

All of a sudden, they both started to yell and swear at me in Swedish. I saw the meter keep running and running as I drove helplessly around the airport. I couldn't turn off the meter because the taxi cab had a "hot seat" feature which turned on the meter as soon as someone sat in the back seat; this was to prevent drivers from taking fares and not putting them on the meter in order to keep the money for themselves.

I felt awful, and they kept yelling and cursing at me in Swedish, but I had no choice except to circle the airport again.

By now the couple in the back was quite agitated, so it didn't help when I sort of spaced out for a moment and passed the Lufthansa terminal yet a third time.

The man was now bouncing up and down on his seat yelling "Lufthansa! Lufthansa! Stop! Stop! Get me police! Lufthansa! Lufthansa!"

At this point, I realized that I really needed to get this right on the next pass, so I focused and drove very slowly, until finally, we arrived in front of the Lufthansa terminal, and a porter came over to help the couple with their luggage.

As I got out of the taxi with my screwdriver in hand to pop the trunk, the man threw a twenty dollar bill onto my front seat and then spit on the back seat as he exited. The fare was $20.35, but I wasn't going to make a big deal about the thirty five cents, not to mention getting no tip.

Since I reeked of pot and had several grams of black hash in my pocket, I just wanted to get out of the airport in case either of them decided to call the cops to talk to me.

I drove for Tone Taxi for nearly three years. During that time, I had my taxi break down in every borough of New York City, usually in the worst weather conditions, and on all of the major holidays.

I had fares to just about every ghetto area in all five boroughs of New York City. Sometimes, we would actually take our taxis to the bad neighborhoods to look for fares. Surprisingly, really poor people seemed to take more frequent taxi rides than regular people. My taxi friends and I called this "driving the ghetto."

It amazed me how many abandoned building there were everywhere, but it perplexed me even more why all of the people living in those areas stayed there instead of just moving somewhere else. However, I had seen from my own experience growing up with my mother and living in a tenement slum that many people stay where they are because of lack of inertia and a general acceptance of their lot in life.

The more I saw, the more I knew that I wanted something better. I didn't need the townhouses, but I wanted something better than to spend my life in old apartment buildings.

Whenever I was driving back to the garage late at night at the end of my taxi shift, I would look at all of the sparkling lights on both sides of the river as I crossed the Brooklyn Bridge. I'd often think, and hope, that one day it would all be just be a memory, and I'd someday be telling people about my experiences as a New York City taxi driver.

I tried to capture the scenery in my mind in order to remember the feeling of driving at night, with the wind blowing through the open windows of my taxi, taking in the sights for posterity.

During the summers, I would usually take the bus to get to my taxi garage in Bensonhurst, from the Midwood section of Brooklyn where Debbie and I were living in our first three room apartment on Ocean Avenue and Avenue J.

Coming home, the bus would leave me off at two or three in the morning on Foster Avenue, about five long blocks from where we lived. To get home, I walked through a number of very pretty tree-lined side streets bordered by large one and two family houses.

The idea of one day owning a home like that was incomprehensible.

All of the houses had a postage stamp sized front lawn, usually with a short fence around it, and a swinging gate door leading into the house. Some houses just had the front lawn outlined in bricks with no fence. Most of the homeowners tried to keep their houses looking nice with well-kept lawns and attractive bushes and shrubs. Many of the homes had flowers or roses incorporated into their small piece of frontage.

I have no allusions that I have been an angel all of my life, but for several years I engaged in conduct that I have always felt badly about.

Each night that I came home late from taxiing, I would scope out the various roses in the different front yards, and then take the prettiest one that I could find to bring home to Debbie. I only took one rose a night, but that certainly doesn't excuse the fact that I invaded their people's gardens, and took their nicest bloom.

At the time, I justified it by thinking that the owner wouldn't mind if they knew that I took their beautiful rose to bring as a tribute to my young bride; but now I know that what I did sucked. And even worse, Debbie probably didn't deserve the roses anyway.

Perhaps as punishment for my rose thefts, I was eventually fired by Tone Taxi for more reasons than I'd care to enumerate, and that finally ended my taxi career.

In Connecticut, I sent dozens of letters and resumes to different colleges and universities looking for a job teaching writing, but never got as far as an interview, just a lot of quick rejections.

It didn't take long for me to realize that the Greater Hartford area of Connecticut was not a hot bed of poetic activity.

There was one bookstore in downtown Hartford that had occasional poetry readings. I read there twice. The first time there were six people there, and two of them were Debbie and her mother. The next time, there were only two people who showed up, and they were me and another poet who wanted to read.

During my search for a job, I noticed that Hartford had an "alternative" newspaper called the *Hartford Advocate*. It looked like a stripped down version of the *Village Voice* from New York City, which I had been reading since I was a teenager.

The *Advocate* was full of articles about art, music, and the pressing left wing oriented social issues of the day. There was an abundance of advertising for rock and roll shows, band appearances, strippers, massage parlors, as well as a significant" personals" section.

It was obviously the "cool" newspaper in the area, and it didn't take look for me to notice that they were always looking for sales reps to sell advertising space for them.

Since I desperately needed a job, and I knew that I gave great phone, I decided to go and apply for the sales rep job. Of course, in the back of my mind, I was hoping that if I got into the newspaper, that maybe I could eventually find someone who would let me write something for publication.

I knew that they didn't publish poetry, but I thought that I could write about one of the things that I knew best, rock and roll music.

But first, I had to get in the door.

My interview was with the sales manager named David who wore a three piece suit and obviously had a strong cocaine habit.

David was totally wired as we sat in his large grey cubicle. He was loud and obnoxious as he spoke; I wondered if he typically disturbed whoever was on the other side of the tall grey partition that separated his space from the office next door.

David seemed to be in a rush, probably to do some lines of coke with the door closed as soon as I left. He clearly didn't like me because I had no real sales experience. He didn't care that I thought that I gave good phone.

I tried to impress him by telling him that I added extra value because I could also write, and maybe I could "help out" by writing some articles from time to time. I told him that while I had written mostly poetry, rock music would be easy to write about, because I knew so much about it.

This was clearly not the right thing to say, so he led me out of his office cubicle, and quickly shut the door behind me. I stood there for a moment, feeling rejected and a little numb when I was approached by a woman with brown hair and a handful of papers in her hand.

She introduced herself as Sally, the editor of the newspaper. She said that she had overheard our conversation. "You think you can write?' she asked.

"I know I can write," I replied. "Let me show you."

She asked me to bring in three articles about anything that I wanted to write about by the following Friday. She said that if she liked them, she would give me an assignment.

I wrote one article about the new "punk rock" movement in music; I reviewed *The Book of Pot*, written by Pamela Lloyd Shakespeare, the editor of *High Times*. The subject of the third article escapes me, but it was something along the same lines as the first two.

The following Friday when I brought the articles, Sally quickly read through them. She punctuated her reading with little mumbles that sounded approving. Finally, she finished the last article, looked up and asked, "What are you doing Saturday afternoon?"

"Writing an article, hopefully," I replied.

Sally assigned me to interview a pair of married artists; the husband was a sculptor, and the wife was a water colorist. She gave me a few pages of background material on the two of them, and told me where and when to meet them.

Except for the fact that I often visited many of the museums in New York City so that I could wander around stoned and look at all of the pretty artwork, I didn't have any depth of knowledge about actual art itself. So I headed to the library in Windsor and took out several dozen books about sculpture and water color paintings. Then I spent several hours leafing through all of the books, copying down key words and phrases that I thought might be useful for the article.

The interview went well.

I showed up with a long list of questions for both each of them, and then tried to quickly write down as much of their responses as I could.

Sally liked the article, and immediately assigned me to another article. This one was an interview with six different photographers who were having a joint exhibit in the nearby town of Bloomfield. I didn't know much about photography, so I headed back to the library.

My first article paid fifteen dollars, and the second article paid twenty dollars. It was the first money that I had ever made with my writing. I wanted more.

I asked Sally if I could do some rock music articles and reviews. She replied that the music stuff was the best job in the place, and asked me why I thought I was qualified to cover such a lofty subject.

"I was raised on rock and roll," I told Sally. "No one here knows more about it than me."

I explained how I had been raised by a single mom who could most kindly be described as a party girl through the 1950's and 1960's. She worked as a barmaid in a dozen different bars, and she always brought home and played all of the 45's from the jukeboxes.

My mom listened to all of the early R&B music before it was fashionable for white women to listen to that kind of music. She had a near complete collection of Sam Cooke and Elvis Presley 45's, not to mention lots of Jackie Wilson, Marvin Gaye, and Smokey Robinson and the Miracles.

In the early sixties, she took me to the famous rock and roll shows at the Brooklyn Fox theater which were hosted by Murray the K. I remember being one of the youngest kids in the audience, watching a motorcycle riding on stage at the beginning of the Shangri-Las' *Leader of the Pack*. I saw Smokey - live, not once but several times, and Little Anthony, Ben E. King; I saw them all.

Sally paused, looked at me with a little smile, and said, "What are you doing Friday night?"

She asked me to cover Country Joe McDonald's show at the Shaboo Inn. Country Joe was best known for his appearance at Woodstock where he performed his memorable *I-Feel-Like-I'm-Fixin'-to-Die-Rag*.

I had heard of the Shaboo Inn in Willimantic, Connecticut. They always had large ads with the band schedules listed in the *Advocate*. At the time, I didn't know where Willimantic, Connecticut was, but over the next few years, I would be spending lots of time at Shaboo.

The building had an interesting history, beginning as a textile mill in 1847. It eventually became a run-down hotel, until in 1971 when it was turned into unique musical venue which hosted dozens of major artists as a stop in between Boston and New York.

Shaboo was a home away from home for dozens of blues acts from Muddy Waters and James Cotton to Howlin Wolf and John Lisa Hooker. The Shaboo Inn also hosted an endless list big time rock names such as Aerosmith, Hall and Oates, AC/DC, and The Police, not to mention jazz icons like Buddy Rich.

I covered dozens of shows at Shaboo.

I had a couple of memorable evenings there getting stoned with Rick Derringer and Joe Cocker after their shows. Cocker rolled enormous English joints filled with chunks of hash, and drank about a full bottle of straight whiskey for each joint that we shared.

One evening I was set to interview Johnny Winter, who'd been drinking steadily throughout the show. He played beautifully, but by the end of the show, he was so drunk that he had to be helped off the stage, and was way too "out of it" for me to interview him.

Writing rock reviews didn't pay very well, but at least I was doing a lot of them. Soon I picked up a writing gig for *Soho Weekly News* in New York City. Them I began writing for a small publishing group called *The Journals* that had local newspapers in four nearby towns.

I began to write articles for money about all sorts of things, but always enjoyed the rock and roll writing the most; that is, except the times that I took Debbie with me to the show. Then it was never was a good experience.

During his *Darkness On the Edge of Town* tour, I was assigned to cover the Bruce Springsteen show at the Springfield Civic Center, sitting in the third row center. I had two seats, so I took Debbie.

Springsteen's first set was one of the most remarkable rock performances that I had ever seen, with one exhausting crescendo after another until finally the last notes were sounded. Before Bruce had even left the stage, Debbie was tugging on me and asking if we could finally leave. Just then, Bruce said something like don't go anywhere because that was just the first set, and they had a lot more to play.

I couldn't believe that she wanted to leave. I pointed out that I was "working," and had to stay for the whole show.

Debbie grumbled all through the incredible second set, then nudged and tugged on me to leave after each of the four breathtaking encores. It was a great show but after that, I realized I probably shouldn't take Debbie to shows where I was working.

But despite her attitude at the Springsteen show, I couldn't help inviting her along on my next assignment.

Growing up, Debbie's favorite band was *The Monkees*, from the sixties' TV show. So when Peter Tork, one of the original *Monkees*, played at the Shaboo Inn with his new band, *The New Monks*, I asked Sally for the assignment.

I brought Debbie to the show so that she could meet one of her teenage idols.

The show itself was awful. There were about ten people in the audience. The band sounded like they had never played together before, and the only song that I remember was Peter Tork singing *Daydream Believer*, while playing on an out-of-tune keyboard. Fortunately, it was a short set, and Debbie and I went upstairs to meet the ex-Monkee.

I tried to ask Tork a variety of questions, so that not everything was about the original Monkees; however, I did ask why he was playing with a new band with a Monkee sounding name.

He was distant and clearly didn't like talking about his previous life as a Monkee. The interview was not particularly interesting, but that's the way it was sometimes.

Debbie sat in a corner, waiting for the interview to end.

When Tork and I finished talking, Debbie came over so that she could to introduce herself. She told him what a huge Monkees fan she was growing up. She was very genuine, and clearly excited to meet him. However, as she went on about having been a fan and enjoying their music, Tork began to scowl, until finally he turned away, ignoring what she was saying, and walked out the door, slamming it behind him.

I felt bad for Debbie.

For several months after we moved to Connecticut, the only money that I earned was from writing music and art reviews. At fifteen and twenty dollars an article, Debbie was not at all impressed, and regularly made it a point to mention that given all of the hours that I put in going to the shows, and then spending even more time typing the articles, that I was only working for pennies an hour. She said I'd be better off working at McDonald's.

CHAPTER 3

FINDING THE DOOR

It took a **full six months** of sending out resumes, some with semi-fictional job histories, that totally de-emphasized my poetry and rock review writing, until I finally landed an entry-level customer service job for a manufacturing company in Hartford, called Arrow Hart.

The building that I worked in was a decrepit brick factory. The administrative and sales people were on the ground floor. The manufacturing of things occurred on the floors both above and below.

Dozens of people worked downstairs in what was referred to as "The Pits." The air smelled of machine oil. Blank greasy looking faces worked in the yellowish florescent light on screw machines, as well as many other kinds of old alien looking machines which formed pieces of metal into different kinds of widgets and strange-looking parts.

There were rows of dark old metal bins filled with little screws, posts, levers, and small metal forms. People moved through the rows picking out parts to be gathered and brought to another area where others would combine them into small subassemblies to be passed on to the next production line.

There were no windows, and it looked like most of the people there had already spent years in the florescent gloom of The Pits.

While I was at Arrow Hart, I realized that I had to do something to elevate myself out of the customer service group I was mired in. There were several other younger people like me who happened to work in some of the other more prestigious departments like Marketing or Sales; They made a lot more money than I did, and walked around like lower to mid-level young executives, while I was just a part of a small, loser-filled customer service crew. I got to know a few of them who said that they either had an MBA or were working on one.

The MBA was a relatively new degree back then. I first heard of it from reading some articles about the new breed of young business people who had traded in Woodstock for three piece suit; they were called "yuppies." Since I really did want to better my lot in life, and I knew that my MFA in poetry and my background as a rock and roll critic wasn't going to get me in to any board rooms, it was about then that I decided to go back to school and try to get an MBA in something.

I wanted to be upwardly mobile too.

The University of Hartford offered an MBA program, so I signed up as a non-matriculated student because I didn't have the classes, grades or background to get in any other way.

Even though the first course was a Marketing course, and I worked in their Customer Service area which seemed to be somewhat marketing-oriented, Arrow Hart refused to pay for any of the classes, claiming that my job was too low-level to be included in their tuition rebate program. Clearly, my services were not held in very high regard at Arrow Hart, and after about a year, I was fired when the company closed down my customer service area altogether.

After being fired from Arrow Hart, I was again dependent on my writing to earn money. That did not sit well with Debbie. She wanted me to look into driving a taxi again for one of the local cab companies. I decided to try to write more articles instead.

When I started telling my writing contacts that I was looking for more assignments because I had lost my full time job at Arrow Hart; one of them, the publisher of The Journals in Windsor, asked me if I'd be interested in doing some general reporting, copy editing, as well as administrative work in the office.

It wasn't full time work, but it certainly helped pick up the financial slack, and it was very close to home.

A few weeks later, I was sitting in *The Journals'* office opening some press releases when I saw a notice from the University of Hartford looking for an adjunct lecturer to teach a course on effective business writing.

Since I had a MFA in Writing, albeit poetry, as well as professional writing experience from the newspaper reporting and rock music reviews, I called the Chairman of the English Department about the position. He asked me to come in to meet him the next day.

It was August, and he must have been really scrambling to fill the position because he hired me on the spot. After all of the effort that I had put into unsuccessfully trying to get a teaching gig in Brooklyn, I finally got a teaching job by the simple act of being in the right place at the right time in Connecticut.

Teaching a class at the University also had the added benefit of allowing me to continue to take my MBA courses for free. For several semesters, I taught and took classes on the same nights. I was keeping very busy.

However, between the teaching, general reporting, and the rock reviews, I was still making hardly any money, and Debbie never let me forget it. But my writing was finally starting to pay off, at least a little bit.

Before being terminated by Arrow Hart, I met a woman who was an administrative assistant for one of the department heads. Her name was Lisa, and she was a green-eyed Irish girl who liked to drink tequila shots after work, and smoke pot in my car in the back of the parking lot at lunchtime. She was also taking some kind of business classes in marketing. At one point, she asked me to read one of her school papers. I remember I found it incredibly intriguing that it began with the word "Mmm."

Lisa left the company a few months before I was fired. She preferred to be unemployed during the hot, sunny summer, rather than be subjected to the depressing factory environment of Arrow Hart. At the end of that year, Lisa and her husband, Patrick, threw a Christmas party, mostly filled with people I'd never met, including the one who gave me the idea to become a stockbroker.

A friend of Lisa's was talking about someone else who had gotten a job as a stockbroker trainee at E.F Hutton. The person they were talking about wasn't even at the party, but I was already impressed by the very concept of being a stockbroker; although, I really had no idea of what it was that a stockbroker actually did, except that they bought and sold stocks for people. I barely knew what a stock was.

Standing on the periphery of the conversation, I remember listening intently, sipping a rum and coke, thinking that I had finally found the road into Wall Street that I had been looking for.

Now that I had a focus, I scoured the Yellow Pages, and over the next several weeks, I sent out a few dozen resumes to every company that even looked like a real Wall Street firm that had a branch anywhere near the Hartford area.

A few months before, I had purchased 50 shares of Chrysler, my very first and stock purchase ever, at EF Hutton. I had read about the Chrysler bailout, and how they were going to modernize the auto industry. I didn't know if they would. I didn't know if they could. But I had read that their stock was three dollars a share. It seemed cheap, even for me. Debbie knew as little as I did about stocks, but I managed to convince her to take $150, and buy 50 shares through E.F. Hutton.

They were the first firm to send me a rejection letter after receiving my resume.

While I had my little stock account at EF Hutton, I had a broker named John Carroll, who was the first and only stockbroker that I had ever known, or even spoken to. He was haughty sounding on the phone, and acted like he was doing me a favor when he set up my account to buy the 50 shares of Chrysler stock.

If I eventually got hired by somebody, I knew that I didn't want to be like him; so, I really wasn't too upset when Hutton rejected me. After all, they obviously employed obnoxious pompous jerks.

After a few weeks, I had received several more rejections, a few no responses, two requests to interview me, and one telephone call.

The telephone call was from Merrill Lynch. They wanted me to come into their office with the next group of people that they would be interviewing, which was in a few days.

Apparently, they did their hiring by filtering through larger pools of prospective candidates. It sounded more like a cattle call than an interview. I called them right back and made an appointment to be in the next group in a few days.

The other two letters were from firms called Paine Weber and Bache, Halsey, Stuart, Shields. I was pleased, almost surprised that I actually had three firms that wanted to talk to me. I figured that I at least had a chance, albeit a small chance, to get in somewhere.

At the time, I only owned two suits, a salmon-colored one, and a grey one, so I was hoping that the interview process wouldn't go on too long since the salmon-colored suit was memorable looking, to say the least.

My first interview, at Merrill Lynch was a sterile affair. There were several nervous looking people in the reception area that seemed to be part of the group being studied that day.

Every fifteen minutes or so, a very properly dressed Assistant Manager named Robert Fisk would come and lead another candidate to his desk are for a preliminary interview. There was a big, open white wall right outside his desk area. I pictured that being the wall that they threw all the candidates against to see who would stick.

Robert had a perfect haircut, suspenders bright white shirt, light brown tortoise shell frame glasses. He looked exactly right; I felt very imperfect in comparison, but at least I was wearing my grey suit, not the salmon one. He asked a few obligatory questions about my unusual background, my degree in poetry, the free-lance job of writing rock music and art reviews, and my part-time teaching at the University of Hartford.

He mentioned that there are many people in the business with "eclectic" backgrounds, and that I shouldn't let it deter me from going forward. But overall, I felt his attitude was condescending and not very encouraging. He said that "they" would let me know if they wanted me to come back for the next step in the interview/testing process.

My interview with Paine Webber was just a few days later.

The Branch Manager at Paine Webber was a middle aged windbag named Harry Whitehouse; I will never forget that name.

He was the very first asshole that I personally encountered on my road to Wall Street.

He looked like Gene Hackman in a three piece suit, waiting to chomp down on a cigar, seeming annoyed that you were keeping him from it. Bad obnoxious attitude flowed out of the man like sewage out of a Superfund site.

His office was this huge wide expanse that stood over this large room full of desks, with smaller cubicles tucked in the background. He acted like he was a Caesar ruling over his helpless obedient minions.

After about five minutes, I didn't know why I was even called in for an interview. Whitehouse was practically making fun of my resume. He asked me why someone who wrote poetry wanted to sell securities. He pointed out my total lack of sales experience.

It was like he wanted me to justify why I was wasting his time.

I wanted to call him an obnoxious creep, but it occurred to me that maybe he was just trying to play with my head to see if he could get a rise out of me. No one could really be that offensive; I felt that maybe it was a ruse to try to draw me out.

"Tell me how you would sell an ice box to Eskimos in Alaska?" he asked me with an imaginary cigar in his mouth.

"I'd tell them that they didn't have to go outside to freeze their meat." I responded, amazingly impressed with my own wit.

He grumbled, and looked down at my resume, and grumbled again. "You see that guy over there?" He pointed to someone in the first row of desks. "He's my hard drinking Irishman." He paused, looking around with a sort of twisted sense of satisfaction. "And you see that guy there?"

Again, he pointed, this time to the middle right section of the rows of desks. "He's my Chink. But you know," he paused, "I'm kind of short on Jews."

I still think, or would like to think, that he was baiting me, but I really didn't like him at all, and even the idea of having to talk to the balding jerk again was offensive. I put some quick sentences together to make an even quicker exit. Paine Webber was out of the question.

My first interview with Michael Green, the Branch Manager at Bache, Halsey, Stuart, Shields, was a quick one. No dumb questions about refrigerators, no disheartening comments about my liberal arts background; he simply just did not seem at all interested in me.

However, for no particular reason that I can remember, I had this feeling that this was where I was supposed to be; and I just had to convince him to hire me.

Michael had the air of someone important about him. Then in his early forties, he had thinning brown hair, an expensive looking suit, and wore a big black onyx ring that kept catching my eye as he moved his hands when he spoke.

Necktie pins, the kind that you wear by your collar button, were very popular back then, and he wore a gold one which accented his red tie. I thought of the T.S. Eliot line about the necktie being "asserted by a simple pin." I finally understood what he meant.

In our brief conversation, our only commonality was that we were both originally from New York City. He was from the Bronx, so I tried to play up to the fact that I grew up in the ghetto of Brooklyn. When the conversation seemed to droop, I asked him how he got in the business, and he told me that he had an uncle who had helped lead him into the industry.

I told him how I had discovered Wall Street through the windshield of my taxi cab. He seemed mildly amused by my taxi stories.

Then he deflated me by saying that he needed to think about my application, and he would let me know if he wanted me to come back for a follow up interview. When his phone rang, he led me to the door and pointed me towards the exit.

With my options dwindling, I decided that Bache, for some strange unfathomable reason, was where I wanted to work. I began to plan my campaign of persistence and tenacity to convince Mr. Green.to give me a chance.

I waited two days and then called him to see if I could schedule another meeting to be interviewed by some of the guys in his office, as he had suggested. At first, I wasn't sure if he knew who I was, but after mentioning Brooklyn, he seemed to remember and sent me over to his secretary to schedule some meetings for early the next week.

The following week, I came in twice; the first time to meet a serious looking guy with a beard, Fred Brighton.

Fred told me he was primarily an options trader. I really didn't know what that was, and he didn't seem particularly interested in trying to teach me anything about it. It seemed like I was an inconvenience that he had to endure for a few minutes. He barely looked at my paperwork; he asked me a few questions about my previous "jobs," and wanted to know why I wanted to be in the business. I answered, but don't think he was ever listening to a single word I said.

My second visit to the office that week was to meet the top "producer" in the office, a large, heavy man with big jowls and glasses with thick black frames. His name was Bob Krohn.

Bob was loud, boisterous, and clearly had an ego larger than the building we were in. He mostly talked about himself, and how much money he made, and how much money he made for his clients, and then again, how much money he made for himself.

While I was in his office listening to him talk, he had two telephone calls from clients. Considering that they had called him, once he knew who they were, they never had the opportunity to say another word. Bob just started yelling instructions at the people on the phone, telling them what they were going to buy and sell. Then, he'd hang up the phone and write some order tickets quickly, while yelling out the door to his sales assistant to come in and get the orders.

His sales assistant was a woman named Patty, about my age, and gorgeous. She was blonde, blue eyes, little wire framed glasses, and an extraordinarily curvaceous body. I didn't want to drool. Bill made some suggestive facial expressions as he stared and gestured towards her very round butt as she exited the office.

I still didn't know what this Wall Street stuff was about, but now I really wanted to get some of it.

Having previously encountered other ego-maniacs like Bob Krohn, I knew that the best way to get Bob to say something positive about me to Mr. Green was to assure him that I realized that he was truly a great man, and I hoped that one day I could only be a fraction of the broker that he was.

Any wisdom or advice that he could offer me would be greatly appreciated, I told him humbly.

I assured him that if I got hired, I would observe him as my role model, but would keep out of his way so as to be an unobtrusive admirer. He gave me a hearty handshake and a big smile, and motioned for Patty, the pretty blonde, to lead me out of the office.

By the next week, when I hadn't heard anything, I decided to call Mr. Green, the Branch Manager, yet again. I coaxed him into letting me come into the office for a fourth time.

During that meeting, he basically told me that he didn't know if I was right for the job.

I countered by saying that I had two other firms interested in me, but I really liked Bache and the people that I had met there. I told him that his firm was my "first choice."

I didn't think that he was buying it at all, and inside, my spirits were definitely sagging, but I didn't want to let it show. Then he asked me if I'd be willing to go down to New York City to meet with a professional evaluator in the personnel department. I had gotten so-so reviews from his two people in the office, but he'd be willing to get another opinion from someone who had the job of making sure that they hired the right people.

I knew that there was no chance that a Wall Street personnel person was going to recommend a rock writing poet for a stockbroker trainee position, but I said that I'd be happy to go to New York to meet with the personnel lady named Kristine Stanton.

I was nervous all the way down to the Wall Street area in New York City. It cost me eleven dollars to park in one of those underground garages. The eleven bucks was most of my money that I had brought with me, but I still had just enough to get back to Connecticut.

I kept thinking about how to position myself in the interview as someone with a suitable background and experience for the job, and not get blown away by my creative writing background. It didn't seem hopeful, but I went into the interview hoping for the best; however, it went about as badly as an interview could go.

The personnel lady named Kristine who I was supposed to be meeting didn't come to work that day. So, I was interviewed by this guy with suspenders who basically looked at my resume and said that my background was certainly not the kind that fit their profile of promising hires. The firm preferred strong business backgrounds with "demonstrated experience" in sales of some sort. The trainee position demanded someone who was a "self-starter" who had already achieved some level of success, and was now willing to take the" next step."

The longer he went on, the clearer it was that he was telling me that it wasn't me they were looking for.

Mercifully, the interview was no more than five minutes. I was bummed, and I knew that Debbie would be pissed by my having to spend the eleven dollars. It was a long ride home.

Two days later, I received an official rejection letter, thanking me for coming in, but that my background did not suit their requirements. It was two or three sentences, very short, but it made a very big hurt in me.

Then, from some deep, dark, scared place in my soul arose this sense that it wasn't over yet. It was like a fantastic comic book revelation. It was like Spider-Man refusing to accept defeat at the hands of Doctor Octopus, or Superboy finding a way to outwit the young Lex Luthor and his green Kryptonite ray gun.

I was defiant, as well as in a state of general denial.

I remembered Bluto in *Animal House* saying, "It ain't over until we say it's over." A strange almost spiritual feeling of determination came over me.

I had nothing to lose.

I was going to call Mr. Green the Branch Manager yet again, and give it still another try. I actually had a concept, an approach that I wanted to try. It was theatrical, and I just needed another round of face time with Mr. Green.

It took a few tries to get him on the phone, and when I did, I thought I'd try some subtle righteous indignation.

I mentioned that I had driven all the way to New York just to find that the lady hadn't shown up for my interview, and then I got a five minute rush job as an interview, which didn't seem very fair after a two hour drive.

Then I pointed out that I had just received a rejection letter signed by the personnel lady, Kristine Stanton, despite the fact that I never met with her. It hardly seemed like a fair shake, I said.

There was a pause, and then Michael said, "Your interview was just five minutes?" He sounded surprised.

"Maybe less," I answered, "and Kristine Stanton wasn't even there!"

Michael asked me to come into his office the next day for a few minutes. I figured that this was the final blow off, but I at least wanted the opportunity to make him an offer that he couldn't refuse, hopefully.

My underarms were starting to sweat under my salmon colored wool suit, even though the sunny March day wasn't particularly warm. I was standing off to the side of the dark blue glass exterior of the Phoenix Building in Hartford, readying myself to walk towards the entrance.

I discreetly moved my tie to the side, opened a button on my shirt and slipped my hand in to reach under my armpit to adjust the large wad of paper towels that I had rolled up into a pad and taped onto my armpits in order to avoid sweat stains appearing on the underarms of my shirt or my suit during the interview.

I just wanted to look relatively calm and collected while I offered one last pitch. This was probably my last shot at getting the stockbroker trainee job, but I wasn't going gentle into that good night. I was wearing my salmon color suit for the second time, but if he was going to give me the blow-off, I wanted him to remember me for more than the color of my suit.

Feeling nervy, I decided to take the initiative.

"Mr. Green," I said emphatically, "I know that you already have a lot of money, but I can make you more." I could feel the sweat droplets running down my sides under my shirt.

I remembered the movie *Kramer vs. Kramer*, where Dustin Hoffman needs to get the owners of an advertising agency to hire him during a Christmas Eve party. In the movie, Dustin Hoffman tries a "one time offer" of offering himself at a discounted salary rate to his potential employers to force their decision. It worked in the movie. I had nothing to lose.

"Mr. Green," I continued, "this is the place where I feel I can be successful. This is the place I want to be. So I'd like to make you a one-time offer."

He seemed interested and was listening. I didn't know if he had seen the movie, or remembered the line, so I went on. "The salary range for the trainee position is $16,000 to $41,000 a year. If you hire me now, I'll take the $16,000."

His jaw dropped and his head turned slightly to the side. "You would take the $16,000 to work here?" He sounded incredulous.

"Yes, because I know I'll make a lot more than that. I'll make you lots of money if you give me the opportunity."

"You want this bad." It was more a statement than a question.

"I know I'll be a success, if it takes living in the office to build my business."

During our conversation, Bob Krohn told me that if Michael was going to hire me, he would ask me to lunch at the Hartford Club, and all I had to do was not throw up on him to get the job. I didn't know what the Hartford Club was, but it sounded fancy. I was hoping, hoping, hoping.

"What are you doing for lunch tomorrow?" he asked me.

I was so excited, I wanted to cry and scream at the same time, but I needed to act cool. "Where are we going?" I asked, pretending to be calm.

"The Hartford Club," he said.

CHAPTER 4

The Odd Squad

April 27, 1981.

That was my first day of work at Bache, Halsey, Stuart, Shields. Their office was located on the fourth floor of the Phoenix Insurance building, commonly referred to as the "boat building" on the edge of downtown Hartford. The building itself was a big blue glass covered structure with two concaved sides that resembled the shape of the bow of an immense blue boat with steps and terraces built around it.

As I walked towards the building, I could feel my heart start to flutter as my stomach gurgled a few times. I was feeling very nervous and a little queasy.

I walked towards the security guards' desk and signed in, hoping they wouldn't send me away as if a mistake had occurred and I wasn't really supposed to be there at all.

There were two guards sitting at the desk; a man and a woman, both in dark blue uniforms that looked like they'd seen better days. I had seen both security guards before when I came for my interviews. I introduced myself to both of them, and told them that I would be working in the building.

They both seemed less than interested in meeting me. The lady guard quickly handed me a stick on label type name tag, and pointed towards the elevators. Rather than stick the label onto my nice new grey pinstriped suit, I held the pass and put it into my pocket as I walked into the elevator, going up to the fourth floor.

There was a moment when I was right outside the front entrance to the office of Bache, Halsey, Stuart, Shields that I felt like I was entering something strange and different from anything that I'd ever known before.

I thought of Alice falling down the rabbit hole, but as I reached for the door handle, it was more like Alice walking through the looking glass into another world. This looking glass was a large wood door that led into the reception area of the office.

A few minutes later, I was standing up against a white wall in the office, and Michael's secretary Linda was taking my picture for a photo ID to allow me to get into the building.

It was a large old fashioned camera with a big round flash on its side. The flash was very bright, and there were two blinding flashes. Then as my eyes were clearing, Linda began to lead me towards Michael's large office on the other side of the room.

There were three office chairs positioned in a semi arc around Michael's desk. The chair on the far left was open. The other two chairs had people sitting in them, a preppy looking white woman, and a very large well-dressed black man in the middle.

I sat in the empty chair, took a quick glance at the other two, gave them both a cursory nod, and turned my attention towards Michael who was already starting to talk.

Behind Michael, there was a large plate glass window, so there was a lot of sunlight coming in from behind him, bathing him in a sort of transcendent back lighting. His big gold and black onyx ring glittered when he waved his hand as he spoke.

He looked very classy and prosperous, the way you would expect a Wall Street executive to look. He even had a fancy sounding title, "Resident Manager," which sounded way more prestigious than just Branch Manager. He wore a gold necktie clip near the knot on his burgundy tie. I wasn't sure of the purpose of the gold necktie clip, but it looked way cool.

I immediately wanted one.

Michael went through a description of the training program which began with a large box of study material which we would be receiving in a few days. The box contained about 35 booklets, quizzes and exams.

There was no failing anything. If you failed one test, you were out.

After all of the study material was completed, we would be taking the Series 7 exam to receive our securities licenses. If someone failed that exam, they would be terminated. After the Series 7 exam, we would be going down to New York City for two weeks of training, before returning to Hartford to begin "production."

In the meantime, he would be working with the three of us, giving us things to learn, and tasks to do around the office. Since the three of us would be working and studying together as trainees, he asked all three of us to introduce ourselves one at a time.

The lady at the other end was in her late twenties, sort of mousy looking in a corporate looking brown pants suit and matching brown platform heels. Her name was Theresa. She had a background in business and library sciences, and had most recently been a sales assistant in an insurance agency. She wanted to try to make it in the sales end of the business. She thought that securities sales would be a lot more interesting than insurance sales, so she decided to give it a try.

Theresa seemed reasonably confident, but really did give the impression that she was more suited to be a librarian than a stockbroker. She held her hands together on her lap, and her legs seemed bound tightly together with her feet flat on the floor. However, she had a much better business background than I did, so I figured that she was definitely going to be competitive, and probably had some contacts through her previous work that would help her to build a business more easily than I could. I knew that I didn't have any contacts at all, not a one.

The person in the middle was a big, tall black man named Raymond G. Patterson III. He was about thirty, medium dark completion with a hint of freckles. I later found out that Raymond had some American Indian in his blood which accounted for his shiny black curly hair.

Raymond had a very nice middle class upbringing in Buffalo; he grew up in big house with a white picket fence, nuclear family, brothers, sisters, family dogs, and the whole all American experience. He went to prep school, then Babson College for Business, and most recently, he had been working in the Trust Department for one of the major local banks, and wanted to move into the investment sales and management part of the business.

They both seemed way more qualified for the job than me, but I tried to position my experience as a poet, rock critic, and part time adjunct professor at the University in as much of a business light and perspective as possible.

I also mentioned that I had grown up in a really poor section of Brooklyn, and I drove a taxi in New York City for five years to put myself through school to get a BA and a MFA in Writing. It sounded a little absurd compared to their backgrounds.

Raymond seemed amused when I mentioned the growing up in poverty stuff because of the obvious irony of the poor white kid growing up in the slums, while the tall black guy went to prep school.

Towards the end of the meeting, Michael handed each of us an S&P stock guide and a bond guide. These were two basic tools that we would have to begin studying immediately. They were booklets about an inch thick, about four inches by eight inches, filled with rows and columns of tiny words and numbers filling up every page. We would begin with the stock guide.

I fingered through the guide as Michael spoke, I was awed by the information it contained. I wanted to master this little book and know everything that it contained. I looked forward to taking the booklet home, spreading it open on the kitchen table, and begin divining its secrets.

A few days later, the box of study and exam books arrived. It was covered in white plastic and about the size of a small file box, durable, with an attached flexible lid that snapped close. All of the books inside were about the size of spiral notebooks, with some a little thicker than others, with all sorts of titles like " Common Stocks," "Municipal Bonds," "Convertible Securities," "Options." As I read through them, I was fascinated by them all.

The booklets seemed like rubies, emeralds, sapphires and diamonds in a treasure chest. I wanted to know them all. I had found all of the knowledge of Wall Street in a big white box.

The study-books part of the training went by pretty quickly. I lived with every individual lesson until I had it down cold. I made sure that I scored 100% on every single exam. I got about 15 perfect scores in a row until I hit a few scores in the 90's on the more challenging topics.

They had a countrywide progress report that the firm put out to show you how you were scoring on the exams as compared to other people in your respective training group around the country. I was in training group 81-I.

For a time, I was first in the country in test scores, but I ultimately finished second to someone from Georgia named Paul Blair, like the baseball player, who only lasted in the business a few years.

Raymond, Theresa and I spent most of our time studying together in the conference room, or helping out around the office, redoing files, updating sales materials, even answering telephones. Periodically, Michael would call the three of us in his office and begin quizzing us on some body of material that we were supposed to be studying. Sometimes, he'd ask us to find him a gold stock to buy, or what utility stock looked cheap?

I found it all very interesting and entertaining.

I was ready for more.

One of the most useful and fun things we did was called the "portfolio game" where Michael would pretend to be the client with a certain amount of money, and you had to find out the client's information, develop portfolio suggestions, and then contact the client (Michael) with your various recommendations.

Sometimes he would take your suggestions, sometimes he would shoot you down; however, if you weren't adequately prepared with your information, you would simply look and feel foolish.

I think that my enthusiasm and determination helped push our little group of three.
All of us did well through the testing and were really getting into the flow of a Wall Street office.

Because we spent so much time moving around together as a group, Raymond began calling us" The Odd Squad," modeled after the 60's TV show *The Mod Squad*, one black man, one white man, and a blonde chick. The name really suited us, and it caught on in the office.

It happened that Raymond and I both lived in Windsor, a town right outside of Hartford, and it didn't take long before we became fast friends. If the three of us were "The Odd Squad," then it was even more strikingly apparent that Raymond and I had a passing resemblance to Bruce Springsteen and "The Big Man," his saxophone player, Clarence Clemons.

I was a little like Bruce, short, white, dark curly hair, and scruffy on weekends. Raymond was "The Big Man," for obvious reasons; a large black man, at a hefty 6'4," he had a booming deep voice, filled with "the almighty power of the American dollar" as Raymond liked to phrase it.

Raymond immediately loved the nickname.

I was on my best behavior until we completed all of the preparatory exams, and didn't realize the depth of our common brotherhood until a bit later.

Finally, it was time for the big one, the Series 7, which we were to take up in Boston.

I don't think that I ever studied that hard in my entire life. I read the books over and over and over. I took the practice tests over and over until I knew the order of the questions on the sample exams. In the back of my mind, I felt the horror of potentially failing the exam, and then being fired.

When I drove up to Boston the night before the exam, I knew that everything I wanted going forward in life somehow depended on what happened at the Series 7 exam.

Debbie, my wife, in what had become her usual demeaning manner, made it clear that she thought that this would be the end of the road to Wall Street for me; and when I failed the exam, she would expect me to go to work for McDonalds, and forget about my Wall Street dreams.

Raymond and I decided that after the exam, we would go over the Federal Reserve building in Boston to genuflect before the large stone steps surrounding the building.

The test was about as difficult as I thought it would be, but I felt uncertain throughout it, even though I knew the material from end to end. After the test, I knew that there was no way I could have failed the exam, but there was no way of knowing for sure.

This was way before the era of electronic online testing. The forms were still made of paper, where you filled in tiny little boxes with the sharp point of a number two pencil. What if I had filled out my answers on the wrong columns or wrong rows, or something stupid like that?

When the test was over, Raymond and I headed to the nearest bar that we could find, and Theresa headed back to the Holiday Inn that we were staying at. I had no idea that there was a Federal Reserve building in Boston, but Raymond had gone to Boston University for a while, and led us right to the hallowed steps.

We were both a little buzzed by the time we got there, so our mumblings were probably pretty nonsensical, but we had, nonetheless, paid homage to the temple of capitalism. All we could do now was go home and wait for the test results.

The next day, Michael called the three of us in to let us know that we all passed. I was so relieved; Raymond and I talked about how the universe had given us "the power." I was starting to feel "the power" and I liked it. We were going to be leaving for our two weeks of training in New York starting the following Monday.

The firm put us up in residential hotel on Lexington Avenue and E.28th Street. Raymond and I were sharing a three bedroom suite with a broker trainee from Miami, Florida named Billy P.

Billy P. had a dirty blonde mullet haircut, and wore clothes that looked like he belonged as an extra in an episode of *Miami Vice*. His previous employment had been as a broker in a commodity trading boiler room operation. He cold-called elderly Miami residents trying to get them to trade something called Mocotta gold options which were an early version of our current types of futures options.

Mocatta options traded out of London, and at the time, were hardly known at all in this country. It didn't sound like Billy P. had made a lot of money trading Mocatta options either for himself or his customers. He remarked that this training program was his way of trying to "go straight," and learn a trade, rather than, as he said, "hustling old Miami Jews with gold trades."

Billy P. also liked to do funny voices, and he would make up strange market related characters as he spoke and do little skits with himself; that is, until Raymond and I started joining in. It seemed like Billy P. was always very up, which I figured meant he was probably stoned on cocaine. We only saw him actually do lines of coke once or twice, though Billy spent a lot of time sniffling and being very animated.

Our training classes were down in the Wall Street area of town in the firm's main headquarters. Classes ran all day from eight in the morning to five in the evening, with frequent breaks as, well as free breakfast and lunch in the building's cafeteria. The class' main instructor was a friendly, animated elderly man named Al Levy, who served as both homeroom teacher and Master of Ceremonies.

Al would make some opening remarks about each product area, and then introduce each presenter. After each presentation, he would tell some amusing story, or discuss appropriate applications for the particular product that he had personally experienced in the field. Al had been a retail broker for over twenty years, and moved to the Training area about ten years before our particular class. Ours would be one of the final classes that he would mentor before retiring shortly afterwards.

One particular thing that Al Levy said that I have never forgotten, and has always turned out to be true over the years, was that our lives would be permanently changed by entering this profession.

Al said that from now on, every time you went into a room, or began a conversation with someone who you just met; people would always be asking your opinion about the markets, and asking you what you thought about various economic topics or individual stocks.

He talked about how people had a fascination with stockbrokers, and that everyone would always want to know what stocks were hot, and would be looking for tips. According to Al, most people perceived stockbrokers as glorified bookies in three piece suits and wingtip shoes.

As Al Levy spoke, I was looking forward to this new way of living. However, training classes were still a long way away from being a successful stockbroker. First, I had to get through the training class, and then the real challenge would begin.

Each morning, the Big Man, Billy P., Theresa and I would take the subway downtown to the home office building, go to breakfast in the cafeteria, and then sit through a full days of classes, which were basically presentations by people from each of the different product, legal and compliance areas.

Afterwards, Theresa would usually drop out, and the three of us would then head for the local bars, as we worked our way back uptown towards our hotel room.

The classes had an international component with a small group of people there from both Germany and Great Britain. There was only one woman in the German group, a broad heavy set woman with dark brown hair, and piercing dark brown eyes that made me feel like a piece of meat on a skewer whenever she happened to look at me.

She had a heavy German accent, a deep voice, and she liked calling me "Liebe."

On the first Thursday of classes, at a break, she asked me if I would be staying in town for the weekend because she would like to go out drinking with me. I noticed that she wore black shoes that were more like boots than women's business footwear. She moved very close to me when she spoke, so that we were almost touching.

I could faintly feel her warm breath on my face.

She gave me the feeling that she wanted to take me prisoner. I pictured myself bound in leather straps while she paraded around me with a whip talking dirty in German. I told her that I would be going back to Connecticut for the weekend, even though I hadn't originally planned to.

It seemed like the safe thing to do.

By the middle of the second and final week of training, we had already finished all of the presentations and lessons from the various product areas, and were well into pretend role playing, cold calling, and group discussions.

As the days became more unsubstantial in terms of content, the Big Man, Billy P. and I would spend our evenings sitting around drinking with our old friends: Jose Cuervo, Jack Daniels, Jim Beam, and Johnny Walker Black.

The dining room table was cluttered with bottles of booze and empty beer cans, surrounded by bottles of Coke, Canada Dry ginger ale, tonic water, club soda, and orange juice.

It hadn't taken long for Billy P.'s funny voices and characters to morph into an endless series of drunken group skits. Some of them were so funny, that I brought a tape recorder to the room to save a few of the best for posterity. I still have the tapes.

My favorite two skits that we put together were the "Second Guesser Meets Mr. Bill," and the legendary "Mutant Broker."

The "Second Guesser" was a concept that evolved out of the fact that no matter what a Wall Street analyst is going to tell you the market is going to do, six months after the fact, they tell you how that they were right, whether or not they were.

Raymond and I came up with a supposed commodity markets call-in radio show hosted by the "Second Guesser" who sounded like the late pitchman Billy Mays on steroids. The skit opened with "Secky" answering a call in from Mr. Bill, the tormented little puppet character from *Saturday Night Live.*

Billy P. played the "Second Guesser," and Raymond changed his voice to a falsetto to play the emotional Mr. Bill. I wrote and sang the theme song that opened and closed every show we taped. Together, we came up with:

"Helllloo, call in, line open. This is the "Second Guesser." Who do I have on my line tonight?"

"Hello, Second Guesser, this is Mr. Bill."

"Well, how are you doing there tonight Mr. Bill, and please call me…Secky."

"Second Guesser, you told me that cattle was going up, up up….and I went long and bought cattle because you said that cattle was going up, up, up…but then, but then…cattle start going down, down, down…and oh, nooooooooooo."

"Hey, Mr. Bill, I said that cattle might go up, yes…it might go up…but hey, it didn't go up at all. Hey….. Instead it dropped like a stone through water, and you lost all of your money…and that's my…*second guess.*"

Mr. Bill replied, "Oh, nooooo."

For the "Mutant Broker" skits, Billy P. would use a voice that sounded like a cross between James Earl Jones and a vampire.

Mutant Broker was based on cold calling for clients. In our skit, Mutant Broker contacts a stereotypical middle- American type retiree named Mr. Jones, played by Raymond.

"Hello, Mr. Jones?"

"Yes, this is Mr. Jones."

"Mr. Jones…this is the….*Mutant Broker.*"

"Um, hello. Excuse me, what did you say your name was?"

"Mr. Jones, this is the…*Mutant Broker,* and I'm calling you about an exciting investment opportunity tonight. Are you interested in making money… Mr. Jones?"

"Um, well sure, Mutant Broker. What do you have in mind?"

"Well, Mr. Jones, I want to talk to you about Mocatta gold options, traded out of London England. You've heard of London, England, haven't you, Mr. Jones? You see, Mr. Jones, we are going to embark on a program of selling out of the money Mocatta gold put options…"

No one would understand this rap; it was nonsense and I was doubled over in the background as Billy P continued:

"Now, Mr. Foster… if you get put the gold, we just turn it around and sell the out of the money Mocatta gold call options, and keep selling the options until we are called the gold., and then resume selling the gold puts. This strategy will make you twenty percent….no….*forty* percent…no….. *seventy percent*….no *ninety to one hundred and twenty percent* on an annual basis, assuming you don't get put the gold.   (pause)…Are you still with me Mr. Foster?"

"It sounds great Mutant Broker. Sign me up."

"I'm glad that you're seeing this my way, Mr. Foster, and remember, I'm the … *Mutant Broker.*"

The three of us would be rolling on the floor, laughing so hard it was hard to breathe. I even composed the musical commercial for the radio shows, and played guitar as we all sang. That night we sang our completed song *"Oh, Mocatta Pinata,"*

Theresa happened to come by our hotel suite to hang out.

She sat there in horror, with her blues eyes wide opened like a deer in the headlights, sitting tensely on a chair, legs tightly pressed together, and her hands in her lap, as the three of us sang the verses and group choruses to the song. It would have been nice if she would have sung along, but Theresa was pretty straight.

That Friday, they let us out early, training was over. The three of us all headed back to Connecticut, saying goodbye to Billy P. I couldn't wait to get some clients of my own, and buy some securities for real.

About two years later, I looked up Billy P. on a trip to Florida. He had already left the business, and went back to trading commodities for a local boiler shop operation. I think he also might have been dealing coke, or something, on the side, mostly because he was always nervously looking around while we were sitting together at an open air bar on the strip in Miami.

I hoped that there wasn't a contract out on him or something criminally weird like that. This wasn't the same Billy P. that I remembered from training. That was the last time that I ever saw or heard from Billy P.

It didn't take long for me to find out that my profession was not for everyone.

CHAPTER 5

GIVING GOOD PHONE

Though it did **not seem like it at the time,** the Summer/Fall of 1981 was a particularly propitious time to start out as a new stockbroker in the business. By then, the job title had already evolved from "stockbroker" to "Account Executive," probably in an early industry effort to deemphasize the stock market part of the job, since the stock market had basically gone nowhere for almost twenty years.

The early 1980's was a time of sky high interest rates, with yields in the mid-teens for tax free municipal bonds, and even higher for U.S. Treasury securities. Despite the fact that these were about the highest interest rates in the history of our country, just about everyone thought that interest rates would continue to rise forever.

The stock market, as measured by the Dow Industrial Average, peaked at around the 1000 level way back in the mid 1960's, and had basically ranged between 500 and 1000 for the past two decades. If someone invested in the general market at the high part of the range in the 1960's, they were probably still negative by the early 1980's. If they had invested in the lower part of the range, they had basically gotten nowhere over the years unless they were nimble traders.

As a result of the inflation in the economy, commodity prices were volatile, with huge price swings in gold and silver, as well as all of the agricultural products like the grains, coffee, orange juice, pork bellies, and just about everything else that lived or grew.

At that time, there were many individuals who speculated in commodities. The regulations and suitability standards for clients was much lower, so trading commodities for clients was a regular part of the stable of products that brokers offered to their clients.

Michael required that we study for and pass the licensing exam for Commodities; it was not a particularly challenging exam considering the complexities of the markets. During that period, many brokers who ventured forth in the Commodities markets destroyed their clients financially because they simply did not have a sufficient understanding of what was going on in the specific commodities markets that they were trading in.

Fortunately, Michael had great wisdom in giving the three of us proper direction when we all returned from our two weeks of training in New York City.

When I walked into the office that Monday morning, the first thing I noticed on the desk was a box of business cards with my name on them. I took one out and just stared at it. It wasn't even one of the really nice embossed type cards. This looked like it was a quickie cheap printing job so that they were ready on our desks when we returned.

They may not have been the fanciest looking cards, but they looked like little plates of gold to me. I was very excited to put a bunch of them in the little plastic cardholder that came in the box of business cards. Then I slipped the valuable little package into the jacket pocket of my suit.

Almost as exciting was the variety of stationary that I had on my desk. There was a small stack of large yellow lined pads, a pack of memo sized pads with the Bache logo, but not personalized, a stapler, two boxes of paper clips, in different sizes of course, and an entire box of blue pens. I felt that I had arrived. I wanted to start to call people right away.

I didn't have to wait long. The first thing that Michael wanted us to do was to begin prospecting using a new tax free municipal bond that was being issued by the nearby town of Bloomfield, Connecticut. This required the three of us to start cold calling right away in front of him.

Michael took a copy of the Yellow Pages and opened it to the section of "Accountants," and then asked us who wanted to go first. Theresa shirked and seems to shrink into the corner of the room. Raymond stood there like a robot with dying batteries, trying to get either his arms, legs, or mouth to move. So I decided to volunteer.

Despite the fact that I was terrified, I knew that I was good at talking to strangers on the phone. I had a lot of unusual phone experiences, and over the years, it had given me the ability to" give good phone."

In 1981, there were no "do not call" lists; there were no "scrubbed lists." States had not yet begun enacting legislation to prohibit certain types of solicitation by phone. You could call whoever you wanted, whenever you wanted, across state lines, at midnight, during dinner, for just about anything. Cold calling was the foundation of the way brokers built their business.

Fortunately, I liked talking to strangers. I'd done it before.

During college, in order to supplement my meager taxi income, I sold Fuller Brush products "door to door" in many of the office buildings in the Garment District of New York City. I had a large awkward tan "samples" suitcase full of different types of brushes, cleaners, soaps, sprays, and all kinds of other Fuller Brush products that I carried around. I went floor to floor, office to office in any of the buildings that I could slip into.

Most of the buildings were filled with small to medium sized apparel producing companies that had sales offices and a showroom in the front, and in the back there was usually an old fashioned looking factory filled with hordes of foreign speaking women working behind rows of sewing machines. Often, I would try to get a friendly receptionist let me into the factory where the dozens of Puerto Rican and European women would stop working on their garments, and gather around me to see what sort of exotic American goods that I was selling.

The Fuller Brush products were all relatively expensive compared to what someone might pay in the store for a comparable item, but all of the sewing machine ladies loved the colorful booklets and fancy looking pictures; they would begin impulse buying tons of merchandise, that I would later deliver and get paid for.

In most of the factories, the biggest selling item was the strawberry air freshener. I would often take out my sample spray and shoot a few blasts around the factory workspace. The sewing machine ladies would all begin to ooh and aah, as they squealed excitedly in their native languages. The Puerto Rican ladies were all very friendly, and would come scrambling over, talking quickly in Spanish to me as they fumbled through their little purses for money to pay me for the sprays.

I also sold a very nice green apple scented spray, but strawberry was always the big seller.

I learned to overcome my shyness by having to engage and sell people who I had just met moments before, even if they didn't speak English. Every Friday, I'd be walking around Manhattan carrying big shopping bags of sprays, mops and brushes to deliver to my customers. I didn't really like the job, but it fit in well with my school schedule and driving a taxi.

The worst part of the Fuller Brush job was the constant rip offs at the storage room that my Fuller Brush manager maintained in one of the office buildings to receive all of the products ordered from the factory. I would order a dozen strawberry air sprays and get billed for their cost, and then there would only be eight of them when I went to pick them up.

There was no system of protecting your merchandise. Everything was delivered to a central room, and the first people in the room took what they wanted from the shipment. When I repeatedly complained that people were taking my merchandise that I had to end up paying for, the manager wasn't interested in hearing about it. After I wrote to the Fuller Brush company to complain, I was fired.

I got fired a lot.

During the 1970's, while I was still living in Brooklyn, one of the biggest telephone scams going involved literally dozens of boiler room operations, mostly located in Manhattan, selling commercial and industrial chemicals to business owners and farmers around the country.

At that time, *The New York Times* was full of ads in the employment section looking for sales people who wanted to make $1000 to $5000 a week, princely sums back then. I was always getting fired from part-time jobs, and was always looking for work, so I regularly noticed all of the ads for the high paid chemical sales people.

I didn't know anything about industrial chemicals so I never considered applying. I was looking for something like an administrative assistant position, which I happened to find, ironically, with Jaguar Chemical, one of the companies that ran some the biggest print ads for chemical sales people.

At Jaguar Chemical, I saw firsthand what the chemical sales scam was all about. The company had the whole floor in one of the older office buildings on Park Avenue, around East 25th Street. The floor was divided into two areas; a large room filled with desks, phones and sales people trying to sell the chemical products. Everyone sounded like a pitchman. Standing on the perimeter of the sales room, it sounded like a dozen Home Shopping Network commercials playing at once.

Farmers seemed to be one of the primary targets of the predatory sales force. The salesmen called and offered to sell the farmers products that they would typically use, like herbicides or weed killers, and then ship them large quantities of the products in eighty gallon drums, whether it had been ordered or not. The salesmen also worked the car wash market with eighty gallon drums of concentrated car wash products; they also did a brisk business in concrete sealers and fillers which could be sold to a wide range of businesses.

Unfortunately, most of the products were pure crap. The weed killer was diluted diesel fuel; the car wash concentrate was dishwashing liquid, and I doubt that the concrete sealer actually sealed anything. The point was to have the stuff shipped out to the customers, because the sales people got paid as soon the items were shipped out the factory door.

Some of the sales people were faking southern or western accents as they spoke to their prospective customers. I could hear that everyone was using extreme persistence and high pressure tactics to get their prospective customers to agree to take a shipment of at least a few drums of some industrial chemical product to try out; they said there was no upfront payments, no obligation, and if they didn't like the product, they could send it right back for a full refund.

When one of the salesman got an order booked, they would put down the phone and let out a howl, or a yell, or some other loud exclamatory sound, and then start trading high fives with all the other sales people around him while strutting down the aisle like an NFL running back prancing in the end zone after a touchdown.

The sales room looked like a big frat party complete with discreetly placed pin-ups and the faint aroma of a beer keg. Almost everyone seemed to be making lots of money selling chemicals by phone.

But I worked on the other side of the office, the administrative side, where all of the orders and paperwork was processed. I made a hundred dollars a week, and it was a full time job.

My job at Jaguar was curious. I opened the mail that contained the payments from the customers, added up the checks on an adding machine that dispensed a tape, gave the total and the tape to my boss, before bringing the checks to the bank for deposit. A few days later, I would go to the bank to pick up a thick envelope of cash to be given directly to the owner of the company, Sidney Samuels.

I also helped to process the incoming orders as they were being received from the sales room. I would gather the hand written order forms that were generated by the salesmen, and then make lists of who sold what for the week, so the salesmen could get paid commissions.

The salesmen were paid on their orders as soon as the items were shipped, not when they were paid for. So obviously the salesmen had an incentive to submit as many orders as possible for processing, whether or not the customer had genuinely wanted the material.

In theory, there were supposed to be chargebacks, but the game really seemed to be to get mountains of product shipped out to potentially unwilling buyers, and hope that enough of them paid the bills to keep the operation going. The refusal of a shipment would leave some indeterminate number of large chemical drums floating around in the trucking transportation system, usually ending up "On Hand" in a terminal or a warehouse, awaiting disposition from the shipper.

The refused shipments generated physical "On Hand" notices which were sent by the shipping companies to the Jaguar Chemical offices, where they were then forwarded to the individual sales people for handling. At that point, the sales person needed to contact the customer and "re-sell" the item, or have their commissions reversed and charged back. The problem was that the sales people would just leave the notices on their desks and ignore them. No one followed up about the notices; they were treated as out of sight and out of mind.

Occasionally, I'd get one of the "On Hand" freight notices in my mail, and would bring it to the attention of my boss, a heavy unpleasant swarthy looking man named Dave, who looked like Tony Soprano with black glasses. Dave wore crumpled cheap suits, and his ties were always partially loosened because he couldn't close the top button on his shirt due to his neck being too fat.

Usually, by the time I got the freight notices, they were second or third requests for action by the shipper; otherwise the goods would be disposed of or sold by the carrier, and the shipper would be charged for all unpaid freight fees and penalties. For some reason, Dave didn't like me giving him the notices and pointing out that Jaguar's shipments were being disposed of by the carriers, and that very large shipping fees were being charged.

Apparently, it was his area's responsibility to take care of freight problems, and he seemed to have piles of "On Hand" notices all around him on the windowsills, with more of them scattered around his desk. It seemed obvious that the freight problem was not being attended to by anyone in particular.

Dave's boss was a big fat slob named Lonnie, who bore a strong resemblance to Jabba the Hut. Lonnie was the sales manager, and constantly reveled in how much money he made collecting a small piece of the action for all of the products that his sales force sold. "On Hand" notices were anathema to Lonnie because it meant that there was money that he and his sales people would have to "give back,"

Lonnie was busy riding the gravy train, and he didn't want any refused drums of chemicals to derail him.

One day when Dave was out, I received a cluster of about a half dozen notices of freight liquidation in the mail. The notices seemed kind of urgent, and there were several of them, so I decided to bring them to Lonnie who was not pleased. He happened to be sitting with the actual owner of the company, a sleazy looking lizard of a man named Sidney Samuels. I didn't mean to put Lonnie on the spot. Sidney Samuels seemed very disturbed, and asked Lonnie why the notices hadn't been handled until then. Lonnie just stammered.

I just wanted to help and try to score some brownie points when I offered that there were dozens and dozens of these "On Hand" notices all over the office, and if they were that important, we should collect them all and find an orderly way of dealing with them. Looking at Lonnie's face becoming a flushed red and orange, I wasn't sure if I was saying the right thing.

Sidney Samuels, the owner of the company, told me to collect all of the notices and bring them into the office as soon as possible. I left Lonnie's office, and Sidney got up and closed Lonnie's door behind me.

In about half an hour, I collected close to a hundred "On Hand" freight notices which seemed to be everywhere in and around the office. There were stashes of them in unused desks and on the window sills all around the perimeter of the office.

There were dozens of them piled on one of the unoccupied desks in the sales area. The sales people apparently used that desk as a depository for their respective notices of rejected shipments. Many of the notices had coffee stains or doodling on them. Most were at least a little crumpled like Dave's clothes.

When I brought the rather substantial pile of messy papers into Lonnie's office, his big round face had a greenish pallor that quickly morphed into a look of extreme dislike. I handed the pile to Sidney, who thanked me and then asked me to leave again, shutting the door behind me.

The next morning, dumpy Dave called me into his office as soon as I arrived and fired me; so much for succeeding in business by trying to help the company do things better.

After Jaguar fired me for being a good corporate camper, I was again unemployed, and would have to tell Debbie, who already thought that I was a loser, and didn't hesitate to say it repeatedly.

I needed a job as soon as possible, so I immediately went and bought a copy of *The New York Times*, and sat on the low ledge of one of the office buildings, and started going through the want ads yet again. This time, I considered getting on the selling end of the chemical sales business, and I spotted a gaudy looking ad for another chemical sales boiler room operation, Crystal International Chemical Company. The ad said to apply in person, and ask for Al. The office was down in the Wall Street area, so I got onto the subway and headed downtown to meet Big Al.

Crystal Chemical had a small suite of offices in one of the much older office buildings tucked into a corner of the financial district. There was no security guard or reception area in the small lobby of the building, and the tiny rickety elevator had one of those old fashioned manual accordion style inner doors that you had to pull across to close before using the elevator.

The building was so old that it still had windows in the offices and bathrooms that could be opened and closed, and window sills that looked like they might give way if you leaned on them too hard. Later on, I would hang out with several of the sales people in the bathroom to smoke joints and blow the smoke out the open windows. A few of the offices had doors, so those sales people didn't even bother to go to the bathroom to smoke pot; they would just close their door and open the window.

The Crystal offices were much smaller than the Jaguar operation. Crystal had a suite of about eight offices for the salesmen, with a huge overly opulent office for the Sales Manager, Big Al.

Big Al was a large fat round man with thinning combed over red hair and a thick red beard. He wore colorfully patterned imitation silk shirts with the buttons opened to his belly button, with his belly hanging over the bottom closed button.

Big Al wore more bling than a pimp. He had a mass of gold chains around his neck with crosses at the ends of some of them, kind of like Mr. T.

Big Al had a huge wall in his office painted black, with the outline of a naked woman set in rhinestones on the wall. At the foot of the wall, he had a fountain with giant goldfish.

Big Al liked to throw money around to people who stroked his ego, and he kept two women on the "payroll" as his personal assistants.

Both women were gorgeous. I think that they were both strippers who needed day jobs because it became clear that seemed to have zero secretarial or administrative skills. They both spent long periods in Big Al's office with the door closed.

When I first showed up at the office in the early afternoon, the place was very quiet with most of the offices empty, and the door to Big Al's office was wide open. When I walked in, Big Al was sitting in his oversized high backed red leather chair, with his arm around the waist of the dark haired assistant who stood next to him, while the blonde woman leaned in from the other side to rub his shoulders and his neck. Big Al's face was sort of nuzzled into the side of the dark haired girl's blouse when he saw me enter his office.

As I introduced myself, I was taking in the decadent depravity of the décor in his office. Big Al's desk was the size of a boat with not much on it but a telephone and some messy looking scattered papers with coffee ring stains on them. I was awed by the large silhouette of a naked woman outlined in rhinestones on the black painted wall. There was a big dark velvety looking couch on the side wall that looked battered and disheveled as if a Boy Scout troop had been jumping on it.

Big Al's big belly was sticking out way over the bottom button of his shirt, almost touching the edge of the desk as he leaned back to talk to me. He wore an oversized gold I.D bracelet with a shiny gold plate near his wrist on which a large "AL" was engraved.

I told Al about my experience at Jaguar Chemical, and he asked me if I had done any sales there. When I said no, he immediately started to lose interest and turn away towards the girls. So I quickly threw in that I knew how to handle the "On Hand" freight notices that used to come in, and maybe I could help him with that. That caught his attention for a moment, and I used that opportunity to try something so schlocky that it could only work with a self-worshipping ego maniac like Big Al.

"Big Al," I said. I had made up that name for him on the spot. It sounded really corny, but he was listening so I continued.

"Big Al, you're the kind of guy that I've been looking to work for. You've got it all, money, beautiful women, great looking jewelry. I can see that. You don't need me, Big Al, but I want to learn how to be a winner like you. Let me work with you, Big Al. Let me learn from you. Tell me what I can do to help you make even more money, Big Al."

Big Al bought it, and liked it. He really did. He liked me too. I was in. He would pay me five bucks an hour to come in during the evening shift to call customers and try to get them to take delivery of the refused chemical drums that were sitting in a warehouse somewhere. He promised me extra money when the customers finally paid for the goods .He was going to pay me all cash, out of his pocket. No paperwork, no applications, no benefits, no taxes, and I could start the next day.

When I got home and told Debbie about my day, she was not impressed that I had been fired from a "real job" to work nights for some red-bearded maniac who had a goldfish pond in his office, and was going to pay me as I went. Debbie was never particularly encouraging or supportive, but I suppose that I was looking pretty hopeless at that point.

The next day when I came in to the office, Big Al wasn't there. However, the blonde girl was sitting on top of the small reception desk near the front of the office, filing her nails. She told me that Al had left a stack of papers for me to work on in one of the offices.

I looked to find about thirty "On Hand" notices on a desk in an office that was totally empty except for a phone. I sat down at the desk, realizing of course, that I had never actually tried to handle the disposition of a single "On Hand" freight notice, which would obviously require me calling the customer and trying to get him to take delivery of the goods.

The addresses of the freight companies and the customers seemed to be mostly in the Midwest, where I guessed most of the farmers were. The top few freight notices were from some small towns in Texas that I had never heard of.

Given my potential audience, it certainly didn't seem like the name Don Goodman and a Brooklyn accent was going to win me any points with the farmers or the ranchers, so I decided to use a different name and try a phony accent, just like the salesmen at Jaguar Chemical.

I came up with the name Daniel Parker, a nice Christian Middle America sounding kind of name. The only accent that I could do was sort of a cross between Andy Griffith and Jed Clampett from *The Beverly Hillbillies*.

But before I started calling people, I needed some basic stationary like a pen to write and a pad to take notes. I looked in the desk. The drawers were empty except for a dried out Styrofoam coffee cup in the bottom drawer.

When I went into the empty office next door, there were no stationary supplies either in or on the desk. In fact, I then realized that the entire suite of offices was very bare looking with no pictures on the walls, no books or sales material, no paper, envelopes or any kind of stationary with any kind of company logo on it.

There were no plants or other decorations, and absolutely no photographs or personal effects of any kind in any of the offices. In fact, the individual sales offices didn't seem to belong to any sales person in particular. It was more like the sales people used any office that was available when they decided to show up for work. At that moment, I noticed there were only two sales people in the offices, working the phones, trying to sell product. I wondered where everyone else was.

The blonde at the reception desk was kind enough to lend me her pen, though it certainly didn't look like she would be needing it for anything any time soon. The only paper that I could find to write on was the large supply of order forms that the salesmen filled out after selling a customer the goods, so that the order could be processed and they could get paid their commissions. The only other thing in the place that even resembled paper to write on were randomly placed stacks of index sized cards that had sales leads with the names and telephone numbers of all of the farmers, ranchers and small business owners that the sales people would call.

Finally, it was just me alone in an office with a phone, calling a farmer down in Texas named Buddy Jones, who had recently refused a half dozen eighty gallon drums of weed killer, which was now sitting in a freight yard in Texarkana Texas.

"Howdy," I said. "This here is Daniel Parker from Crystal Chemical. Might I kindly speak to a Mr. Buddy Jones?" I tried to drawl on all of the words so they sounded thick and heavy like grits sticking to a spoon.

"This is Buddy Jones. What can I do for you, son?"

As soon as I realized that Buddy wasn't going to call me out on the phony accent, I decided to pile it on, which entailed repeating phrases like "that's mighty nice, mighty nice," or "that's good, real good," or I'd appreciate it, sure would appreciate it." I tried to mix in a few "I reckons" and "sure enough."

After about ten minutes of wondering if my new down home friend Buddy Jones knew that I was really faking it, he agreed to take delivery of the eight drums of weed killer and "give the stuff a try." I thanked him profusely, and gave him a "that's real gentlemanly of you, real gentlemanly to help me out here, Buddy."

It didn't take long for me to get comfortable in my new job, real comfortable. I didn't get everyone to take delivery of the merchandise, but I sure got enough of them to take in the goods so Big Al was happy with me, real happy. Each Friday, he'd pull out a big wad of bills and pay me between eighty and a hundred dollars for my week's work. I could come in to the office pretty much whenever I wanted. The office was usually open. There was nothing in there to steal.

I made hundreds of telephone calls to people all around the country, using all kinds of variations to my southern-western accent, incorporating new phrases every day. I started doing a "Howdeeee" like Minnie Pearl, and an "ooooooh doggies" like Jed Clampett. I was so funny that I sometimes had to take a break between telephone calls to stop laughing at my ridiculous sounding accents.

I began to realize then that I gave "good phone," real good phone.

It might have been a great and lasting career, sitting with the window open, blowing smoke out of the window, being Mr. Daniel Parker for fun and profit. Unfortunately, Big Al wasn't doing his part.

After a while, there were hardly ever any sales people in the offices. New people would come in for a few days, and then decide not to come back. Al really wasn't bothering to replace them; he was too busy playing with the girls in his office. Crystal Chemical had the look of a failing dysfunctional office. I knew it was just a matter of time.

I liked to work in the evenings, from about four in the afternoon to near midnight. It made it easier to catch the farmers and whoever else I needed to reach after they were done for the day, in whatever time zone they were in.

Many nights in the office, it was just me and this weird guy named Richard who seemed to be the office's primary source of revenue. Richard was in his late-forties, salt and pepper hair, huge dark puffy circles under his eyes. He always had a very dour, almost anesthetized sort of look, like he was on downs or Quaaludes. Richard always seemed to be in the office; sometimes it looked like he stayed there all night. Hour after hour, he would sit at his desk, chain smoking cigarettes, and calling sales leads. His phone approach was a totally monotonous short sales script that he repeated in exactly the same way for every telephone call. Richard said that he figured it was a "numbers game," and he "needed the money" so he had to keep working as much as he could.

However, Richard alone was not enough to keep the office afloat. As the sales revenues dried up, Al stopped paying me, and then he stopped paying Richard.

For about a month, it was like pulling teeth to get the money that I was owed, even a little at a time. Big Al started coming into the office less and less, and soon the two hot girls disappeared. Then, the only real piece of office equipment, the copier machine, was removed. The end was near.

A few days later, Big Al's fate was sealed when two elegantly dressed men came into the office to talk with Big Al. One was Abe Crystal, the owner of Crystal Chemical; the other was his right hand man, a tall muscular looking bald man named Joe Malucci. To this day, I have never seen a bald head shine like Joe Malucci's. The florescent lights reflecting off of his head looked like a flashbulb as he walked by.

Clearly, this office was not the only "satellite" sales office that Abe Crystal had, and he certainly didn't look happy about the way things were going. When he walked into Big Al's office, Al got up to let Abe sit in his big chair, with Joe standing like a guard soldier at his side. I saw Al squirm as he tried to fit his big fat ass into the little office chair on the other side of the desk.

Joe saw me looking in, and came over to shut the office door. It was like a scene in *"The Godfather."* I figured that it was a good time to go outside and have a cigarette, just in case they didn't want any witnesses.

When I came back to the office, they were all gone. The next day when I came in late that afternoon, all of the furniture was gone. All that was left in the corner of the room was the remnants of the goldfish pond with one last living giant goldfish struggling to stay alive in the inch of water that remained. I looked around the office and found a small clear glass vase, and put the fish and some water in it.

I took the goldfish home on the subway, holding the vase with the goldfish in it for everyone to see. I named the fish Big Al, and actually had him in a fish tank at home for several years. Debbie used to say that Big Al knew that I saved his life because he always acted excited when I came near the fish tank to talk to him. When Big Al, the fish, finally died, I took him to the beach in Coney Island to bury him near the shore in between two large clam shells.

At Crystal Chemical, I had learned a lot about talking to people on the phone, and it actually led into the final job that I would have before moving to Connecticut from Brooklyn.

I got a job as the Assistant Adjustment Manager for an established old line furniture distributor company named Krebs, Stengel and Co, They were located in the American Furniture Exchange which used to be on Lexington Avenue near East 28th Street.

Krebs, Stengel had salesmen on the road all over the country. Each salesman handled a specific territory, servicing all of the furniture stores and department stores that sold the Krebs' furniture lines. The Krebs salesmen were all older, mostly Jewish guys who had been with the company for years, and had developed relationships with all of the retail furniture dealers in their territories.

The company did business with several dozen furniture manufacturers all over the country, handling mostly lower to mid end lines of furniture encompassing everything from rocking chairs and roll top desks to more modern modular couches, and even some progressive lines like easy to assemble boxed furniture which is now so prevalent in department stores.

The company shipped millions of dollars of furniture all around the country from the different manufacturing operations; and when that much furniture is shipped, there are bound to be many broken, damaged items in the mix that have to be dealt with. That was my job. I called all of the store owners that had problems, and tried to resolve them.

Because it was so expensive to move furniture around the country on common freight carriers, I had a number of tools that I could use to entice the store owners to take in the shipped furniture, including steep discounts, extended payment terms, free freight, repair allowances, and the like. It didn't take long after I started to work the phones for me to see exactly what I had to offer a store owner to get the job done.

I didn't do accents any more, but instead, I modeled myself after the game show host for *Let's Make A Deal*. My boss, Matt, nicknamed me "Big Wheel, Big Deal, Monty Don Goodman."

They loved me at Krebs, Stengel, and by then, I was giving great phone every day, saving the company thousands of dollars. I even had a very good friend at the company named Trudy, who was an extreme pothead. At lunch, she would take me upstairs to one of the floors that were under construction, and we'd find a place to hide out and smoke joints.

I had finally found a company that liked and appreciated me; they even gave me four raises in salary during the year and a half that I was there.

Being "Big Wheel, Big Deal Monty Don Goodman" was way better than working at Crystal Chemical. Now I had something legitimate that I could make a career of. I probably would have stayed at Krebs, Stengel for quite a while, but it was about then that Debbie and I decided to move to Connecticut so she could take the higher paying job in the foreign place called Hartford Hospital.

And now, just a few years later, there I was standing in Michael Green' office, getting ready to call some accountant that I didn't know to try to get them to spend thousands of dollars to buy a tax free bond issued by the town of Bloomfield Connecticut.

As I picked up the phone on Michael's desk and dialed, I could remember all of the calls that Daniel Parker and Monty Don had made. I totally believed in myself. I knew that I gave the best phone around.

After about five minutes, the accountant agreed to buy ten thousand dollars' worth of the Bloomfield municipal bonds. I had my first customer. I wanted to keep dialing for dollars.

CHAPTER 6

DIALING FOR DOLLARS

Fortunately, the Great **Bull Market of the 1980's** did not lift off for nearly a year after Raymond, Theresa and I started in production.

During that first year, the three of us practically lived in the office, calling strangers all morning, all afternoon, and usually into the evenings. Raymond and I referred to it as "Dialing for Dollars."

We called people in Connecticut; we called people in Massachusetts and New York. Then I came up with the idea of calling across the time zones. We asked Michael to have us registered in California so we could prospect on the West Coast on nights when we decided to stay in the office and work until nine or ten in the evening. There were no phony accents, no wheeling and dealing, just dialing and more dialing, looking for people who bought tax free bonds.

I quickly found that many people out there didn't even know what a tax free bond was. Some even questioned how anything could be "tax free." I didn't bother pursuing those people. Rather, if someone indicated that they knew what I was talking about, and asked a question about the bond that I was calling about that led me to believe that they had previously purchased municipal bonds, I knew I had a live one. I'd keep those people in my follow up file until I either sold them a tax free bond or was told to go away.

Within the first year, I had over a hundred clients who bought muni bonds, most of them being company owners and accountants.

I discovered that people who had experience in business and investing understood how unique the very high tax free returns available at the time were. It really didn't take much selling ability to get someone to buy a fifteen percent insured tax free bond; the bonds sold themselves; you just had to find the people who had the money, and then present the product in a clear, unambiguous and knowledgeable way.

As a result of having taken accounting in grad school courses I always did particularly well prospecting accountants because I understood their language; they understood the concept of tax free returns. Accountants were also my favorites because they would refer their clients who needed tax free bonds to me. In fact, the accountant who I sold that very first Bloomfield, Connecticut tax free bond ended up becoming what we call a "center of influence." The accountant's name was Herb F., and over the years we enjoyed many breakfasts together at the greasy spoon diner that was situated below his office in a little strip mall in Bloomfield.

Herb had a nice clientele of small businessmen and semi-affluent people from the local community. Many of them were perfect candidates for high quality, high paying tax free bonds.

After years of being solicited by stock jock fakers and penny stock hustlers, Herb had finally found someone who knew all about tax free bonds, and who he could trust to do the right thing for his clients. Through Herb, I began relationships with many families which ultimately became multi-generational relationships, with me handling the accounts of everyone in the family, from the great grandparents to the great grandchildren.

About a month into prospecting, I thought that my new career was going to come to an abrupt end one day after Raymond and I spent an excessively long lunch, drinking tequila and bourbon, at out new favorite downtown bar, Brown Thompson; after which, we went for a walk on a deserted little bridge that was a few blocks away, and if someone happened to pull out a joint, we smoked it.

By the time we got back to the office, we were both a little overly mellowed, which would have been just fine except that the moment we ambled in and were walking towards our desks, Michael called us both into his office. A few moments later, I was sitting next to Raymond in front of Michael's desk.

The first thing I noticed is that Raymond reeked of marijuana smoke; I, of course, realized that if he stunk that bad, I probably didn't smell any better. Given that realization, combined with the smell of our tequila and bourbon-saturated breath drifting towards Michael, I thought it was curtains for both of us,

Michael sat there tentatively for a few moments, probably wondering about the weird kaleidoscope of strange odors that were filling his office. Then, he expressionlessly said,
"I smell burnt leaves. Do either of you smell burnt leaves?"

I didn't know what to say. I offered, "There could be a fire outside, or a tree burning somewhere." I tried to keep a straight face. I thought that he might fire us on the spot.

Michael didn't say anything.

Raymond didn't say anything; his eyes were glazed red, his lips were pursed and dried out; he looked like he was going to have a stroke.

Michael looked at Raymond, and then looked at me before half rolling his eyes. "Maybe…I'll talk to you two later. Go back to your desks."

I went to the men's room and washed my face and hands with lots of soap to get rid of the marijuana smell. I even flushed some water through my mouth to rinse it. Then I went back to my desk and stayed on the phone without a break until the end of the day.

Michael didn't call us back into his office, and he never mentioned it again.

A few weeks later, our branch office was on the move. The branch was relocating into the newest office building in Hartford, called One Corporate Center. The building immediately became known as the "Stilts Building" because it looked like a giant flashcube on concrete stilts.

The orange marbled lobby floor was bathed in sunlight from the huge skylight window above. In one section of the lobby, there were tropical plants and fountains, all beautifully landscaped. One of the best bonuses of our new location was that we were now directly across the street from Brown Thompson.

In the new building, Michael had a glassed in corner office. He positioned Raymond and I in the two desks immediately outside of his office, with Theresa sitting in the desk right in front of Raymond. When I looked to my right, I saw Michael. When I looked to my left, I saw Raymond. When I looked around the office in general, I saw all of the people that I knew I would have to overtake in order to survive.

In the old office, everyone was visually cramped together. During the few months that I spent there, it was difficult to see all of the people who were there. Except for the few brokers that I had met during the interviews, I didn't get to know very many of the people in the office until we moved.

Once we were in the new place, it was a different story. I probably spent more time in the new space than anyone else. Typically, I'd be in the office by 7:30 in the morning, and didn't leave until eight or nine in the evening, except on those days when I had to either teach or take classes at the University of Hartford.

Raymond and I would usually come in together on Saturdays, and sometimes even Sundays to prospect. A few times, I thought about buying a small dorm sized refrigerator to keep near my desk, but with Brown Thompson right across the street, it wasn't necessary. They had lots of things to eat and drink.

We were only in the new office for a few weeks when Michael had to "clean house," and fire a number of the underachieving brokers who were not cutting it in the business. This left large expanses of empty desks in the "board room" where the lower level and newer producers, like Raymond, Theresa and I, were situated.

Raymond and I called the emptiness "Desolation Row." We wondered if one day we might be next.

There was something within me that was still frightened, and scared of the possibility of washing out of the business. I resolved that I would not succumb to darkness of failure. I did not want to think too much about Desolation Row.

As the months went by, I was steadily rising in the office ranks. Raymond was doing well, but seemed to be branching out into handling more speculative clients, and doing much more stock trading than I was. Theresa was floundering, primarily because she was just too quiet, and not outgoing enough to gain the confidence of prospective clients. She always acted uncertain about what to do, and that did not encourage people to hand over large sums of money for her to invest.

As directed by Michael, who we'd taken to calling the "Wise One," we prospected exclusively for municipal bond clients. I was resourceful enough to buy a directory published by the Greater Hartford Chamber of Commerce which listed every business in the area, and included either the name of the president of the company, or the name of the head operational or financial person.

However, as Al Levy from the training class had predicted, all kinds of people were finding me, including a number of new clients who didn't want to do any investing at all; they wanted to be traders and speculators.

Within three months of going into production, I had about six clients trading options on an almost daily basis. It wasn't the kind of business that I wanted to do, but at that point in my career, I wasn't going to turn any kind of business away.

At that point in time, most branches were filled with brokers who did nothing but trading and speculating for clients in many different types of financial markets, from equity options to stock futures to commodities, and even leveraged bond trading.

Our branch had two older Italian brokers who sat together in the boardroom and did nothing but smoke Marlboros, and trade speculative equity options for clients; their names were Paulie Marsico and Angelo Trincellito.

Paulie was clearly the ring leader, and had brought Angelo in to work with him. While many brokers might have had a pack or two of cigarettes on their desk, the two of them had enough packs of Marlboros in front of them to fill a vending machine.

They would both spend hours every day, smoking, staring intently at the computer monitor, and leaning in towards each other to exchange commentary about the current market action.

Paulie was a small, skinny, swarthy looking guy with thinning short gray hair, and a deeply wrinkled and lined face that could have been a poster for a stop smoking campaign. Angelo was a short fat guy who dressed like an undertaker, usually in a black three piece suits with a white shirt and dark tie.

A few times, I went over to their area to hang around and ask questions about what they were doing in the options market. Paulie always seemed to have gum in his mouth, making odd chewing clucking kinds of sounds as he spoke. I never understood anything that he told me; it sounded like double-talk. After he finished explaining something about an option position or strategy, Angelo would nod in agreement, and I would wonder what it was that he had said. I figured that they must have kept their clients guessing as well.

I once asked Michael about the two of them. He told me that a few years before, Paulie had been a huge producer in the branch, just trading options. That was when he brought in Angelo, because Angelo was well connected with more speculative money in their "community."

However, over time, the two of them eventually blew away all of their biggest, most active trading clients, creating huge losses in their clients' accounts, and generating several pending lawsuits. Michael said that neither of them would be in the business very much longer, and they weren't.

One of my favorite people in the office was Elliot, our dedicated commodity trader. Elliot was a few years older than me and had already been in the business for over ten years trading the different commodities, all of them. Elliot traded everything, and it fascinated me. One day, he would be trading gold, cattle and soy beans, and the next day it would be pork bellies, sugar and copper.

Elliot's office was a huge mess, filled with books everywhere, charts, graphs, market information, and anything else that was commodity related. He had his own private squawk box that was connected to the main commodity trading floor, and was hooked up to all of the up to the minute commentaries on the action in all of the commodity markets.

He used a second computer monitor which displayed an array of historical commodity charts that only a specialist in the field would ever require.

Even though Elliot was already a Vice President and had a private office, he would often be in the office at night prospecting for new clients. He used a totally different approach than me, and repeatedly mentioned to the people who he had cold called that he was looking to work with them and their "higher risk capital."

After hearing his quick telephone presentation, it was abundantly clear that he was looking for clients who wanted to go for the gusto, live *la vida loca*, trading commodity markets with money that they "could afford to lose."

Elliot must have been a decent commodity trader simply because he had survived for so long in the business, and obviously some of his clients must have survived as well. He didn't have many clients at any one time, but he had one particular client that was far and away his biggest customer, and generated most of his substantial commission revenue. Elliot had nicknamed his client "God."

"God" was a retired postal worker who decided to give commodities a try after he stopped working. In the early 1980's, just about anyone was thought to be suitable for trading commodities if they could both meet the margin requirements and sign their name.

Initially, things did not go very well for God, and he lost all of his life savings trading all kinds of commodities, and being wrong all of the time.

But God persevered, and decided to cash out of his retirement accounts and use that money for another try trading the wild and crazy world of commodities. But again, he failed, and lost all of his money again.

God then sold his house, using almost all of that money to trade his way into oblivion. Elliot told me how God called all of his own shots, and Elliot just entered the orders. Elliot felt bad that God had lost so much money, but he felt that God was onto something big.

God finally stopped trading all different commodities, and started focusing on only trading orange juice futures, or "zee juice of the orange," as Elliot would say in a mock French accent.

But, it didn't help, and God lost so much of the house money that he had to go back to work, and get a full time job.

God spent several months working, accumulating more trading capital, before putting it all on the line yet again on another orange juice trade; this time, he got lucky. He was long the juice of the orange when a huge frost hit the orange crop in Florida. Orange juice futures rocketed up, up, up.

God applied even more leverage to the trade, and the orange juice futures prices continued to rise. God pressed his advantage and squeezed and squeezed and squeezed until the orange juice trade had made him eight million dollars.

That's when he became God.

God then re-retired and bought four condos on the eastern seaboard from Connecticut to Florida. Elliot had God take a few million dollars and put it into tax free muni bonds for income. The rest of the money remained in his trading account with Elliot where he used it all as "higher risk capital."

Then there was Benny. Benny was old school; he did a little bit of everything. He traded on margin for clients, sold naked options, traded some commodities, leveraged government securities, and even bought tax free mini bonds for his well healed clients.,

Benny was from somewhere in New York City. Everyone told me that they used to call him "Benny the Whip," because of the way he used to "whip" clients in and out of stock positions.

By the time I met him, Benny was already in his mid to late sixties, and rarely wore suits to work, preferring more casual attire like chino pants and flannel shirts.

Benny knew a lot about a lot of things, but trying to get him to share the information was like pulling teeth. When asked a question, he would offer a minimalist answer, colored with the clear impression that he didn't want to be bothered. Benny generally showed a clear disdain for the newer brokers and trainees in the office,

I saw Benny as a fountain of knowledge that I wished to draw from. I had no problem taking his berating and verbal abuse if I could get him to answer my questions. I usually used our New York City connection to engage him. After about a year, I could see that I was starting to grow on him.

But I wasn't old school, and I didn't want to trade commodities or options. I wanted to emulate the more down to earth successful brokers who bought tax free bonds and blue chip stocks for their clients, set up custodial accounts for their children, and managed the trusts of their clients' parents. I didn't want to be a bookie.

So, I just kept dialing and dialing, looking for more clients, and I kept finding all kinds of them out there.

CHAPTER 7

BE MY EYES, RAYMOND

For a few years early on, Raymond and I sat next to each other in what was called a "quad," which was four broker desks set up in a square. The two front desks were separated from the two back desks by a low divider with glass on top of it.

Our quad was right next to the branch manager's large office which was enclosed in glass. Michael, the branch manager could always see us, and we could always see him. Seeing him sitting there kept us working and busy. That was a good thing.

The back of our quad was like a little spaceship where Raymond and I were co-pilots, navigating through the swirling darkness of the stock market. We did all sorts of dumb things to have fun while we were practically living in the office, working amazingly long hours, and trying to build up a client base.

In between endless cold calling, we'd sit back and watch our screens, observing all of the movements in the market universe. Way before there was a CNBC, we would sometimes take turns acting as commentators of the stock market action. However, our commentary was more like little funny skits, often with horse-racing announcer voices.

I might start with something like, "Raymond, I can see definite selling action in the pits in Chicago from here...yes I can *indeed*...the futures are diving...*yes diving*...lower and lower and lower they go...the traders are being *crushed*... I see bodies being carried out."

Almost everybody smoked. Sometimes certain areas of the office would be enveloped in a smoke cloud when four smoking brokers sat together in a quad. Raymond smoked menthols; I smoked regulars. We always had variety.

Working so closely together, we both got to know a lot of each other's clients. When one of us was away from the desk, the other one would take any calls that came in. Since we both had a number of actively trading clients, we often entered client orders for each other.

In the financial markets, when a speculative position becomes profitable, someone needs to be available to take action to grab the profit, because markets rarely give you a second chance.

One of my favorite clients of Raymond's who I never actually met, was a retired guy named Russ. Russ was in his 70's and fairly wealthy by 1980's standards. He had a stock portfolio with Raymond of about two million dollars, and he traded it in an insane and totally out of control manner.

It didn't help that Russ was also a habitual alcoholic; he was drunk by 9:00 in the morning.

Russ would do things like buy ten different stocks in the morning at the open, add five more before noon, sell off half of all the positions after lunch, and then buy five totally different stocks at the close.

His stocks of choice were always blue chip issues like GE, IBM or AT&T, or any other major company that you might find in the Dow or the S&P.

Russ did not trade small quantities; he preferred 500 to 1000 share lots of moderately to high priced stocks. Russ' account gave "trading velocity" a new meaning. The guy turned over thousands of shares every day; Raymond was making a fortune in commissions, even after giving him all kinds of discounts.

Russ was far and away Raymond's biggest client in terms of revenue generation. I didn't have anyone even close in terms of generating the volume of business that Russ did.

Fortunately, Russ did not trade every single day; most days, maybe, but not every single day. This allowed Raymond to handle his other clients.

The truth is that some days Russ was just too drunk to trade, and he'd be sleeping all day. Sometimes, Raymond would try to reach him about some position which needed tending, but when Russ was gone, he was way gone.

Russ was fun to talk to. He definitely enjoyed our racetrack kind of commentary throughout the market day. Since this was the era before the advent of financial news TV stations, most active market participants got their market information directly from their brokers, either during, or after the trading day. It was commonplace that after the market closed each day, a number of clients would call their respective brokers to get end of the day quotes on the stocks that they owned or were "watching."

Russ would have loved CNBC, and the ability to get quotes on his home computer and so would Raymond, because Russ would call just about every day to get closing quotes on all of his stocks. Sometimes he would own fifty or sixty issues at a time; sometimes way more. Raymond would patiently go through the positions one by one, taking notes as to what trades Russ wanted to enter before the market open the next morning.

Even when Russ was totally polluted, and could not make any trades during the morning or afternoon, he would usually muster up enough consciousness to call Raymond at the end of the day for quotes. Russ was fond of saying, "Be my eyes, Raymond; be my eyes."

I guess that's what they mean by being blind drunk. Sometimes, Russ did in fact make money; and then again, sometimes he didn't. During some days, there were so many trades happening that it was hard for Raymond to keep track of what was going on.

At one point, Russ had been doing a lot of buying, but very little selling for a few days, so he owned nearly a hundred different stocks.

It was about then that Raymond was out of the office for a few days, and I had to deal with Russ on my own. Russ took it easy with me for the first two days, only putting in a handful of orders here and there. He usually sounded tipsy on the phone, but seemed to have a handle as to what was going on. I pointed out to him that I wasn't that familiar with many of the stocks in his portfolio, so I preferred not to make any sort of buy or sell recommendations, but Russ didn't need my opinion to do whatever it was that he was going to do anyway.

The third day that Raymond was out of the office, the market was having a bad day. It wasn't a cataclysm, or anything like that, just your garden variety ugly, down market day. But Russ didn't see it like that.

When he called me after the stock market opened that morning, he was already totally wasted, don't light a match near him, drunk as a skunk.

Russ seemed to think that this was the beginning of a great market apocalypse. Whatever had spooked him, he thought the end was near. I thought it was the whiskey talking.

He said, "Don...be my eyes...Don....I need you to be my eyes."

I said, "Russ... but maybe we should wait...."

"Be my eyes, Don," he repeated more emphatically.

"Russ...Russ...what is it you want me to do?" I pleaded.

"Don...Sell me out. Sell everything!"

"*Everything?* But Russ, you have about a hundred positions. All of them? You mean *all of them?*"

"Don, sell me out...be my eyes......*help me, please.*"

"Um, sure Russ." I felt bad for the guy. I wanted to do whatever he wanted me to. "Let me start writing up the orders. I'll call you back as soon as I get the executions."

"Don...thank you for being my eyes."

"Glad I could help Russ."

So I sat there and wrote all of the tickets, and entered all of the orders, and then reported all of the trades to Russ. He was relieved, and then went to bed.

When Raymond got back the next day there was a pile nearly six inches high of confirmations on his desk. He made about $15,000 in commissions. I don't know how Russ did.

Raymond asked me what happened, so I told him the whole story. He thanked me. And then the phone rang. It was Russ wanting to enter some orders.

CHAPTER 8

Gurus, Granville, and Gann Angles

Just as **The Beatles had their guru**, Wall Street participants have had a long succession of their own of gurus over the decades; all of them promising profits and financial success from the financial markets if only you will follow their methods, and in most cases, subscribe to their respective market newsletters and telephone market update services.

When I began my career in 1981, one of the most powerful market voices was that of Joe Granville.

Joe combined the talents of a stock market technician, and a showman. Sometimes he came to speaking engagements dressed up as Moses. Sometimes, Joe would emerge from a coffin, or even appear to walk across water.

My first year in the business, our Bache branch in Hartford sponsored an investment seminar featuring Joe Granville. Hundreds of people came to hear Joe speak at the Bushnell Memorial Coliseum in Hartford.

Granville was in his prime. He grabbed everyone's attention when he walked out onto the stage with a giant iguana lizard on a leash.

We were "lucky" to be able to get Granville as a speaker. Joe had come to small town Hartford, Connecticut primarily because a relative worked in our branch as an aspiring young stockbroker.

Joe Granville's initial claim to fame had been the development of his *On Balance Volume* theories which basically used "volume," the amount of shares traded, to predict future price moves by both individual stocks, as well as the overall stock market itself. By identifying patterns of "accumulation" (buying) and "distribution" (selling), Joe had apparently made some right-on the-money market calls in the 1970's and very early 1980's. He outlined and expounded on his theories in his manifesto entitled *Granville's New Strategy of Daily Stock Market Timing for Maximum Profit* published in 1976.

But Joe's ego soon eclipsed his sanity, and he began predicting natural events like earthquakes, which didn't occur. He once claimed to have predicted six of the past seven major world quakes. His predictions went far beyond the narrow worlds of the financial markets, which he claimed to have conquered when he said "I don't think that I will make a serious mistake in the stock market for the rest of my life."

As you might expect, it didn't take nearly that long for Joe to be wrong, very wrong.

Unfortunately, this coincided with the period where his cousin, Burton, was a relatively new stockbroker trying to build his career on the coat tails of the great Joe Granville. For a brief time, Burton was like the surrogate voice of God, interpreting and disseminating all of Joe's writings and utterances for an eager audience of investors who wanted to hitch their money onto Joe Granville's star.

Burton had been with the firm for two or three years, and his clients were mostly Granville devotees. He was likable, but haughty, based on his connections with what he saw as a higher power.

Burton looked a lot like Groucho Marks, bushy black hair, a big dark mustache, thick black eyebrows; but he didn't wear glasses, and he wasn't funny.

Raymond, the Big Man, and I had both read Granville's book, and while it was fascinating and actually did create an entirely new methodology in stock market technical analysis, it certainly didn't seem to relate to predicting earthquakes, or any of the more esoteric pronouncements for which Granville was getting most of his press.

From my inner city Brooklyn perspective, I liked Joe's *On Balance Volume* theories, but I knew a huckster when I saw one; so it wasn't surprising to me when Joe Granville quickly became the clown of Wall Street.

A little over a year after I arrived at the firm, Joe Granville's rapid demise from grace commenced when the Great Bull Market of the 1980's began to roar in August 1982.

I can actually remember the exact day of the stock market liftoff. The Big Man and I were watching what appeared to be an unusually strong stock market rally. The stock market volume was exploding upwards at a record pace. Stock prices were jumping like catfish in a dried out pond. There was something going on in the stock market that the Big Man and I had not yet seen, and could not fully comprehend.

Bob Krohn earned his nickname "Krohny's-no-Baloney" that day when he came over to the quad where Raymond and I sat, and stated confidently that this very day was the beginning of a great and thunderous bull market rally that would go on for years. He proceeded to tell us all the reasons why, from falling interest rates, to the economy which was finally showing signs of beginning to recover from the recession.

I didn't fully comprehend all that he was saying, but the market was definitely going up like a mother. By the end of the day it had made an historic move in terms of both prices and stock market volume.

Ironically, Joe Granville's theories were all based on the volume patterns in the stock market. When Raymond and I saw the magnitude of the stock market volume that day, almost all of it on the buy side, it was clear that this would generate a huge *On Balance Volume* "buy signal."

We all awaited Granville's observations and conclusions, which soon came, with surprising results.

Joe saw the historic market move as a huge fake out, a con, a false signal. He urged his followers not to buy, but to sell, and then to short stocks, which is to play them to profit on downward moves in stock prices.

I sure didn't get it.

The Big Man remarked, "Say it ain't so, Joe." According to our amateurish interpretation of the tenets of *On Balance Volume*, it sure looked like a brave new world to the upside, but Joe said it wasn't, and of course, Burton said it wasn't; and that wasn't good for either Burton's or Joe's clients.

The lift off of the Great Bull market was not of huge relevance for either Raymond or me at the time because we were much more focused on building our businesses with clients who wanted to buy tax free bonds, and not stocks. There were double digit tax free interest rates available on the municipal bonds of the era, and it was far easier to get someone to buy an insured ten percent tax free bond than it was to get them to buy stocks in an uncertain market to get an uncertain return.

In contrast, just about all of Burton's clients were involved in trading stocks, on both the long side and the short side. So, when the market started going up, up, up, and Burton kept positioning his clients totally opposite the strong trend in the market, their account values started to go down, down, down. Very soon, Burton started losing clients who had lost substantial amounts of money, as well as their faith and belief in the wisdom and judgment of the Granville guru.

Things went from bad to worse over the coming months for the Granville followers as the market moved ceaselessly upwards with barely a pause. Each Granville pronouncement became more and more bearish. Not only did he want his minions to short the market, and play only the downside, he suggested that they now use margin to leverage their positions to quickly make back their substantial losses.

That definitely didn't work, and Burton began hemorrhaging clients who had lost significant amounts of money, with several threatening to sue both him and the firm. It hadn't taken long. It was clear the end was near for Burton's career. Not long after the market had risen hundreds of points and pierced upwards to never before seen new highs in the stock market, Burton's desk in the office was empty; he was gone; the first victim of a guru gone bad that I had ever personally seen.

Interestingly, Joe Granville stayed bearish through most of the violent uptrend that characterized the first few years of the bull market, absolutely destroying and annihilating his followers in the process. His performance was so abysmal for so long that in "Wikipedia" it states that *The Granville Market Letter* "is at the bottom of the Hulbert Financial Digest's rankings for performance over the past 25 years – having produced average losses of more than 20 percent per year on an annualized basis."

In 1986, I found my own guru; one who had been right about the market going up, up, up.

My guru's earthly manifestation was Robert Prechter who wrote a newsletter called the *Elliot Wave Theorist*. But it wasn't Prechter that intrigued me, as much as it was the Elliot Wave Theory itself.

Briefly, Elliot Wave theory relates the movement of prices in the financial markets to the natural mathematical relationships that are inherent in nature. For example, relating the patterns of a rising market to the patterns inherent in things like sea shells or the spirals in a galaxy,

As an ex-hippie, a theory that related the behavior of the financial markets to the cycles and patterns in nature really appealed to me. Elliot Wave was something that seemed to make more and more sense when you studied it by candlelight with incense burning, listening to *Kashmir* by Led Zeppelin playing in the background.

Prechter did not create the Elliot Wave Theory, he only popularized it by using it with astounding success from the 1970's into the 1980's, with his ultimate peak in popularity coming soon after the Crash of 1987.

Unlike Granville, Prechter was on target with his market predictions for years before I had even heard of him. If anything, I was an extreme Johnny come lately, because by 1986, Prechter had been very right for a very long time.

As the Dow Jones industrial average soared through 1000, then 1500, then 2000, Prechter had long pointed to Dow 3686 as the precise end point of the great bull market run.

Though I might have been late to the party, I still had plenty of time to make money for both myself and my clients.

I began when I started to subscribe to Prechter's *Elliot Wave Theorist* newsletter. It was just about then that I began a personal speculative trading run that was the talk of the local broker community for years.

Utilizing the wisdom and guidance of the interpreter of the cosmic wave patterns, as channeled by Bob Prechter, I began trading stock index options for both myself and my clients on a daily, sometimes hourly, sometimes minute to minute basis, with astounding results.

I was making so much money for both my clients and myself that I decided to invest a larger sum of my own money to subscribe to Prechter's telephone hot line service which was updated daily, and sometime more often, if market conditions dictated. It was a direct line to hear the words of the man himself.

No intermediaries, no interpreters, just the actual voice of the prophet offering trading guidance and market enlightenment for a substantial semi-annual fee. There were also live personal consultations available via private telephone call-ins for a rather substantial minute to minute charge. I never went quite that far.

For several months, the Elliot Wave and I were in sync with the forces in the market universe. In my personal account, I had a streak of 29 trades that began with 18 winning trades in a row, a single break even trade, and then 10 more profitable trades in a row. On some days I was so busy counting the waves and analyzing the small undulations in the stock market that I did little, if any, business with clients. I was my own best client.

It was thrilling to make tens of thousands of dollars at a time trading, as well as getting to keep the substantial commissions that were being generated. I ultimately ran about eight thousand dollars into over six hundred thousand dollars. No one was more impressed with me than me. I went and bought a silver Porsche 924, and planned to get a license plate that said WAVE1.

The first sign for me that things were about to turn was near the end of the streak when each morning a crowd of brokers would gather around my desk to hear the wisdom of the Elliot Wave from both myself and the call in service that I shared with others.

One day, I looked around and saw six wanting greedy faces staring at me when I realized that I had now become the office guru. I realized that I had become the new Burton, and it made me very uncomfortable. I began to feel the possibility of impending doom coming my way.

Once again, it didn't take long for the tide to turn, and when it did, it began with a two hundred thousand dollar loss on a single trade in my own account. The wave had hit me in the back of the head, knocked me down, and was going to try to finish me off.

All of a sudden, I couldn't make a profitable trade if I was on both sides of the market, which I tried on several occasions. The wave wasn't working. My own analysis was worthless because I had no idea where we were in the wave structure. I couldn't tell if we were in a primary wave down, or a sub wave up, or were experiencing a change in trend through an X wave.

I was messed up wave wise.

The crowds around my desk thinned away to nothing. When you're hot, you're hot, and when you're not; you are an office leper.

There is an old market saying that one should "never confuse brains with a bull market." In retrospect, I made money simply because I rode one of the strongest and dynamic up trends in the history of the stock market. If you were long, you almost couldn't help making money. Once the market became choppy, the waves became murkier and harder to interpret. It was like trying to swim far out in the ocean during a storm, and you can't see which direction shore is; all of the waves are splashing and breaking around you, as you struggle to stay afloat.

I eventually recovered from the pounding of the surf, and slowly crawled back onto the shore of solvency, fortunately, with some of my money still in my possession. I hadn't lost it all; a good chunk of it, but not all of it.

To Bob Prechter's credit, he soon made one his best stock market calls when he told his followers to get out of the market shortly before the Crash of 1987. To his detriment though, once the market finally did crash, he became even more bearish, predicting that the Dow Industrial Average would wall to the ungodly low level of 32, a level commensurate with the end of human civilization on the planet as we know it.

Then, in blinding Granvillian similarity, he remained bearish for years as the Dow rose thousands of points. He subsequently destroyed and annihilated the portfolios of his followers by having them short the next huge up phase of the continuing great bull market.

As Yogi Berra once said, it was like "déjà vu all over again."

A year or two later, the firm recruited a slimy looking broker from another firm named Joe P. who coincidentally had the same name as a famous guitar player. But this Joe wore cheap three piece polyester suits, and had a thin wispy mustache, a slightly pockmarked face, greasy looking dark hair, and a sleazy quality that reminded me of some of the strung out hustler types that you'd see hanging out in front of the seedy bars in Brooklyn.

Joe was a chain smoker extraordinaire, with a huge ashtray filled with a small mountain of cigarette butts, with burnt out cigarettes balanced all along the large rim of the ashtray. There were always several red packs of Pall Malls on his desk, along with several large cups of colored pencils, different kinds of measuring and drawing tools like rulers, compasses and protractors, as well as several different kinds of graph paper.

Joe needed all of the equipment because he was deeply into "Gann Angles," a barely remembered market theory named after W.D Gann who described the use of angles in the stock market in his *The Basis of My Forecasting Method*, a 33 page course published in 1935. According to Wikipedia, calculating a Gann Angle is "the equivalent to finding the derivative of a particular line on a chart in a simple way."

I spoke to Joe P. about Gann angles, at length, at least ten times, and really never understood what is was all about. Even when I did my own independent reading of Gann's theories, I couldn't make heads or tails out of how to use the angles to predict stock market movements going forward, but then, either could Joe.

Joe had several sheets of large graph paper spread in front of him, and each sheet would be covered in artistically dazzling displays of multi-colored lines, angles, channels, and market patterns in a wide variety of colors. For hours each day, Joe would be sitting at his desk, smoking cigarettes, drawing strange lines with his red, blue and green pencils that intersected other lines of brown, orange and black.

Sometimes, he would show me charts filled with more colors that the aurora borealis, and would then ask me if I could see what it all meant; but I couldn't see it. I didn't understand it then, and I don't understand it now.

Joe may have understood it, but the problem was that he didn't seem to have very many clients who wanted to trade stocks based on Gann angles. He wasn't getting paid to sit, draw and smoke; it was expected that he would be using his "insights" to make money for his clients, which he seemed to have very few of.

Apparently, most of his clients that he had at the previous firm chose not to follow him when he moved to our firm. This usually happens when a broker loses money for their clients. Whether or not Gann Angles worked, it didn't matter if it didn't translate into making money for people. From the moment he arrived in our office, Joe P. struggled to survive.

While I didn't pay close attention to whatever Joe was trading, I did notice that there was nothing distinctive about his results; he seemed to lose money just like everyone else. The angles did not seem to provide any additional edge to Joe's trading results. As the months rolled on, Joe's production steadily dropped, as more and more of his clients moved on, looking for the next hot hand.

However, instead of trying to maintain or expand his business, Joe seemed to spend more and more time each day drawing and smoking. Often, he would have this wide eyed obsessed look at he sat in his quad crushing out cigarettes in his ashtray and muttering to himself. His behavior seemed somehow familiar, but I didn't realize why, until the office Christmas party arrived that winter.

The party was at a beautiful country club in the hills of Avon, Connecticut. Most of the people from the office were there, everyone dressed to the nines. Near the end of the cocktail party before dinner, I went into the Men's room to find Joe standing there with a wide manic look in his eyes, holding open the door of one of the bathroom stalls.

He called to me and asked me to look inside the stall. I couldn't imagine why, until I looked and saw at least half a dozen thick long lines of cocaine neatly arranged on top of the toilet tank.

Joe invited me to do a few lines.

I could not believe what I was seeing. Apparently, Joe had gotten so lit that he lost all common sense and had no grasp of reality or remembrance that I was also the Assistant Manager of the office.

I personally cared less if Joe wanted to do coke, or anything else, but to bring it to the office party and flagrantly offer it to whoever might have wandered into the bathroom was beyond insane. I told him to immediately remove the drugs and get back to the party. But of course, he didn't listen, and must have offered the blow to other people who were not as open minded as I was.

It was no surprise that by the time I got into the office on the following Monday morning, Joe had already been fired. No more colored pencils, no more Gann angles; no more gurus, at least for a while.

CHAPTER 9

A New Way of Living

When I was first hired by Michael, Debbie didn't think I had a prayer of being successful. Quite to the contrary, she espoused the much more practical, but demeaning view that "at least you'll collect a salary for a while."

Certainly, the sixteen thousand dollars a year that I was being paid during training wasn't the most impressive salary. The salary only lasted for up to a year, and then it was strictly commissions. Any supplementary income from writing rock reviews quickly dried up when I joined Bache.

Like most Wall Street firms, Bache had very specific rules regarding their brokers writing for any outside publications. All articles had to be reviewed and edited by the Legal and Compliance Departments prior to publication. There was a whole process that needed to be followed; even the branch manager had to be involved.

I did not want to bring unnecessary and unwanted attention to myself, as I was training and trying to make a good impression, so very shortly after joining the firm, I put the writing on the back burner.

My focus was on doing whatever it took to succeed in the business; there was no way that I was going to let myself fail. I didn't care how many hours a day or how many days a week that I had to work.

I lived in the office. I prospected all of the time, and most importantly, I found that I genuinely loved the business. It was like it wasn't even work. I entertained myself endlessly by calling strangers all day and into the night, opening accounts, buying tax free bonds, and I continued to learn all about of the financial markets.

My interests extended outside of the realm of the office. I began reading and studying the history of the financial markets. I bought books about the different historical periods in the stock market. I read about the stock markets of the early 1800's, the Civil War era, the Great Depression, the World War II era, and everything before and after.

I was struck how the markets never really change; they, as one broker once told me, "just change the names of the players and of the companies to protect the innocent."

I read about how the "great man" J.P Morgan saved the banks. How Jesse Livermore shorted the stock market after the San Francisco earthquake in 1908 and made a fortune. I read about the great traders and speculators of the different eras; how they all had their own theories about divining the direction of both the stock market and of individual stocks.

I discovered that while the stock market Crash of 1929 is widely known and written about, there were also panics in 1819, 1837, 1857, 1873 and 1893 that no one ever talks about, but were blindingly meaningful to the market participants of those eras. I learned that, if you stick around long enough, you will have the opportunity to see financial markets collapse quite regularly. Further, sometimes, it will seem like the system is about to self-destruct and, crumble as civilization is thrown back to the Dark Ages.

However, as history continually demonstrates, it never actually happens that way. The panic comes, and then the panic wanes. This is eventually followed by complacency, until some conflagration of events begins to rouse the animal spirits of investors. Then, suddenly the markets again begin to rise, inciting yet a new cycle of opportunism, enthusiasm and greed. In other words, same as it ever was.

The cycles of creation and destruction in the financial markets are analogous to the tides of the ocean, with the waves rising above and then falling below the shoreline. Over the first few years in the business, I learned much market wisdom. I didn't see my profession as so much of a job, as much as a way of life.

The number of clients that I had developed multiplied rapidly. The revenues that I generated grew steadily and strongly with each passing month, until, just a few months into production, I decided to ditch the training salary and go on straight commission; it was time to sink or swim, and there was no way that I was going down.

I never stopped working; I never looked back. That first year I made over fifty thousand dollars, followed by a long string of six figure incomes.

After about three years in the business, I was already in the top ten in the office. What amazed me was that it didn't even seem like work. I looked forward to coming in every day and playing on the phone, buying securities, watching the markets, meeting new people. It was like being in a professional playland, and getting paid a lot of money to be there.

I used to say that I was having so much fun at work that I would do it for free.

A short time after I completed my MBA in 1984, Michael called me into his office.
Michael wanted me to take the Series 8, which is the licensing exam for people who want to be Branch Managers. I asked him why he wanted me to take the exam, and he told me that he needed someone else to be his back up in the office.

Up until that point, the broker in charge when Michael was out of the branch was Benny the Whip. However, Benny could be rude and abrasive, and was prone to drinking from the bottle of booze that he kept stashed in his desk. Sometimes he became downright belligerent to anyone who came into his office.

I liked Benny, and I knew that this wouldn't go over well with him. .I told Michael that I had no particular interest in running a branch. I liked just being a broker.

Michael responded by telling me that I "owed him" for hiring me, and he wanted me to take the exam, period. Then he handed me a large package that had all of the study material and practice tests for the exam.

He had his new assistant, Michelle, make an appointment for me to take the exam in a few weeks. His reasoning was that the business was changing, and I represented the new guard, armed with an MBA in Finance, and a fresh approach to the markets.

To Michael, Benny the Whip represented the old line brokers of the 60's and 70's who were basically glorified bookies who churned and burned their clients' accounts for commissions, and spent their off time at the race track or OTB. Benny wasn't anything like a classic churn and burn broker, but he certainly did like spending his days off at the casinos in Atlantic City, and at the racetracks in New York.

Over the next few weeks, I studied the exam material the way a reformed sinner studies the Bible.

I took my study books everywhere I went, reading them in every corner of every moment that I could squeeze in. I repeatedly took every sample test exam, until I saw the questions flashing by my eyes as I fell asleep. The material was challenging, and there was a lot of it.

The exam itself was quite lengthy, taking several hours to complete at the computer testing center. When it was finally all done, I pushed the button on the computer to get my score. It was a 93.7; I was disappointed, I was going for 100.

As I walked out of the testing center, the lady at the front desk asked me how it had went. I told her my score and how I was disappointed. It made me feel better when she told me that it was the highest score that she had seen in this testing center, and that she had seen grown men leaving that test in tears.

When I got back to the office, Michael mentioned at the next office meeting that I had passed the Series 8 exam, and I would be "helping" him out in the office, effectively becoming the Assistant Manager. I don't think that anyone particularly cared, except for Benny, who later told me that I had "stabbed him in the back."

I tried to explain that I hadn't done anything of the kind, but Benny was mortally offended, and did not talk to me for over a year. In the meantime, I soon began to find out what a pain it is to try to supervise a branch full of supposedly bright financial professionals.

My first test was when Michael was out of the office for the day. As the stock market close approached, I could see one of the younger brokers in the office, Evan, leading several other brokers towards the conference room. I guess that I was preoccupied at the time so I really didn't think anything of it until Evan came over to my desk and said, "Hey, Don, come on into the conference room; I've got something that I want to show the guys."

As I followed Evan into the conference room, I asked him what he was showing, thinking that it might be some product or seminar presentation.

"*Debbie Does Dallas.*" he replied.

I was astounded. I had never seen the film, but knew that it was a hard core porn flick. It just didn't seem possible that anyone with any sense at all would bring a porn flick in to work to play in the conference room during business hours. No one could have so little common sense. I was wrong.

This would not be either the first or last time that Evan would demonstrate an absurd level of stupidity

As soon as Evan started the film, there was a woman on the screen sucking on some guy's dick. I stared blankly at the screen, numb, for a few minutes, taking in the reality of what was going on. The conference room door was still open, and right outside the door sat a sales assistant named Carol. From the look on her face, I'm sure Carol hadn't gotten laid in years, and deeply resented anyone who had.

As the groans started emanating from the screen, Carol looked into the conference room and saw what was going on, as her face became flushed. She gave me the look of death, and then proceeded to slam shut the conference room door, and turn her back to the glass wall which separated the conference room form the rest of the office.

Evan walked over to the glass, and pulled the curtains closed across the glass wall so that the people outside couldn't see in. "Fuck her," he said, "What a fucking bitch."

I realized that he obviously shouldn't be playing a porn movie in the conference room, and told him that he had to stop the movie and put it away.

"Fuck you, too," he responded, "You're not in fucking charge."

I looked at the four or five other brokers who were in the conference room and told them that this was totally inappropriate, and Michael was going to be very pissed when he found out.

"He's only going to be mad if you squeal on us." Evan replied defiantly.

"I don't have to," I replied. "She will." I added pointing to where Carol sat on the other side of the curtained in conference room wall. With that, I walked out of the room, with two of the other brokers following me.

The next day, I saw Carol walking out of Michael's office as I was walking in towards my desk. Michael motioned for me to come into the office, which I did, and related all that had happened in the conference room, without offering a recap of the movie.

I never understood why Michael didn't fire Evan that day. It was probably because he knew that Evan's wife was pregnant with their first child. Evan survived his meeting with Michael, and lived on to screw up many more times.

While Evan may have seen the office as a movie theater, several other people saw it more as a hotel room.

One night, I had a particularly nasty argument with Debbie, and I needed to escape to somewhere quiet so I could just gather my thoughts; so I decided to go into my office at about ten in the evening.

Our office building was always open if you had a pass to get in. There were several companies in the building that ran night shifts, so it wasn't unusual to see people coming and going at odd hours. Everyone who worked in the branch had their own key to get into our office whenever they wanted to.

Although I often worked late, I had never been in the office quite that late at night. It was very quiet as I got off the elevator and approached the locked front door of our office, but the door wasn't locked.

When I opened the door and looked into the darkened reception area, I could see two people lying together on the plush wide brown couch. When they saw me, they began scurrying to put on their clothes. I could see in the shadows that it was Jason, a young married broker in the office, and a long haired blond woman who I recognized as a receptionist for another company in the building.

I decided not to say a thing, and walked right past the two of them, and headed to the far side of the office area, to my own office in the corner of the building. I sat there staring at the empty street below for about an hour, and then headed to Brown Thompson for a drink, before returning home.

The incident didn't seem to me like it was a "reportable event," so I decided to forget about it, but it didn't want to just go away.

The following week, Michael was out of the office again when Sharon, the Operations Manager, asked me to come into her office to see what we had received in the mail.

At any branch office, there is always someone who opens, inspects and sorts the mail when it comes in. Since every branch office receives a lot of checks and securities in the mail, this is a necessary procedure to make sure that no one has sticky fingers with negotiable securities and the like.

Sharon showed me a long five page letter to Jason, handwritten in red ink, ostensibly from the blonde woman who was in the reception area with Jason. The letter outlined, in vivid detail, her expectations of their next meeting, and rambled on about her love and passion for Jason, and how she wanted him to leave his wife and come be with her.

There was quite a bit of graphic description and language in the letter. I had never received a letter anything like it in my life; it was hot.

The issue was what to do with the letter. It certainly didn't simplify the situation when Sharon showed me a second letter just like the first that had come in the same mail shipment. It looked to both Sharon and I that there were likely to be a lot more letters like these coming in the future, so we had no choice but to bring the matter to Michael's attention.

Michael was not pleased. He told Jason that if the branch received one more letter, he would forward them all to Jason's wife. The branch did receive another two hot torrid letters the next day; however, after that, Jason somehow made them stop.

Perhaps, it was the stress of the job, but it seems that there were always a lot of illicit romances going on in the office. Even Michael had met his own second wife Lois when he hired her to be his executive secretary and sales assistant. Through the years, he has said that I was his second best hire ever, next to Lois. I've always said that's just because he got to sleep with her.

But Michael was certainly not the exception. There were at least two or three other brokers in the office who married people who were at one time their sales assistants.
Many of the office relationships were just flings, though.

One Sunday afternoon, I happened to come into the office to weed through all of the paperwork and reports that had piled up around my desk, when I saw Sharon, the Operations Manager scurrying out the side door of the office with Fred, the smooth talking options trader with a beard and a sports car.

They were both, of course, married to other people. They both had obviously heard someone come into the office, and quickly finished whatever they were doing. They saw me, and offered only the quickest of passing hellos as they ducked out the side door, with Sharon giggling about something.

A little later, I happened to pass by the conference room and noticed that the door was open, so I looked inside. It was hard to miss that one end of the conference room table was angled down to the floor as if something had caused the legs on that end of the table to collapse, as if perhaps someone had leaned a bit too hard on that side.

The room smelled of perfume. There were a number of chairs in curious places. Now I knew why Sharon was giggling. I thought that the table legs would have been stronger than that.

My only involvement with anyone that I had worked with came about several years later when the firm, hired a young woman named Susan to be the receptionist. Susan was about twenty one, and chewed gum a lot when she wasn't talking on the phone.

Susan was one of the most beautiful women that I've ever seen. She had long brown hair, dazzling blue eyes, full lips, and looked like Carmen Electra, but with a better body, if such a thing were possible. She had the most striking blue eyes…so blue that when you spoke to her, you felt enveloped in the blueness, like an aura surrounding you.

I was over ten years older, and not her type at all. She liked biker guys, not married older stockbrokers. Nonetheless, we developed a strange friendship based on drinking tequila shots and eating warm brie cheese with crackers and apples at Brown Thompson.

The only physical relationship that we ever had together was one Christmas season, when after excessive amount of Cuervo Gold shots, she gave me a big wet kiss in the parking lot before sending me home to my wife.

During one drinking session, the song "Suzie Q" started playing in the bar. Susan really liked the song, and started singing along out loud at the bar.

It was about then that I began calling her "Q," a nickname that would stick for a long time.

Q and I were to end up having some interesting times together, but those was later on, after I left Debbie, still another life away.

CHAPTER 10

OPTION EXPIRATION AND THE EMERGENCY ROOM

Prior to the **stock market crash of 1987**, everyone traded index options; this included clients, brokers, branch managers, and even the back office staff. Index options are "derivative" securities which are essentially a bet on the direction that the overall stock market will go; either up or down. The simplicity of the up or down concept attracted many types of traders and speculators.

Trading index options required very little analysis compared to buying the stocks of individual companies which tied the investor's fortunes to the earnings and profitability of the companies being invested in. As the stock market continued to climb in the early and mid-eighties, the volume of index option trading exploded across Wall Street and Main Street.

At that time, the most popular index option was the OEX, which was really the S&P 100, an index of the top 100 stocks in the S&P 500. Buying call options on the OEX was a bet that the market would go up, and buying puts on the OEX was a bet that the market would go down.

Another index option that became very popular with traders called the XMI, nicknamed "the rocket." The XMI was an index made of 10 stocks from the Dow Industrial average. The price of the XMI index moved with amazing volatility when the stock market went up or down. If you were on the right side of the market, it was Heaven; if you were on the wrong side of the market, it was Hell.

In the spring of 1986, my son Ethan was almost two years old, and I had become a high stakes option trader for my own account. I used to trade the XMI almost on a daily basis.

The reason that I was trading the XMI on such a regular basis is that I was on one of those once in a lifetime streaks that all gamblers dream of. I had started a few months prior with about $8,000 of what we used to call "risk capital." And all of a sudden, I had parlayed the eight grand into over a hundred thousand dollars, and it appeared at the time that I was just warming up.

I had read a few books about gambling theory. One book discussed "streaks" of good luck or bad luck. It said that when gambling, it is important to determine whether you are on a long streak, a short streak, or a streak of indeterminate length. If you can identify that you are on a long winning streak, ride it as far as it will take you. If you are on a long losing streak, go home and come back another day.

I seemed to be on one of those long winning streaks, and I wanted to reach up and touch the sky. Strangely, the trading streak all started with something that I had seen on TV one morning while I was watching Sesame Street with my two year old son, Ethan.

Sesame Street would always feature a letter and a word of the day for the little kids to learn. This one particular morning, I was watching with Ethan, both of us sitting on the big red sectional couch. I will never forget that the letter of the day was M, and the word for the day was UP.

It was one of those things that you realize is a sign as soon as you see it.

As soon as I got to the office, I hit Raymond with the news. The letter of the day was M, and the word of the day was UP. Raymond didn't quite get it, so I made it clearer.

"Raymond, the M stands for 3M (symbol MMM), and UP means it is going up."

Raymond looked at me like I was on drugs.

"Raymond, we need to buy call options on 3M; lots of them, all of them."

Options on a particular stock are referred to as "equity options." These kinds of options tie your fate, not to the market's ups and downs, like index options, but to the ups and downs of the stock in a particular company. In this case, it was 3M Corp., most widely known for their Scotch Tape.

Call it a leap of faith, call it blind dumb luck, call it the magic of believing in silly things, but Raymond and I bought several hundred 3M call options at ¼ ($25 each) and sold them for 4 ($400 each) within a week or two. I had about 200 options, but Raymond only had 50.

I cleared nearly $75,000 on the trade. All of a sudden I had a pile of "their money," and I was willing to risk it all to make even more.

Now, I was reasonably well capitalized to do some far more aggressive trading, and index options were the forbidden fruit. I started trading the index options, cautiously at first. However it quickly began to appear that I was on one of those long winning streaks. I continued to watch Sesame Street every day.

They say that when you're hot, you're hot; and I soon discovered that when you're *really* hot, even mistakes can turn in your favor. Well, I had one of those. It was the first time that I had bought as many as 200 index option calls.

I thought that the market was going to go up, up, up. But minutes after I entered the order, I was horrified when I went back to my desk and saw on the monitor that the market had suddenly turned sharply down. A voice from the squawk box on my desk started yelling that there were "sell programs" hitting the floor. It was Vinnie Vitale, my firm's trader/"spokesperson" on the floor of the New York Stock Exchange.

This period in time represented the advent and proliferation of what was referred to as "program trading." This consisted of institutions and/or large traders buying or selling large "baskets" of stocks, as they sought to benefit from the price discrepancies between the prices of S&P futures contracts and the prices of the underlying stocks in that index.

The specifics of the mechanisms and methods of effecting those kinds of computerized trades is not that important, but what is important to know that these programs were becoming more common and larger in size as each trading day went by.

Sometimes, a series of buy programs would hit the floor, and in minutes the stock market would start rising like a beach ball released under the water. When a sell program hit, the market could go from up 50 points to down 50 points in seconds. It had nothing to do with what stocks were "worth," or how the companies or the economy were actually doing.

It was an endless tide of mechanical waves of buying and selling that bounced stock prices and market direction around like Mexican jumping beans on steroids.

The newspapers referred to the computerized program trading as "the tail wagging the dog."

That kind of volatility can mean instant gratification if you are on the right side of the market in an index option trade; but, that day, I wasn't on the right side, and it looked like I was going to get killed in my first big trade.

I scurried back to the order window to pick up my order execution from the wire operator, who in those days was responsible for sending orders to the various exchanges, and then reporting back the prices that the trades were executed at.

I did a double take when I saw the report. I had accidentally checked that I wanted to buy puts and not calls. I had never made that kind of mistake before.

If a broker makes a mistake in their own account, they own the trade no matter what it is, and are totally responsible for the consequences of the trade, with absolutely no do overs.

In this case, I had made a big mistake, but all of a sudden I was on the right side of the market. I rushed back to my desk to fill out a ticket to sell the options that I had fortuitously and accidentally bought. It looked like that the downward movement in the market had abated, and the averages were beginning to recover; I had to move fast.

I handed the wire operator the sell ticket, and she entered the order. The executions were coming back very quickly that day. I hovered around the window for a minute or two, and then the order execution came back. I had made $40,000 by accident. I was *invincible*.

A few weeks later, at the beginning of the week that index options "expired" that particular month, I took my biggest position to date, 400 index option calls. I had four days to be right or wrong.

Options, unlike most other securities, have a very short and finite life. They are essentially like bets that end when the market closes on a certain day. If the market or stock has not moved sufficiently in the desired direction, the option "expires" worthless, and you lose all of your money. No do overs.

While some options can run for months, the most aggressive option trades required buying options that expired in days or even hours. My 400 options had four days until expiration, and I needed about a two hundred point move in the stock market, right away.

The options cost me about $15,000, a pretty large sum to put down on the equivalent of a two hundred to one long shot in horse racing.

Luck was really a lady that week, and she was hot as well. The market rallied strongly every day fueled by an explosive parade of high octane computerized buy programs.

Every time Vinnie Vitale reported from the floor of the exchange, it sounded like you were at the horse racing track. Vinnie had a nasally voice that jumped up with excitement. I could picture him leaned over one of those big old fashioned microphones that sports announcers talked into in old black and white movies.

Even though he was indoors at the stock exchange, I could picture him with a cigarette in one hand, the microphone in the other, and a Sinatra-style hat slouched over his eyes as he made announcements like,

"Solly is on the floor with a *big buy program*. It looks big, really *really* big." Then his voice would rise in pitch and excitement. "Oh, *my god*, yes, it is! Right behind Solly, here comes Paine Weber and Merrill Lynch…We are going to explode….*explode!*"

I was in awe of myself. My options had exploded up in value, they were at about 2 ($200 per option). The next morning was option expiration day, where absolutely anything can happen, and often does.

It was a very choppy, highly volatile day as both buy and sell programs were hitting the floor all day long. The market would swoosh up seventy five points, and then swoosh down a hundred points. In the span of a minute, my options would rise to 3 and then collapse to ½. Getting a profit out of this position was no longer assured.

I could have just thrown in a market order and ejected at whatever the prevailing price was, but the market was moving so fast that by the time my order hit the floor, it could be in the middle of a huge sell program, and the trader on the floor might stick it to me at the low price of the day, right before the market went the other way. When trading options, if you leave yourself open for being fucked over, you will get fucked over bad, real bad.

On that day, if the market had declined far enough, I would have lost even my initial investment. In speculative trading, when you are ahead by lot of money and then you lose it, it is the ultimate feeling of being a chump, a schmuck and an asshole all rolled up into one.

By early afternoon, things seemed to be picking up. The market started to rally. All of the program traders on the downside appeared to have shot their load. Vinnie had made so many announcements that he was starting to sound hoarse and worn out, like a lame horse trying to hobble over the finish line.

There was about fifteen minutes to go before the bell. My options were at 3 1/2. I was feeling lucky, so I entered an order to sell my entire position at 4, figuring that if just one or two buy programs hit before the bell, the market would jump up enough to get me out at 4; and if not, I could move quickly to change my order. Then the phone rang.

It was one of those calls that you never want to get, let alone ten minutes before an option expiration where you might either make a hundred thousand dollars, or get busted.

The phone call was from Cindy, the lady who took care of my son Ethan during the day at her home day care. She started her sentence with the terrible words,

"I don't want you to worry…but Ethan has gotten hurt."

My mouth opened, my eyes immediately welled with tears. Cute, little mop-topped Ethan had run into the edge of a door and gashed himself above his left eye. She said that he was OK, and Debbie had just picked up Ethan to take him to Hartford Hospital. Cindy said that Debbie would probably be there in a few minutes.

It wasn't life threatening but I was beside myself. I needed to leave. I needed to run. I needed to get there right away, when a huge sell program hit the floor. My options were melting down.

I needed to change my order, but I was frozen. I needed to call the Emergency Room to see if Debbie and my injured little boy had gotten there, but I had to do something about the index option position first.

I got up from my desk and then I sat down. I grabbed an order ticket with one hand, and the phone to call the emergency room with the other.

The seconds were like hours. The minutes were like an eternity. I figured that I needed to stay for the five minutes that it would take to deal with this. I was in agony. Then Vinnie Vitale came on the squawk box with a new sense of vigor and energy and started screaming:

"I *do not believe this!* Solly has come to the floor with not one, but *two huuuuuuge* buy programs! We are going to explode…yes *exploooode* into the close."

I looked at the screen. My options were at 3 7/8, close so very close. "C'mon Solly baby…hit it big," I prayed.

Then the option hit 4, then 4 ½, then 5, then 6. It was an amazing move up into the close.

The traders on the floor of course executed my order at 4, not a cent higher, even if I might have deserved it. I made $145,000 on the trade. It hardly mattered. I booked out of the office and headed to the Emergency Room.

When I got there, Ethan was sitting on the chair in the waiting room with Debbie holding a big bandage over his eyes. When he saw me, he smiled.

I hugged him and started to cry.

The doctor examined Ethan, and assured us that he was going to be just fine. A few weeks later, there was only a faint scar above his eyebrow.

The option expiration and the emergency room were already a memory, but Ethan and I continued to watch Sesame Street together for some time to come.

CHAPTER 11

WORST TRADE EVER

I've seen people **make some horrifically stupid trades**, and of the ten worst trades that I've seen over the decades, five of them have belonged to me personally.

However, there is one transaction that demonstrated such lack of forethought, abysmal market timing, and utter disregard for common sense that I have always referred to it as the worst trade ever.

The trade was not by a client or a market speculator; it was not by some dummy trading with a nefarious broker. The trade was by a licensed broker in my office who did the trade in his own account, and should have known better; a financial professional who did the transaction for one of the stupidest reasons ever.

I should know, because I signed off on the trade.

It happened in the days that led up to the great stock market crash of October 1987.

The crash was on a Monday, but the week before, it was clear to most observers that something was sorely amiss in the markets. The previous Monday before the crash there was a sharp drop in the market of about 90 points, probably the equivalent of about 500 to 700 points today. The market had been weak and failing for weeks before, but when that drop hit the averages, there seemed to be dark forces brewing, and the sense that the ugliness was just beginning.

Bob Prechter, of Elliot Wave fame, had been telling his clients to get out of the market for weeks. The Friday before the crash, Marty Zweig, a *Wall Street Week* regular, said the he thought the market could plummet. The middle of the pre-crash week was filled with confusion, as the pundits jockeyed for time to espouse their predictions.

There were so many Wall Street people were filled with such dread and foreboding that I took a small speculative contrarian position on the long side. I was not all that smart back then either.

While I mostly believed in the coming apocalypse, it just seemed too obvious. There is an old Wall Street saying that "if it's obvious, it's obviously wrong." So I obviously wasn't short anything when the shit hit the fan. Sadly, I may not have been very committed on the long side, but I should have been short something…anything.

On the Tuesday before the Monday crash, Evan., the broker in the office who played *Debbie Does Dallas* in the Conference Room, came to me to sign a ticket for an option transaction in his own account. He was "shorting" four way-out-of-the- money OEX index put options at 3 to take in a premium of $1200.

Without going into all of the technical jargon, this position made money if the stock market went up at all, or even stayed flat. If the market went down, it would have had to go down a huge amount before Evan would lose money. The only thing that would really kill him was if the market absolutely dive bombed; any normal sell off wouldn't be enough to hurt him. Nope, it would take something really unusual, something profoundly bizarre.

The stock market had been breaking and accelerating downwards for weeks. When Evan asked me to sign the ticket to allow him to enter the order, I asked him why he was doing the trade. He told me that he wanted to get a new stereo system for his car, and as soon as he could clear $300, he would cover the trade. The option premiums were so large that he felt he could cover the position on any up day in the market.

Trying to be a responsible Assistant Manager, I, of course, pointed out to him that it sure looked like the market was breaking downwards, and his trade was a very dangerous and silly way to try to make a lousy $300. I suggested that he reconsider before entering the order.

Evan was offended that I would even question an order that was for his own account, and not a client's. Evan shrugged me off, and shoved the ticket in front of me. I signed it.

If all that Evan needed to make money was an uptick, a small rally, a cessation of the decline, or absolutely anything that did not begin with the word disaster, he never saw it.

The next day, the market took another huge header downwards. Evan sat transfixed, staring at the monitor with a pinkish flushed look on his face, and beads of sweat forming on his brow.

Evan sat in sight of my desk, and at no time during the day did I ever see him on the phone with a client. He just stared and stared and stared at the declining market. The price of his options was rocketing upwards, which might have been a good thing if he hadn't been totally on the wrong side of the market. His position was such that he would make money if the price on his options went down, not up, and as the market cascaded downwards, the option prices went higher and higher.

I was also watching his options, and began getting concerned when the price went through about 10, which meant that he was now down about $2800 in his attempt to make $300 for a stereo.

The next day in the market was a reasonably flat day. Nothing bad happened to the position, but nothing good either. If anything, the position continued to get marginally worse because it was clear that there was no relief rally happening anywhere or anytime soon. And then came Friday.

The Friday before the Monday crash was an ugly, ugly market day. The market went down about 100 points, building downward momentum like water cascading down the sides of a toilet bowl, swirling downwards into the dark hole.

Evan looked absolutely green all day. He barely moved. His head was still and locked into position to soak up every nanosecond of market movement, A few times, I passed his desk on the way to the men's room and saw him barely breathing, literally holding on to the edge of his desk. At least once, I thought I saw tears in his eyes.

Without appearing unsympathetic, I knew that Evan was falling deeper and deeper into the abyss, but it was not my job to play his Daddy. In the frame of mind that he appeared to be in, I don't think he would have even heard me if I tried to talk with him as a friend, a father, a supervisor, or anything else. Further, it was always understood that brokers are totally responsible for anything that occurs in their own accounts.

There are no do overs on Wall Street

That weekend, the financial media, as limited as it was back then, was all abuzz about the breaking, sliding, and self-destructing market. I remember a few pundits saying that it was all just a normal correction, and that they had been buying all during the previous week. If someone pointed out that their positions were already deeply underwater, they would, of course, respond that they were in it" for the long term."

But options are anything but long term instruments. Trading options can make seconds seem like hours, and minutes seem like days.

Evan's weekend before the crash on Monday must have seemed like a millennium in the lowest level of Dante's Hell.

Monday was the Big One.

It looked like the world was going to end as stock prices melted like ice cubes on hot asphalt. The prices of already depressed blue chip stocks kept going lower and lower and lower. By mid-day, the atmosphere was turning into sheer panic. I could see my entire fledgling business evaporating before my eyes, as I watched the prices of every stock that I had bought for my clients drop into the market sump hole.

I glanced over towards Evan's direction a few times. He looked absolutely green. He was leaning oddly, clutching the side of his desk as if for leverage to pull himself out of the chair quickly. I wondered if he was going to puke as the price of his options went past 100, then 110, then 120, then 130, and suddenly Evan was springing up from his desk heading towards me with a ticket in his hand. I signed the ticket and moments later Evan covered the position at 156, which meant that he had lost $60,800 trying to make $300 for a car stereo.

When I saw the utter panic during the middle of the day, I started buying anything that wasn't nailed down for any of my clients that would listen to me. I figured that if the world was going to end, it didn't matter; but, if it didn't end, we could be heroes.

That turned out to be one of my greatest moments as I negotiated my clients through the apocalyptic storm; but not everyone got out alive.

The next day, Michael, the Branch Manager, called me in the office to discuss the situation. Evan owed the firm about $50,000 that he didn't have. His small accounts had been totally wiped out. Michael asked my opinion, and I offered the fact that Evan had just fucked up himself, and not a client.

We briefly discussed firing him, but that didn't seem to accomplish anything except to put him out of the business, probably making him unemployable by any other Wall Street firm, leaving us permanently in the hole for the $50,000. I suggested that we make him work it off.

The firm made Evan take out a third mortgage on his house, though I was not privy to all of the specifics of the agreement.

Ironically, Evan had been trading options with a client who he referred to only as Margarita, as in the cocktail. This client had a long history of losing money, probably because Evan always had him on the wrong side of the market. During the decline, Evan was having him buy call options which would make money if the market rebounded; however as the market kept declining, Margarita just kept losing and losing.

But Evan and Margarita had both apparently forgotten that Margarita had bought a large quantity of very cheap puts way before the market started breaking downwards. These options had already declined to near zero and were virtually worthless, unless something big, really big, happened on the downside; something gigantic.

After Evan covered his own position on the crash day, he realized that Margarita still had the put position. When the market dropped the 500 points on Monday, Margareta made about $600,000.

At least someone made some money.

CHAPTER 12

Penny Stock God

There is something about penny stocks that is irresistible. I love penny stocks. You love penny stocks. Everyone loves penny stocks. But why?

Perhaps the answer is that penny stocks are kind of like lottery tickets, but they don't become worthless when the drawing is over.

Penny stocks are like buying raw land and hoping that gold or oil is discovered on the property, except you don't have to go through all the trouble of a real estate transaction, and there are no property taxes. If you happen to buy the penny stock of a company that actually explores for oil or gold, the company does all of the legwork involved in finding the stuff.

You just have to wait, wish, and pray for the big payoff that you hope will come someday.

From a stock market standpoint, penny stocks are appealing because it is easier for a penny stock to go from fifty cents to five dollars than it is for a blue chip company's stock to go from fifty dollars to five hundred dollars. There are many reasons for this.

The primary one is that the world is full of momentum-based penny stock players who are constantly looking for small cheap low priced stocks that are experiencing large volume and price moves. The stock prices of small low priced "microcap" companies can be greatly influenced by hordes of small time traders piling in or out of the stock.

The unfortunate reality about penny stocks is that many of them are financial trash; while others are the products of boiler room scams set up to separate penny stock fools from their money.

Two of the most important characteristics of the trash penny stocks are when the company has no revenues, and/or a huge amount of shares outstanding. If a company has no revenues, then it has no sales; that means that the company isn't doing any business.

While there are many development type companies that at least have the promise of one day producing revenues, most of the scam-type penny stocks have no real possibility of making any money because they have no actual operations.

The other red light is when a tiny company with little or no sales revenue has billions and billions, and sometimes tens of billions of shares outstanding. Shares outstanding are all the little pieces that the company "pie" is cut up into.

When penny stock companies have billions of shares outstanding, and little if any revenues, it is impossible for the company to generate any perceptible earnings per share, and earnings per share is one of the foundations of stock valuation.

Some penny stock companies are merely "shell" companies, with no real existence other than a stock symbol. These are often set up as part of a stock promotion scheme. Unscrupulous stock promoters will create a shell company for the purpose of trying to exploit a hot stock market theme or buzzword.

For example, during the internet bubble, there were hundreds of different "fledgling" internet concept companies being brought to market by stock promoters. The mania for internet stocks was so pervasive that investors only needed to hear that the promoted company was "the next big thing." Then, the greedy investors would go rushing in to buy the stock, hoping for the next Microsoft or Yahoo.

In the 1990's, there were seas of biotech companies being promoted, many of the companies claiming that they had promising cures for different diseases. In the 1980's, the oil and natural resource companies were being touted.

An elderly client once brought me a certificate for an obsolete penny stock that he bought in the early 1960's. It was a uranium stock, which was not surprising given the era it was purchased.

Penny stock promoters create products to satisfy the investing appetite of the time period that they exist in.

Many penny stocks have a brief moment in the sun when volume rises, the stock price rises, and there is great excitement about the issue. The promoters sell their stock to the late-to-the-party chumps. The speculators, who got in early, start getting out as soon as their short swing profits begin to erode.

Finally the people remaining, often called "bag holders'", are all of the dummies who heard about the stock from somebody who knew somebody, who knew somebody else, who got a hot tip from an inside source.. Then the balloon pops, never to re- inflate, as the stock price dives.

However, despite all of the hucksterism and imaginative stock concepts out there, it is possible to make real money in penny stocks.

In my branch during the early 1990's was the best penny stock trader investor that I have known; an experienced successful broker I referred to as the Penny Stock God.

The Penny Stock God was a very tall man, in his early sixties, with dyed jet black hair. His clientele, for the most part, was made up affluent investors who utilized him for what he did best: buying penny stocks. He was the best at what he did because he personally found, researched, and often went to "kick the tires" of the companies whose penny stocks he planned to accumulate.

During the Penny Stock God's personal due diligence process, he talked to company management, poured over the financials, and in some cases, even visited the company to actually see their facilities. I recall him going to visit the mining site of a gold company that he was interested in; he told me that he needed to see the gold before investing his clients' money.

If a prospective company was looking to sell a billion widgets, the Penny Stock God wanted to assure himself that the company had the physical and financial capabilities to achieve that level of production. He also tried to meet with other large shareholders to get their input about the company. He tried to cover all of the bases.

My first real encounter with the Penny Stock God was shortly after he was recruited over from another firm. Sometimes, as the Assistant Manager, I had to sign certain transactions for large block purchases or sales of penny stocks. The Penny Stock God, as one might expect, always had all of the proper authorizations and forms. Everything was always in order.

The list of companies that he was buying or selling was always fascinating. I never heard of any of them. They ran the gamut from precious metal mining companies, to aerospace high tech, and sometimes, just mundane manufacturing companies.

Over the months, I noticed that the Penny Stock God's clients generally made money; sometimes lots and lots of money. One day. I was walking by his office when he called to me.

"Hey Don, got a minute? I want to show you something really interesting."

When I walked into the Penny Stock God's office, he turned the monitor towards me and showed me a stock chart unlike any I had ever seen before. The chart showed the stock price rising from about thirty five cents a share to over eight hundred dollars per share, and this was in about the past two years. I gasped. "What company is that?" I said as I moved my face closer to the screen to make sure that I was seeing the correct numbers.

"The company is Northern Saskatchewan Diamonds Ltd." He puffed out his chest a little.

"What made the stock go up like that?" I queried with envy.

"They found diamonds. What else would it be?"

The Penny Stock God discovered the stock when it was about two dollars a share and rode it up to about two hundred dollars a share, where he and his clients made boat loads of money by selling out way too early, instead of the mountains of money that they might have made if he held onto the stock for a little longer.

"What a bitch" he said. "I totally missed the big spike up. What a bitch." He repeated. We both laughed.

Over the next few weeks, we exchanged a number of penny stock ideas, but none seemed to have the jazz we were looking for. Then, one afternoon, he called me and said that I should look at a company that he liked, and was starting to buy.

I didn't like all of the Penny Stock God's picks, but this one I liked. The company was called MegaVideo, and was based in California.

The Penny Stock God had already been out there to visit. He was telling me about their state of the art facilities, and how they manufactured multimedia computer monitors that were way better than the crappy computer screens that we were using at our firm.

I didn't know much about monitors, but "multimedia" was like the advent of color television over black and white. I read about the company. I liked it. I bought some. Over the next three days, I purchased 47,000 shares at an average cost of about thirty eight cents a share. Then, things began to happen.

Over the next week, the stock rose to about sixty cents. Each day the volume was increasing. By the next week, the stock was about ninety cents a share. The stock which had typically traded about fifty thousand shares a day was now trading five million shares a day.

Something was up in Whoville.

Usually, when a stock makes a run like that, it is a good idea to sell out when it approaches a big round number like a dollar a share. I figured that I'd blow at about ninety five cents a share so as to avoid the crowds. But I never got a chance.

The next morning, when I arrived in the office, I was heading towards the men's room when I heard the Penny Stock God call my name. "Hey Don, did you see the news on MegaVideo? The stock is *gonna explode!*"

"Let me go look in my office," I answered. I forgot about the bathroom, went to my computer and waited while the system logged me in. Finally I saw the news headline: "MegaVideo Changes Name to MegaVideo *Multimedia.*"

The stock price was indicated higher, way higher. However, the only thing that had really happened was that the company changed its name to incorporate the hot new buzzword, *Multimedia*. The stock opened at $1.10 and just kept going. I was so profitable that I was actually able to focus on my clients' accounts.

By about 11:30, the stock had risen to $1.40 a share. I had enough. I reached for the phone to call the Penny Stock God and tell him that I was going to blow out my position, when my phone rang. It was the God, himself.

"I think it's time," he said.

"I was just about to call you." I said.

We both laughed.

"How about lunch down by Max's?" I said, "My treat."

"Sure. Come swing by my office at noon."

We both had meatloaf. I made about $45,000, and the Penny Stock God made $200,000.

A year later the stock was back at thirty five cents.

When the market offers you an easy one, it is usually wise to take it before it goes away.

CHAPTER 13

BAD INVESTORS KILL THEIR LOVED ONES

Sometimes the biggest **danger to a good investor** is the bad investor that happens to become a significant part of their personal life. Bad investors are like a disease. They spread their bad habits, bad ideas, and ultimately their bad investment results to those who most closely surround them.

By professing a greater knowledge and greater experience in investing than the companion investor, who is actually making money, the bad investor slowly alters the behavior of their companion investor, like a parasite eating away at the finances of its prey.

Unfortunately, this is not an uncommon phenomenon. It happens most often in mature adult relationships where either the man or the woman happens to be successful and prosperous as an investor, and then they hook up with a new "soul mate" that comes along, and tells them that they are doing it all wrong.

From my perspective as an investment professional, is it very frustrating because it leaves me trying to debate, stifle, or diminish the lousy investment recommendations and suggestions that are being made by the financially inept partner.

Typically, the parasitic mate attempts to alter or destroy the existing portfolio that has been constructed, whether or not the portfolio has performed well. The predatory partner usually has a much smaller portfolio than the partner who had invested more wisely.

Sometimes the influence of the new devouring mate is slow, subtle and creeping like the mold rising from the base of the sheetrock in a damp room. Other times, the new partner will try to seize control like a coup d'état, coming on with guns blazing and large vociferous promises of impending financial success.

Then, the new partner will begin acting like a surrogate portfolio manager, initiating numerous buy and sell orders to reconfigure the portfolio, until it is decimated by their influence.

One of the most memorable examples of this predatory phenomenon was when a very nice soft spoken middle aged client named Harold, unfortunately, hooked up with a black widow spider of a woman named Ethel Matson.

Harold was a salesman for a company that sold commercial printing supplies to large print shops, business or organizations that do massive amounts of printing. One his major clients was Wesleyan University, which is where he met Ethel, who was a minor administrative person at the university.

I guess that Harold was pleased with his financial relationship with me because he told Ethel how well we had done together through the years trading stocks and buying tax free bonds. Harold encouraged Ethel to call me to see if I could help her with her small portfolio.

When Ethel first called me on the phone, I immediately noticed that she had a stand offish skeptical tone in her voice, but she didn't know me so it was understandable. It sometimes takes a little while to win the heart and mind of a client; that usually comes over the years with demonstrated success and consistency.

I began asking Ethel about her investing experience, and she told me how she kept losing money with other brokers because none of them knew what they were doing. Whatever had gone wrong, it was their entire fault, she said, and she could have done better without any of them.

When I asked her about the sort of stocks she had traded, the names certainly didn't sound like the sort of companies that most brokers would have recommended. They were all very obscure speculative stocks; the kind of stocks that that go up and down based on rumors and hot tips.

When I asked her how she had happened to select those stocks, I wasn't surprised when she told me that she had picked most of them. She quickly emphasized that a few of the stocks went up in price right after she bought them, but her brokers didn't tell her to get out in time before the stock prices dropped sharply; therefore, she had picked them right, but she had lost money because of the brokers.

I didn't want to insult or hurt her feelings, but it was obvious that she was one of those people who invested in rumor stocks that were being pumped up by someone. Ethel was fed the hype, and would then go and buy the speculative stocks through a broker, just before the stock price bubble would burst. Then, she needed someone else to blame for her losses, so pointed to the broker who purchased the stocks for her.

Normally, I shied away from clients who harbored anti-broker sentiments. I wanted to be judged by how well I managed a portfolio, not by a client's past experiences with hot stock tips that went badly. However; Ethel wasn't all that intolerable, at first. I'd seen worse.

Ethel was reasonably bright, and I thought that I might be able to get her to see the investment light of day. Also, she was getting into a more serious relationship with my client Harold, who I liked.

Harold had been my client over ten years, so I didn't want to blow Ethel off, and make it appear like I didn't want to handle her account. So I decided to give it a go with Ethel.

I told Ethel about the types of investment securities that I had bought for Harold over the years for his portfolio. In particular, I thought that she might be interested in some nice, safe, boring tax free municipal bonds. At the time, high quality tax free bonds yielded about seven percent; an excellent return without dealing with all of the risk and volatility of the stock market.

Tax free bonds seemed like a good way to start the relationship. Nice predictable financial instruments which were easy to build a sensible portfolio around. But Ethel wasn't having any of it.

Ethel was totally uninterested in safe tax free bonds. She wanted to buy stocks. She didn't think that Harold should be buying bonds either, and she was going to tell him that. She said that she had some of her own stock ideas that she wanted to get back to me on, and in the meantime, she felt that she really needed to work with Harold on "improving" his portfolio.

I felt bad for Harold. I could see it coming, but I was hoping that his conservative New England common sense would prevail; but given Ethel's clearly bossy bitchy attitude, I wasn't hopeful.

I wasn't surprised when a few days later when Harold called up wanting to buy a Mexican cement stock that had already quadrupled over the past year, and a bio tech stock that I had never heard of. The bio tech stock was a developmental company which had recently made a lot of headlines for a niche cancer drug that they were developing, but had not actually yet developed it enough for either testing or production.

I can, and have, turned people down when they wanted to make transactions that I strongly felt were not in their interests, or were just downright stupid, but I didn't want to have to turn Harold down. I tried to reason with him, but got nowhere, so I bought him the two stocks. Within a week, they were both down over thirty percent. The Mexican cement company proceeded to drop by ninety percent over the next year before Harold eventually sold it.

At about the same time, Ethel called me wanting to buy her first stock with me. It was decent smaller to mid-sized New York Stock Exchange listed company named Albanall. I asked Ethel why she chose this particular company. She told me because it started with the letter A, and she wanted to buy stocks alphabetically because nothing else she had done in terms of picking stocks had worked.

She wanted her next stock to start with the letter B, and then the third stock should begin with the letter C, and so on. Ethel said that one day she wanted to be able to read the stock quotes in the newspaper, and see one of her stocks under each letter in the stock listings. This didn't seem like a good way to begin a relationship with a client.

When Raymond and I had bought stock options based on Sesame Street featuring the letter M and the word UP, it had nothing to do with buying stocks alphabetically. That inspired transaction was more like a one-time divine message being sent through the Sesame Street channel. Clearly, buying stocks alphabetically was silly. Raymond and I were just lucky.

I carefully and tactfully tried to explain to Ethel why investing alphabetically was a silly idea, and she might want to reconsider buying stocks "by the letters." I tried to talk to her about more balanced ways to construct a portfolio, and how it was best to see investing in the financial markets as a business, and not a game.

Ethel wasn't interested in anything that I said. I didn't know why she had even bothered to call me in the first place if she was just going to do whatever she wanted to do, and really didn't want any help or advice.

She wanted me to buy her the Albanall stock, which I had no reason to refuse since it was a real enough company. Then, she wanted me to come up with a recommendation for a stock that started with a B and a C. I bought her the Albanall stock, and told her that I was it was ridiculous to buy stocks by the letters.

Over the next few months, Ethel found and bought her letter B and C stocks. At the same time, she was having Harold sell all of his stocks which were winners to buy more of her bizarre picks, all of which seemed to plummet almost immediately after Harold bought them.

A short time later, in accordance with Murphy's Laws, Harold needed a large chunk of money out of his account to help pay for his divorce settlement, at the worst possible time.

Harold's portfolio was being absolutely crushed by the weight of Ethel's interference. Rather than raising the money from selling some of his losing stock positions, Harold had me sell his seven and eight percent tax free bonds. His portfolio which had averaged an impressive eighteen percent annual return over the past three years was now down over forty percent for the calendar year, wiping out all of the good work that I had done for the past three years. What was left was a convoluted portfolio of garbage stocks that Ethel had chosen, and massive unrealized losses.

Love was not only blind, but it was also moronic. And even worse, as Harold's portfolio value started to plummet, he began acting like it was my fault. After all, I was his financial advisor, and it was my job to make him money. If he lost money, it must be my fault; a familiar theme which I've heard said over and over by people who cannot face their own accountability in the deep dark truthful mirror of investment results.

At that point in my career, I still believed that I could save everybody from drowning in the swamp of their own stupidity.

So when a genuinely promising speculative stock opportunity came by, I thought that I would use it to try to generate some quick short term capital gains in Harold and Ethel's portfolios in an effort to show them the "right way" to be aggressive, without being foolish.

The stock was called GSI Enterprises, and for a very short time, they were in the forefront of the emerging video conferencing industry during the early 1990's. The only reason that I had even heard of the company was because the son of one of the senior brokers in the office worked for a company that competed with them. He told his dad about the company so the dad could buy the company's stock for both of them; if you can't beat them, buy their stock. It seemed like a good idea to me.

After I read all about the company's history and products, and then looked at their financials and potential contracts going forward, it looked like the company had the potential to experience explosive growth going forward. However, like many emerging technology companies, they weren't making any money yet, and the promise was in the future, and might never be realized.

From a trading standpoint, the GSI stock was only two dollars a share, and the stock price had been relatively stable to trending mildly upwards for several months. It was a reasonable bet that if the company's news remained positive for a little while, I might be able to get my clients a high percentage trading return in a short period of time.

Low priced stocks can be excellent trading vehicles. When a two dollar stock goes up fifty cents a share, and you sell it, that is a twenty five percent return. However, you have to remember to sell the stock when it does go up because the future promise of the company is still in the future, and stock price is here and now. In the financial jungle, you have to seize the profits when they appear, and if you don't, someone will take them from you.

I suggested to Harold that he buy five thousand shares; he bought two thousand. He was clearly becoming very gun shy and risk averse. I suggested that Ethel buy four thousand shares, which she did, probably hoping that the stock would go down so she could validate her belief that brokers didn't know anything.

Well, sometimes in life, things actually turn out better than you think, and even faster than you could have imagined.

In this case of GSI, it was a series of press releases announcing more potential contracts with several Fortune 500 companies, new product lines, and new financing. Soon after, three Wall Street analysts picked up coverage on GSI with speculative buy recommendations, but not overly ambitious price targets. The company was still far from becoming profitable.

Future promise only goes so far if you can't take it to the bank.

From a professional standpoint, I love it when I have the opportunity to make dozens of clients significant short swing profits. A few great trades a year can make the difference between terrific annual returns, and nondescript returns in a portfolio.

Over the next month, GSI stock doubled to about four dollars a share. The first one to call me to sell the stock was Harold. I suggested that he not sell the stock because it was going up, and going up is what we wanted. I suggested that he let me make the call as to when to sell the stock.

I had positioned the stock in about thirty client accounts, and hadn't sold a share. Harold wanted the quick four thousand dollar profit to offset some of the significant losses on his other stocks, which he never once referred to as Ethel's ideas. I, of course, told him of the old Wall Street axiom of letting your winners run, and cutting your losers short. But he made me sell the stock anyway. It didn't seem like he had consulted with Ethel about it, though. In fact, I hadn't even heard from Ethel in a while.

In about another month, the stock was starting to bounce and fluctuate between six and seven dollars a share. The stock price had quickly gone way beyond the reality of the company's fundamentals. From a trading standpoint, it was clear that the stock was getting toppy with a lot of selling coming in, and a waning new supply of buyers. From a financial perspective, nothing had happened, but the stock price had more than tripled. It was time to start selling it, and harvesting the fruits of the money tree.

It was a joy to call everyone to sell their GSI stock, and to take their impressive gains. I encouraged my clients to go buy some toys, or go on a Hawaiian vacations. I believe that if you make a windfall profit in the market, you should do something nice for yourself. Enjoy and savor the moments of victory, because they come so infrequently.

Call it an educated guess, but I did not think that Ethel was going to revel and celebrate in the joys of our stock market victory, so, I wasn't surprised when she simply refused to sell any of the stock.

Ethel said that she had been reading about the company, and now she knew *everything* about it. She thought that the stock was going to go way higher, incredibly higher. She said that she wanted to keep the shares forever, and one day, pass them on to her grandchildren.

I knew it was going to be a waste of time, but I spent twenty minutes on the phone with Ethel telling her all of the obvious things, like the stock price had already tripled, nothing had really changed with the company, and we had a twenty thousand dollar profit on an eight thousand dollar investment in a few months. I said all of the right things. I said of all the logical and rational things.

She wouldn't even sell a part of her shares. Finally, she said in an absolutely contemptuous way, "A monkey can do what you do. You don't know anything."

With that, I said goodbye to Ethel, and would have just ignored her from there on.

However, the next week GSI stock started spiking upwards and began vacillating between eight and nine dollars a share. The stock had all of the looks of a classic technical blow off where a stock's price peaks, and then sharply starts dropping like a rock falling out of the sky. The stock had hit an intraday high of about 9 ½, and it was now a little over 8, and coming down fast. I decided to give Ethel another try. After all, what reasonable person would refuse to take a quick twenty four thousand dollar profit?

Not only wasn't Ethel reasonable, but she said she was telling all of her friends and family about her wonderful stock. Ethel was encouraging them all to buy it before it went to twenty dollars a share. I told her that I wouldn't be surprised if the stock was back at two dollars a share in a few months. I urged her to take the money, or at least part of it, off the table. Of course, she didn't.

A week later the stock was back at four dollars a share. Three months later the stock was back at two; easy come, easy go. Twenty four thousand dollars gone as quickly as it appeared, like a daydream or the memory of a particular sunset.

For the next few years, I saw the stock decomposing in Ethel's account. Two years later, it had slipped below a dollar a share. The company subsequently did a name change and a reverse spilt, falling to a few pennies a share within the three years, before finally going bankrupt.

I didn't have any further contact with Ethel. I saw no need to call her to either rub it in, or to be verbally abused. A few years later, she transferred out the shattered remains of her portfolio to some discount brokerage firm. It was about the same time that Harold told me that they had split up as a couple, but the damage had been long done to Harold, in so many ways.

Harold became a fetal investor, never doing anything again it terms of buying, selling or even just maintaining his sharply diminished portfolio. It was like he had been poisoned and left paralyzed by the bite of his giant black widow spider.

CHAPTER 14

PLUMBER GONE MAD

Money changes people, and I never saw it change anyone more than Chuck Kowalski, who I like to remember as the plumber gone mad.

Except for the fact that I knew that Chuck was a plumber, I hardly ever spoke to him for the first ten years that I handled his joint account that he had with his wife Agnes. It was Agnes who I always did business with. It was Agnes who I always discussed the portfolio with. It was Agnes who had originally asked for the branch manager to reassign her account which was being handled by another broker in the office named Brian Dunn.

The account was then assigned to me.

Brian was only with the firm for two or three years. He was a quiet, soft spoken, lanky guy who seemed overwhelmed by the markets, and clearly did not have the communication skills to reach out and sell people intangibles like bonds, stocks, or anything else. Brian was too introverted and unsure, a fatal combination in the financial services industry.

Agnes' account was assigned to Brian when another washed out broker left the firm, and his accounts were distributed. Obviously, a domineering

Agnes didn't like dealing with a spineless insecure Brian, so she eventually ended up with me.

Agnes reminded me of a non-entertaining version of the Wicked Witch of the West form *The Wizard of Oz*. She had a raspy voice and a crabby demeanor. Whenever she came into my office, she wore drab clothing, and usually wore an old fashioned hat.

Agnes regularly complained about commissions, and repeatedly asked for bigger and bigger discounts. She was never pleased with the service of any of my approximately five sales assistants that I went through during that period. She made at least two of them cry. She thought that everything I suggested had an ulterior motive to it.

When I spoke to Agnes, even on the phone, it felt like she was pinching me on my lower rib with her curled fingernails digging into the flesh.

It made me feel uncomfortable doing business with Agnes. I felt that eventually she was going to try to sue me for something. It was just a matter of time. But then one day, time ran out on Agnes.

I received a call from her husband Chuck telling me that she had passed away. He seemed sad, but not all that sad. I expressed my regrets and muttered something about how I "enjoyed" our long business relationship. I said something about Agnes' "keen investment savvy." I didn't know if I sounded sufficiently remorseful, but I was relieved, for both of us.

Not much happened for the next few weeks while we put together the paperwork to move all of the assets from the old joint account into a new individual account in Chuck's name. Things went smoothly as Chuck provided us with everything we needed. Soon, the money was all his, complete with a credit card that had a credit line equal to the entire net value of the account, about $400,000.

It appeared that Chuck's remorse was fading when he called me a few weeks later and told me how he was going to make some investments into his own plumbing business. He wanted a check for $25,000 to buy a pump that he needed a long time. I thought that it was a good thing that he wanted to get back to work. I knew that work was good for the soul, and through his work, he could find comfort and focus.

I've always been interested in my client's businesses, so I asked Chuck about the world of a professional plumber's pumps, and how much they cost for the different types of pumps that were used in commercial applications. Whatever he said seemed kind of vague, so rather than pursue it, I told him that we'd get his check right out, and I hoped that he enjoyed the pump.

About a month later, I happened to be looking at different client accounts when I remembered about the $25,000 check. I decided to go look at Chuck's account to see how the account was doing performance wise. I hoped that Chuck was happily plumbing somewhere, displacing immense amount of water with his new super water pump, making the world a better and drier place.

I generally kept a well trained eye on account values, given that client accounts fluctuated wildly during different types of market movements, either up or down. Nothing of consequence had happened in the markets for the past few months, so I expected to see Chuck's account about $25,000 lower, give or take a few thousand dollars. However, when I looked at his account, it was nearly $50,000 lower.

Wall Street computer systems may change with the seasons, but even back then we were able to see all of the individual activity on clients' credit cards. So, when I looked at the activity in Chuck's account, I saw dozens and dozens of credit card charges, mostly from liquor stores, but also from at least a dozen "adult entertainment" related businesses with names like Ace

Entertainment, Black Cat Entertainment, and Pleasure Resources. It was easy to see that the formerly repressed plumber was breaking out like a super nova. Better late than never.

Unfortunately, it soon became clear that this was not just a short term fling. By the next month, the account had dropped below $300,000. On some days there were at least two to four charges just from liquor stores. It wasn't surprising that, one day, when I called Chuck about a maturing tax free bond, it sounded like he just got off the red eye.

At nearly 70 years old, Tom obviously still had a lot of wild oats to sow. The credit card charges kept coming in hot and heavy. I didn't understand how one man could party and drink that much, but after being married to Agnes for nearly 40 years, he clearly had a lot of unmet needs.

When Chuck's account fell to about $200,000, I gave him several telephone calls, without being able to reach him. I just left messages. He had used up all of the available cash and credit lines of the account. In order to spend more, he needed to liquidate some securities to free up the cash.

After a while, Chuck finally called me back sounding like a sailor who has been in port for too long, and needs the MP's to take him back to the ship.

I mentioned to Chuck that his account was dropping rapidly, and we needed to sell some securities if he was going to keep spending money at such a rapid rate.

Chuck told me that he knew that he was getting a little out of control. He said that he was going to try to get everything in his life straightened out by paying off his house as well as all of his personal and business debts. He said that he needed about $60,000, sent to him as soon as possible.

Without mentioning that I could see all of the massage parlor, strip club, and liquor store charges on his credit card, I tried to express my concern about his dramatically falling account value. When I indicated that we would have to begin selling off some very attractive tax free bond holdings, he simply said that he needed the $60,000, and I should sell whatever I could to raise the cash.

Over the next few months, I saw many odd transactions show up in his account activity. It didn't appear that Chuck was doing much plumbing anymore. Soon the account dropped below $50,000, and Chuck called to say that he needed all of the rest of the money in the account. I could see that talking to him wasn't going to do much good. Instead, I pointed out to him that if he zeroed the account, all he had left was about $75,000 in his IRA account. That was a bad move.

Chuck asked if he could get to the IRA money. I pointed out the tax consequences. He didn't care. I could see what was coming next.

But I was wrong, because a few days later I was reading the newspaper when I saw a headline in the newspaper covering towns in the area. The headline read, "Manchester Man, 70, Busted."

Chuck had been busted in a motel room with an ounce of cocaine and not one, but two hookers. There was a picture of him in the paper. I remember thinking that he looked tired, very, very tired. But who wouldn't be under the same circumstances?

Chuck's individual account was toast. I knew that if he got out of jail, all that I would be doing is overseeing the liquidation of whatever was left of his IRA assets. $400,000 was a lot of money to spend on booze, coke and hookers, but at least Chuck didn't waste it on nursing homes.

CHAPTER 15

Mr. Dick and the Aliens

Raymond and I **were sitting in Brown Thompson one afternoon**, having an unusually long liquid lunch, even by our often excessive standards. We were probably up to our sixth or seventh cocktail. This was during Raymond's scotch on the rocks period, and he was clearly bummed about something, so he was drinking a lot of them.

I was beginning my exploration of tequila mixed with diet Coke, and a splash of vodka on the top. Raymond sat half on, and half off the bar stool, with his head leaning precipitously forward over his body.

Raymond seemed stable only as long as he held onto the brass bar rail with his left hand, while sipping his drink with his right. I ordered another drink from Melissa, the very blonde bartender. Melissa had freckles, a little turned up nose, bright sparkling blue eyes, and a curvy little body that made you want to hug her, and pull off her clothes at the same time.

I loved hanging out at the old Brown Thompson's in downtown Hartford. Brown Thompson had an eclectic air and décor that always had you looking around.

In one corner, there was a giant stuffed bear. Hanging on the wall was a giant tiger skin that supposedly was real. Suspended high above the bar was the biggest pair of bull horns that I had ever seen.

There were all kinds of different pictures, posters and signs hanging all around the bar and restaurant areas; everything from old-time ads for soap and shampoo, to a pawnbroker sign. The bar area was separated from the restaurant tables by wood dividers that had a variety of stained glass panels. There were a few suggestive pictures hanging on the walls, things like 1920's lingerie ads, and drawings of Victorian ladies in certain states of repose.

The bar itself was a huge square, partially open on one side for service. The bartenders worked around a center island, on which stood all the bottles of booze, with beer and wine coolers below in a glassed in case.

During the bull market of the early 1980's and well into the mid 1990's, BT's, as everyone called it, was the grand meeting place for the enormous wave of young yuppie stockbrokers that were hired as the markets roared upwards.

At any given happy hour, there might be a dozen or more stockbrokers, from all of the different firms, clustered around the bar. It was like being a baseball player, and after each game, meeting the guys who played for the other teams in the league.

Raymond and I were regulars, mostly because our office was directly across the street from the bar. We would go there for lunch. We'd go there for happy hour.

I've always said that I celebrated my greatest victories and agonized over my most miserable defeats at the bar in Brown Thompson. Happy or sad, if I wasn't in my office during market hours, I wasn't hard to find.

One of my favorite features about the bar was the wide brass rail that ran around the edge of the top of the bar. The rail had elephant heads every few feet along the span. It was a good rail to hold onto while drinking, just as Raymond was doing as we spoke that afternoon.

Raymond was lamenting about the accelerating decline in the fortunes of a friend of his, and an acquaintance of mine from BT's, named Dick. Raymond's nickname for Dick was Mr. Dick (no kidding). If anything, it was a sign of genuine respect and/or fear for Dick who had a certain unstable, almost unnerving quality about him.

Mr. Dick was in his early 50's, about 5'10," wiry, but very strong looking. He was mostly bald with a halo of light brown hair speckled with a few gray flecks. Raymond told me that he had recently seen Mr. Dick dunk a basketball in a schoolyard, several times. Raymond was at least 6'4" and couldn't dunk a basketball if he was standing on a chair.

When you had a conversation with Mr. Dick, he would stare intently back with his large blue eyes which were always opened wide. His intense gaze made it seem like he was getting ready to pounce on you to beat you up. His gaze reminded me of the gaze of the raptors in *Jurassic Park*; sharp focused, and deadly.

When Mr. Dick began losing a lot of money in the market, he started drinking monstrous amounts of liquor. He drank to the extent that he became one of those people who would walk into a bar so sloshed and aggressive that it seemed like was going to pick a fight with someone, and would then start a fight with the police when they showed up. On one occasion, Mr. Dick did get into a fight with the cops.

Mr. Dick had recently quit his long time administrative job with a local manufacturing company to become a full time market speculator, and part time casino gambler. His wife had recently inherited a reasonably large amount of money, about $800,000, and that, combined with his life savings and retirement accounts, had become the fuel for Mr. Dick's new life of being a professional trader, and general high roller about town.

In order to spread his risk, Mr. Dick had set up speculative trading accounts with several of the brokers who hung out at the bar, with the biggest account being the one that he had with Raymond. With the help of the Big Man, Mr. Dick was trading everything in sight; index options, stock options, stocks on margin; he even set up a commodity account.

You could usually find Raymond and Mr. Dick hanging out at the bar, talking loudly and laughing about their latest market score, or sometimes, more seriously discussing what went wrong with a trade, or their interpretations of the current stock market action.

It didn't help that Mr. Dick began subscribing to all sorts of market letters, espousing all kinds of strange market strategies and trading advice.

Sometimes Mr. Dick made his own trading decisions; sometimes he would take the advice of Raymond and his other brokers. For a while, he had so many things going in so many places that I knew that it could not have a happy ending.

In the financial markets, if you bet on nine out of ten possible outcomes, you can count on the outcome not covered to occur. If you bet on all ten possible outcomes, the system is set up so that you will only lose a little money because you have essentially hedged your way out of profitability.

Generally, the way to make a lot of money speculating in the market is to have a lot of eggs in one basket, and then watch that basket very carefully, while praying that you are right, very right about the basket that you have put your money into.

Unfortunately, Mr. Dick was on a long run of being wrong, wrong, and wrong some more.

Very soon, Mr. Dick had lost a lot of his wife's money; lots and lots of it, about $600,000. Apparently, he was doubling and tripling down on losing positions which is a cardinal no-no in trading. Never add money to a losing position because the fact that you are already losing money shows that you were wrong about the position in the first place.

Doubling and tripling down says that you refuse to accept that you are wrong. Throwing more money at losing positions rarely works out. There are endless ways to lose a lot of money quickly in the financial markets, and Mr. Dick was finding them all, everywhere he was trading.

After telling me the latest unfortunate Mr. Dick news, Raymond asked what I thought he should do with Mr. Dick.

At that point in his career, Raymond had moved to another firm so that we were no longer working together. I told him that I would cut off Mr. Dick from further trading, and Raymond should talk to his branch manager about calling Mr. Dick to tell him that his trading account is being shut down.

Raymond was apprehensive about doing what needed to be done, but Mr. Dick was his personal friend, and he didn't want to be responsible for the destruction of any more of Mr. Dick's money.

Raymond hoped that Mr. Dick wouldn't kill him, or do something rash. However, we did not know at the time that Mr. Dick's wife had caught wind of the huge trading losses, and was way more than pissed.

I heard that one night she came into BT's looking for Mr. Dick, and confronted him right in the bar, screaming, cursing, and threatening. Supposedly, she dragged Mr. Dick out with her, presumably, so she could take him home to the castration that she had planned for him.

"The markets and what they do to people is amazing Goody," Raymond sighed, after we had concluded our conversation about Mr. Dick. "I just can't freaking believe it sometimes."

At that point, after hearing about the magnitude of Mr. Dick's latest market disaster, I ordered another drink, and downed what was left in my glass. The tequila was starting to give me a nice warm glow that spread from the center of my eyebrows up into my head.

I was beginning to feel reflective, and almost philosophical. "But, Raymond," I began, pausing to gather my thoughts.

"Yes, Goody?"

"What's left?"

"What do you mean, Goody?"

"I mean, what's left? What's left to see in the markets? It seems like we've seen it all."
I was on a roll.

Raymond gazed at me.

"Raymond, we've seen inflation, recession, stagflation. We've seen rising interest rates, falling interest rates, stock market crashes, wars, invasions, space shuttles blowing up. We've seen bull markets, bear markets…..Raymond… Raymond," I continued, "What's left? What is it that we have not yet seen?"

Raymond G., the Big Man, was always one the brightest, quickest wittiest people that I have ever known. He took a sip of his scotch, let out a satisfied "Aaaahhh" and answered resolutely, "The aliens, Goody…. We haven't seen what happens when the aliens land."

I was stunned. It was so right, so obvious. *The fucking aliens.* That is what we hadn't seen yet.

Using the vast wealth of knowledge and experience that we had accumulated, we began to develop the market scenario that would unfold if the aliens did land. Melissa put down two more drinks in front of us as we discussed the matter.

We surmised that when the aliens were first spotted, the world markets would go into a devastating free fall. The markets would have to discount the possibility that the aliens were going to eat us, or enslave us, or steal all of the water and air from the planet, or that they would just want to fuck us up.

The market decline would continue unabated, characterized by extreme panic and hysteria until such time that the aliens actually landed.

Once the aliens touched down, a huge swelling gigantic stock market rally would begin, in order to discount the possibility that they weren't go to eat us, fuck us up, or do anything bad at all. Maybe, they just wanted to be friends, and give up the secrets to eternal life or anti-gravity, or something really cool like that.

From that day on, Raymond and I knew that if the aliens ever came, we were ready.

CHAPTER 16

LEADERS OF THE PACK

When Michael decided **to step down** from the branch manager's position to return to being a broker, it began a several year period when the firm sought to replace him, with very uneven results.

Bache had been acquired by the Prudential, and soon morphed into Prudential Securities. The old ways of doing things were yielding to a larger, more distant corporate structure, which was learning by doing. Prudential's first three tries at installing a new leader failed miserably, as three different branch managers were quickly given the boot.

Michael's departure roughly coincided with one of the most publicized Wall Street scandals of the late 1980's, the failure of Drexel Burnham Lambert, the firm made infamous by the junk bond scandal. From the wreckage, Prudential Securities bought some of Drexel's retail brokerage operations, which included the Drexel office in Hartford, which would be merged into my Prudential Securities branch.

Most of the employees from the local Drexel office fled to other firms in town, but a few went reluctantly forward to join us at Prudential, among which was their Branch Manager, Reggie Pinkerton. When Michael stepped down, the firm had Reggie ready to step in.

Reggie Pinkerton supposedly had relatives on the Mayflower which helped found the Plymouth colony in early American history. He wore bow ties, had a deeply furrowed brow, and carried himself with a pretentious attitude, which was only amplified by the fact that he was also a drunk.

From the beginning, things did not go well with Reggie Pinkerton at the helm. It didn't help that Reggie genuinely hated the Prudential organization for a plethora of reasons. He felt that they had cannibalized his previous firm, Drexel. He resented the new industry model that Prudential Securities represented, combining a common insurance carrier with an old line Wall Street brokerage firm.

Reggie was steeped in the traditional Wall Street models. Drexel was old school; Prudential Securities was not.

Reggie had absolutely no interest in learning anything about the operational systems within the branch. He barely knew had to use his own computer. His office activity was limited to watching his monitor to follow stock prices. He learned about the order entry system so that he could trade stocks, primarily for himself, although he did do some trading for clients as well.

Reggie neither held meetings nor attended meetings. Some days he wouldn't bother showing up; other days he left the office at about the time that the bars opened, and then came back sloshed for a little while in the late afternoon.

At the time, we had a very experienced Operations manager who, fortunately, knew everything there was to know about how to run a branch office. Between the two of us, we tried to keep anything routine that needed to be done, or signed off on, as far away from Reggie as possible. That was fine with him, because he did not want to be bothered to do anything for the firm that he clearly despised.

However, sometimes things happen that actually do require a Branch Manager to handle the problem or issue. When things like that started to pop up with a number of the large producers in the office, several brokers began calling the Regional Manager for assistance, complaining that they had a drunken absentee manager who was not helping them with their problems.

To make things worse, a number of different Compliance related issues and deficiencies began seeping upwards like bureaucratic sewage. In no time at all, the firm sent Reggie Pinkerton packing on his personal Mayflower, where he could regularly be seen at the local pubs sitting with other men who wore bow ties, talking of the past.

When things started to go wrong at the Hartford branch office, the firm took strong action and sent in the Wall Street equivalent of a decontamination clean up squad, but without the bright yellow and orange Haz-Mat outfits.

In this case, they brought in Joseph Denton., a manager from out west to come in, straighten out procedures, and reestablish the rule of law. Joey D., as I liked to call him, was an older, no nonsense disciplinarian type manager who had a reputation as a go to guy for these type of clean up assignments.

Joey D. was about 60 years old, who looked like an elder David Hasslehoff, but with curly white hair. While he certainly didn't have the Hoff's physique, he was about 5'10, and in good shape. Joey D. looked like the men in the Sunday newspaper ads who modeled suits, expensive watches, ties and shirts.

During one Christmas party which he hosted, Joey D. wore a tuxedo with a bright red, wide cumber bund. I'd never actually seen someone wear a cumber bund, but instead of making Joey D. look like an over the hill matador, the cumber bund actually looked good on him. It made me feel woefully underdressed in my simple pinstriped suit. When I went over to say hello and shake his hand, I noticed that he had perfectly manicured and polished nails.

Joey D. came to the branch with his personal assistant Alicia. riding by his side. Alicia was about 30, blonde, gorgeous, and without a doubt, one of the sexiest women
I'd ever seen. Her body was perfect, and she wore beautiful dresses and skirts that were all on the short side. Her clothing always showed off her perfectly defined legs and tight lower thigh muscles as she walked by.

One day, my office door was open as she passed by in a particularly short skirt that made me gasp and sigh out loud. I called to her, and when she came into my office, I picked up my pitcher of ice water and asked her if she would pour it on me slowly. She didn't seem particularly amused, and called me a nasty name, with a scornful look in her flashing green eyes, before turning and walking away. I knew that she really liked me but was trying to keep her composure, at least in my dreams.

It was immediately clear that Joey D. did not travel with this beautiful blonde Tonto just because of her looks; Alicia was one of the most talented branch manager's assistants that I had ever seen. She knew everything about the firm's systems, and could handle just about any problem in minutes, where others might take hours or days.

Working together with Joey D., they cleaned up all of the mess that Reggie Pinkerton had left behind, and then began instituting their own brand of branch discipline.

When it comes to Wall Street branch managers, there are two general types; there are the broker friendly managers who see the brokers as the ones that produce the revenue that butters the bread of the firm.

Michael used to refer to the brokers as his "book of business." and he needed all of them to be successful, and he was willing to work with them towards that goal.

Then, there are the managers who are droids for the administrative, compliance and legal requirements of the firm. They see the brokers as undisciplined children who need to be beaten down and kept in their place. They usually begin by firing all of the lower and under achievers in the office to establish authority, and then proceed to establish oppressive procedures to assure compliance with all of the rules.

Joey D was obviously the latter type, and it didn't take long for him to start alienating almost everyone in the office with his Hitler Youth Group sort of attitude.

The brokers began hating him because Joey D. would tell them what parts of their business he did not approve of, such as trading options, trading on margin, trading commodities, or trading just anything which was speculative.

The sales assistants hated him because he did not see them as having any particular worth beyond answering phones, sorting mail, and filling out routine forms.

From my standpoint, Joey D. was an intense micro-manager who left me very little to do as Assistant Manager. He wanted to do everything himself in order to have direct control of everything that went on in the branch. That was fine with me. It made my life easier and kept Joey D. on my side of the playing field the entire time he was there.

I've always believed that you never really know someone until you go and get loaded with them. To my initial surprise, Joey D. was all for going out for drinks, either at lunch, after work, or sometimes even mid-day. In a bar setting, he became a very different person who enjoyed sexist humor, and had an amazing tolerance for booze.

Sometimes, we would down for or five Long Island Iced Teas or margaritas during lunch at BT's. After a while, Joey D's cheeks would get all red and flushed; he reminded me of a little of Santa Claus, in a well-tailored business suit, with his twinkling blue eyes and his big smile. But when we got back to the office, his cheery glow would disappear, and it was back to the grim grey business of running a branch by the letter.

I later found out why Joey D. was so happy once he got outside of the office. He and Alicia were apparently having a torrid affair which everyone except for me seemed to know about. I found the thought of the two of them together somewhat disturbing.

However, I didn't have to contemplate such sordid visions for very long. Once again, the complaints and dissension in the ranks began to mount. Once the cleanup was completed, the two of them were shipped out of Hartford, heading off to some other branch that had gone astray.

At this point, the firm knew that they needed to bring someone in who was a "people person" to calm down and assuage the rumbling crowd in the office. That is where Roland Jameson came in. He was a lifetime Merrill Lynch person who had managed a small satellite branch for them, but was not being given the opportunity to manage a full sized branch there.

Roland was a very friendly and pleasant guy, two qualities which were not desirable in a Merrill manager.

So Roland decided to move on, and ended up managing my branch at Prudential Securities.

Roland may have been nice and charming, but once he was away from the structured folds of Mother Merrill's skirt, he quickly floundered administratively. Most of the people in the branch liked him, but the Regional Manager didn't. In less than a year, Roland was returned home to Merrill, where he became Assistant Manager in the Hartford branch.

Finally, on the fourth attempt, the firm got it right when they imported Charles Beauregard from his branch in the Deep South to act as branch manager in Hartford.

Charles Beauregard was not too hot and not too cold; he was just right.

CHAPTER 17

PEOPLE SAY THE DUMBEST THINGS

Over the years, **I've had the opportunity** to deal with many people from so many walks of life that I've learned a lot about people. I've seen how the personal temperament and professional background of a client affects the nature of my relationship with them, as well as the investment results in their portfolio.

I've particularly enjoyed my clients who are smart and interested in learning about investing, because of their ability to absorb information, interpret it, and make good investment decisions.

That is not to say that the smartest people are the best investors, not at all. One of the brightest clients that I ever had also has the distinction of having made one of the dumbest investment decisions that I've seen.

Her name was Wilma. She was a Ph.D. and a full professor at one of the local universities. I "inherited" her small IRA account when another broker left the firm, and her account was reassigned to me.

When I first contacted Wilma to introduce myself, and advised her that I would be handling her account, she asked if she could come into the office with her husband to meet with me.

While I have not personally met all of my clients, I've tried to meet as many as I can, whenever possible. I've found that it helps to be able to put a face together with a voice. I can tell a lot about person when they are sitting with me, talking about all the things in life that matter to them.

Late one morning, Wilma came into the office with her husband Nathan.

I don't recall what I was expecting, but when she walked in, I began feeling goose bumps on my arms when I reached out to shake her hand. She was about 40, short brown hair, a cute turned up nose, and brown eyes that I could see through her thin wire framed glasses.

I was surprised by my reaction, because while she was attractive, I wouldn't have called her goose-bump material. I tried to act cool as I felt my cheeks get a little flushed.

I shook Nathan's hand, and did a quick half turn, leading them towards the conference room. I hoped they wouldn't notice my mojo rising.

Soon, we were all were sitting in the conference room talking about Wilma's twenty thousand dollar IRA account. I was happy to be sitting down, tucked under the conference room table.

Nathan sat very quietly while Wilma and I spoke.

Now, not that Wilma was some kind of stripper goddess, but I just didn't understand what she was doing with Nathan. He was much older looking than Wilma; severely balding, very skinny, haggard looking. For some reason, he reminded me of the custodian in my elementary school.

In between sentences with Wilma, I started to get flash images of Nathan and Wilma together, in an intimate, personal way. It was distracting, even as a momentary mental picture. I pictured Wilma in a black leather dominatrix outfit standing over a tied up and blindfolded Nathan. She was digging the heel of her black boots into the back of his neck, when the image dissipated.

For a moment, I pictured the scene the other way around, with Nathan in the leather outfit. That was beyond disturbing. I shut the images out of my mind.

During the conversation, I discovered that Nathan installed fire alarm systems in businesses. He and Wilma apparently knew each other since they were kids. That explained a lot, especially to me, since I had met Debbie when we were kids in high school. I understood the bond created when two people grew up together.

Before we finished the meeting, Wilma mentioned that her mother was going to start gifting her money from different CD's that would be coming due over the next year. I told her that I looked forward to working with her in the future. By then, it seemed safe for me to get up and walk them to the front door of the office.

A few months later, Wilma and Nathan split up and Wilma moved to Chicago to work as head of a school of nursing. This happened to coincide in that period in my life where I made several trips to Chicago for "due diligence" conferences.

Over the next year, Wilma's mother sent about $60,000 into a new individual non-IRA account that I had established for Wilma. It happened to be good time to be adding money to a portfolio. The world markets were moving upwards, and the mutual funds that I had bought for Wilma began rising sharply in value.

There was nothing particularly special or unique about the asset allocation that I had set up for Wilma. It was a mix of domestic and foreign stock funds, with a high yield tax free bond fund added in. It was a nice, classic portfolio. No rocket science involved.

About a year later, Wilma's account was up about 15%, and I happened to be traveling to Chicago for yet another "due diligence" conference. I arranged to meet Wilma for dinner, and fantasized about taking her back to my hotel room.

We met at a restaurant that was enclosed in glass on one of the corners of the Golden Mile in Chicago. Wilma looked very preppy in a light sweater with a cross around her neck, brown pants, and large dangling gold hoop earrings. Her cheeks looked very pink. She said she had been doing a lot of running and roller blading.

Actually, she looked like she had put on some weight, but I could still feel a physical reaction brewing. I considered inviting her back to my hotel after dinner, but thought it way too inappropriate and unprofessional, if she wasn't into it.

Dinner was pleasant, filled with the kind of small talk that I would typically share with a client. She didn't seem the least bit interested in me as a person. It was more like a business meeting with food.

I kept noticing how cute she was, so I asked her if she wanted to do some shots of tequila. She passed. I was disappointed. I tried to entice her to try a shot or two. She passed again.

We were heading towards dessert when she asked me if I wanted to come over to her place for coffee. Soon, we were in a taxi heading towards her apartment in a tall building overlooking the river.

I'd like to be able to tell how I began unbuttoning her blouse as soon as we got into the apartment; about how I took off her little wire framed glasses, and led her into the bedroom.

Wilma didn't go in the bathroom and come out wrapped in a little white towel. She didn't go to put on something "more comfortable." She didn't ask me if I wanted to snuggle up on the huge leather couch and watch a movie.

It wasn't like that at all. Absolutely nothing happened.

I have learned that you never have to ask a woman if she wants to have sex with you, because she will always let you know. Wilma didn't let me know anything.

Wilma offered me a glass of wine. We made some more small talk about the nice view of the water from her apartment. I told her how much I enjoyed the Art Institute in Chicago, and that perhaps we could go there during my next trip to the Windy City.

Then I left and headed back to the hotel.

I was pleased that I had acted properly and professionally. After all, why would I have had any sort of expectation of anything different? I was obviously the one who had the hots for her, not the other way around. I sighed, and thought about it during the taxi ride back to the hotel.

I didn't speak to Wilma again for a few weeks when she called to let me know that she was sending another $10,000 that her mother had given her, but this time, it was like talking to a totally different person. Her sweet, quiet intelligent voice sound crabby, mean and absolutely scornful.

Wilma told me to leave the money in the account, and not to invest it for her. She said that she was completing a course in investing, and would let me know what she wanted to do with the new money. Wilma didn't even want to hear any of my suggestions.

They say "Hell hath no fury like a woman's scorn,"

but I wasn't sure what it was that I had done, or had not done to be so scorned. Could she have been offended that I didn't try to take off her clothes?

I was, after all, still married to Debbie at the time, even though our relationship was obviously showing definite cracks.

Should my approach with a brilliant professor been different? Was I supposed to have started reading poetry to her, or offered her a back rub, or at least made a verbal offer to have sex with her? I just didn't know, but it certainly seemed way too late to find out.

Two weeks later, Wilma called back again, and indicated that she was very displeased with her portfolio. I, of course, pointed out that the portfolio of three mutual funds was up over 15% in about a year, an excellent return which had also outpaced the market's return. She responded that the investments were inappropriate, and she wanted the previous mutual fund trades rescinded.

In the securities industry, "inappropriate" and "rescission" are two buzzwords that indicate that the client had either spoken to a lawyer, or has spoken to someone who has spoken to a lawyer. These words are usually used in cases where a client has lost money in a transaction, and wants the transaction cancelled, as if it never happened, kind of like a do-over for losers.

However, in this case, the mutual funds purchased were plain vanilla, nothing exotic, nothing unusual, a classic mix of domestic and foreign blue chip stocks. In addition, she had a profit of about $9,000 on a $60,000 investment.

I pointed out to her that if she didn't like the funds, she could either sell them out and take the large profit, or exchange them free of charge into other funds in the same respective mutual fund families. She wanted no part of either. She wanted the trades cancelled as if they never happened.

Feeling exasperated, I pointed out that she was entitled to the $9000 profit, and by rescinding the trade, the profit would go away, and her account value would drop by $9000. It simply made no sense to do that. No one ever rescinds profitable trades.

It was like talking to a boot. I could not believe what I was hearing.

After a few more futile minutes of trying to reason with her, she indicated that if I didn't take care of it, she would be contacting the Branch Manager. My first thought was that Charles, the branch manager was not even going to believe this.

I assured Wilma that I would not only take care of it, but would also advise the Branch Manager of the situation. I mentioned that she was certainly free to contact him if she wished, but I was confident that he would give her the same analysis and advice.

At that point the conversation ended abruptly and I started printing out the account's activity and position information so I could bring it to Charles to show him what it was that she wanted done.

When I entered his office, Charles was watching the screen. He had an option position that was going the wrong way.

"Fucking bullshit market," I heard him grumble.

Charles was in his mid to late forties, and was a very talented branch manager who grew up in Alabama and recently transferred to Hartford from a branch in Louisiana. He had a deep southern drawl which took a little while to get used to.

Charles and I got along very well. He and I were two of the few people who had no problem occasionally using four letter words in Wall Street type discussions. Sometimes, four letter words can add a certain extra emphasis, when used in environments where no one would expect it.

All of the other brokers in the office liked Charles because he was what we used to call "a broker's manager," meaning that he understood that the brokers who produced all the revenues were his bread and butter, as opposed to the Compliance Department which often acted like an anti-sales department.

Charles' attitude towards the sales assistants in the office (who were all women) was sometimes a little rough. I'd often heard him make some crude remarks about some of the sales assistants, and two of his favorite words to use in that context were bitch and cunt, which he pronounced "beeeetch " and "cuuuunnt." He, of course, never said it in front of any of the sales assistants. I found his whole general attitude unusual, but amusing.

After I explained the situation, his first remark was, "Are you sheeeeting me Don? This beeeetch wants us to break profitable trades?"

"Yuuuuup," I answered with my best Southern-Brooklyn accent.

"Is this beeeeetch fucking stupid?" He was still watching his screen.

I answered that she was actually a brilliant professor, but she had taken some kind of investment course. I didn't know what they were telling her in the classes, but this is what she wanted to do.

I suggested that he call her, which he did later that morning.

Then he called me back into his office.

"That is one fucking dumb ass beeeetch. Give her what she wants Don. Take the information to Scott in the Operations Department. Tell him to bust the trades. *Damn*, that was a stupid ass woman."

The $9000 profit went into the branch's "error account" where it was used to offset any unprofitable trades that the branch might have to absorb.

Wilma left the money in the account sitting in money market funds for about six months, and then called Charles to complain that the money wasn't growing. She transferred out the account soon after that. I never heard from her again.

CHAPTER 18

DON'T MAKE ME COME BACK AGAIN

Being a supervisory **person** in a large Wall Street branch is not easy. Most of the broker/financial advisors have egos the size of Brazil. As a general rule, the biggest producers have the largest egos.

As in life, there are all types of brokers in the business. Some are "Type A" guerilla marketers who walk around wearing headsets, talking to prospective clients, even as they sort and stuff sales material into envelopes to mail out to their prospects. These are the people who tend to drive the Mercedes or BMW's, hang out at the local upscale bars, and hustle willing sales assistants to local hotels after an early evening of drinking, before going home to their wives or girlfriends.

Some brokers approach growing their business through social networking, whether it is through their synagogues, churches, fraternal organizations, or most often, at country and golf clubs. They hang out in places where they are likely to find stable professionals with normal families, and reasonably sized portfolios. Since many prospective clients go to these types of places to find other people who share their same religious, cultural, or social backgrounds, if they can also find someone to help them invest their money, all the better.

Then, there are the preppie type brokers. They are usually from old money families, often Ivy educated, whether or not they are smart. Many of them project an attitude that they are better than you because they made their money the old fashioned way, by inheriting it.

Most of the preps have a relatively small number of clients, but large amounts of assets under management. Usually, their biggest accounts are their own, and the accounts of family members or close friends of the families. Often, the preps appear to have gone into the business for the sole purpose of managing the family money, while earning large amounts of commissions at the same time.

My office had a few of these prep types. The preppiest of them all was this guy named Percy. If you were to construct a mental stereotype of what Percy looked like based on his name, you would probably be dead on. Percy was tall, thin, and frail looking, usually wearing suspenders, a bow tie, or both. His glasses were tortoise shell on the top half, and gold metal on the bottom of the frames.

Percy's hair was a sandy brown, always impeccably neat and well groomed, with a very clean part in his hair that reminded me of a photo of T.S. Eliot on the cover of one of his books of poetry that I owned. I never met T.S. Eliot but always imagined him as being incredibly pompous, based on hearing him read his poetry on tapes. Percy didn't look like Eliot, but emitted the same kind of haughty obnoxious attitude that I would have expected from Eliot.

During our infrequent interactions, Percy always acted like I was some kind of street urchin. He was utterly indignant that someone like me could be supervising someone like him. Percy felt that if he was primarily managing his own family's holdings, why should anyone be allowed to interfere in any way, let alone an occasionally potty mouthed Assistant Manager who was raised in a place like Brooklyn?

Clearly, Percy thought himself smarter than anyone else on Wall Street. Instead of investing in normal things like tax free bonds or mutual funds, he preferred to find his own obscure stocks which he would presumably research on his own before building significant large sized positions in various accounts. I'd seen a number of the portfolios that he managed, and it struck me that he was always looking for securities where he could gain some kind of edge over other investors on the basis of his own intellectual and research abilities.

I had no problem with the way Percy, or anyone else for that matter, chose to run their own businesses. My view was that as long as you made money for your clients and didn't break any laws, it was all good. Different strokes for different folks. No one ever had a monopoly on ways to consistently make money in the financial markets.

Sometimes, the path least taken is truly the one that leads you to the Promised Land.

As for Percy's haughty and self-righteous attitude, it was no skin off my back. Assholes abound on Wall Street.

Most of Percy's business came from about a dozen accounts, with four or five of them being family related trusts. For the most part, he just did his thing without bothering anyone, or causing any kind of trouble from a supervisory standpoint. Percy marched to a different drummer.

That was fine with me because I was always very busy trying to handle my own clients, while covering my supervisory duties in the office as well.

One afternoon, the Branch Manager was out, and the phone rang. It was a lady from the Compliance Department. She wanted to talk to me about Percy.

As an Assistant Manager, I always tried to act friendly and chummy with the Compliance and Law Departments, under the philosophy that it is best to keep your friends close and your enemies closer. The lady's name was Jane, and I had never spoken to her before. I started to turn on the" love-me-cause-I'm-Donny" charm, but she wasn't having any part of it.

She was from the monitoring area, and they had detected what appeared to be "front running" by a broker in the office named Percy.

"Front running" is when a broker buys a security for their own account, and then proceeds to continue buying the same security for different client accounts in an effort to push up the price of the security in the marketplace through the demand that they are creating.

Ideally, the frontrunner then sells out his position at the higher prices which result from the artificial demand. Sometimes, the frontrunner will actually sell his shares directly to his own clients, pocketing both the profits and the commissions.

Purposefully trying to move the price of any of the major large or mid cap stocks on an exchange is difficult on the institutional level, and almost impossible on the retail level. The markets for those kinds of securities are very deep and liquid, with many large players ready to jump on any outsized moves, on either side of the market.

In contrast, when it comes to very small, thinly traded stocks, creating stock price movement is not only possible on the retail level, it is sometimes hard to avoid.

Many obscure and thinly traded stocks exist in a sort of twilight market world where any sudden spikes in either buying or selling can cause huge price swings in the stock price. If a stock only trades a few thousand shares a day on average, then someone trying to buy 100,000 shares at one time will likely have to pay higher and higher prices for shares if they are trying to buy the position all at once.

Subsequently, the first thousand shares bought are likely to be at a far lower price than the last thousand shares of the 100,000 share lot. The potential for front running brokers to make instant profits off of the backs of their clients is huge, as long as they don't get caught.

However, since front running is one of the oldest illegal practices in the book, there have always been numerous systems put in place to prevent it.

After Jane gave me the particulars about the trades and accounts in question, I walked over to Scott's office where I could access the Operations Department's systems to check out the activity in the different accounts.

It certainly had the appearance of front running, with Percy buying stock for his own account, and then buying much larger amounts for other client accounts at higher prices.

The only difference was that Percy wasn't selling any of the stock; he was just accumulating more and more of it. While it was technically front running, as long as he wasn't selling out ahead of his clients, it was more like piggish unprofessional behavior than it was genuine front running.

But the rules are the rules, so I went to talk to Percy about it. After I explained the
situation, I immediately saw that Percy was not going to be either cooperative or agreeable about the matter. Instead, he began telling me that this was none of my business, none of Compliance Department's business, and that he knew exactly what he was doing. Further, he indicated that his clients had absolutely no problem with what was going on in their accounts.

Rather than belabor the matter, I simply told Percy to not do anything that was going to cause an issue with the Compliance Department while we were on my watch. I was hoping that it would end there.

Of course, it didn't.

Early the next week, I received another call from Jane of the Compliance Department. She seemed less than friendly, and even bitchy, when she asked me why I hadn't spoken to Percy. I was annoyed at both her attitude, and her presumption that I had not addressed the issue with Percy.

"Percy is continuing to buy the stock in his client accounts, while he is selling the same stock in his personal accounts," she said.

Now, I was starting to get pissed.

I quickly explained that I had, in fact, spoken to Percy, clearly explaining to him that he needed to stop this questionable activity. But, as I said, I was getting pissed, so I gave Jane short shrift, and said that I needed to go talk to Percy, and I'd get back to her later in the day.

After I hung up the phone, I took a deep breath, stopping whatever I had been doing, and headed to Percy' office. His door was open.

I knocked sideways on his open door, and said something like "Excuse me Percy, but I just got another call from the Compliance Department, and I need to talk to you."

He immediately became an asshole. I told him what the Compliance Department had told me.

Percy proceeded to lecture me about his family trust, and how under the terms of the trust, certain monies had to be distributed, and his liquidations were all in accordance with the terms of the trust…and on…and on…and on he went. He began telling me how he was going to contact his family's attorney to prevent the firm from stopping him from fulfilling the terms of the trust document.

He continued to ramble until I finally said, "Percy, stop whatever you are doing that is causing the Compliance Department to call me. If you, or your family, have any issues about anything, please take it up with the Legal Department. Percy, I am not interested in having to come in here again to deal with this. "

Then I walked out, hoping that he had gotten the message.

But no....Percy had to continue to be an asshole.

When I received a third call from Jane a few days later, it happened to be after a long drinking lunch at BT's where I had consumed several Long Island Iced Teas mixed with tequila.

Again, as it happened, Charles, the Branch Manager, was out of the office for a few days.

I don't recall if Percy's door was open or closed, but I specifically remember barging into his office, leaning over his desk so he could smell the booze on my breath, and saying, "What the fuck do you think you're doing?"

He looked at me incredulously, and said something stupid like, "Where do get the nerve to come marching into my office? "

I was drunk and angry at the time, so I leaned in even closer and said, "Percy, don't fuck with me. You haven't listened to a word that I've said to you, and now, I'm really tired of dealing with this bullshit issue. "

"I don't have to deal with your....bullshit...either, Don. "

There was something so forced, so fake, so bitchy about the way he said "bullshit." I wanted to take the pen off his desk, and stick it up his ass. I tried to remain reasonably calm and professional, probably realizing that the tequila was starting to talk. "Don't make me come back here Percy," I said sternly, as I backed off towards the door.

"Or what, Don? " Percy sneered as he backed away in his desk chair.

He said it in such a contemptuous way that I wanted to pound his head into the office wall.

"Percy," I said. "The next time I have to come in here, I'm going to pick up your skinny ass, and throw you face first through the fucking window to watch you fall 16 floors down……and while you're falling, I'm going to throw your desk chair out the window after you, so it hits your dead body on the ground." (That is an almost exact quote.)

"You can't threaten me," he answered meekly, almost under his breath.

"That's not a threat," I replied. I turned around to head back towards my office.

I learned a long time ago that if you can threaten really well, you will probably never be called upon to actually deliver the goods. That is what seemed to have happened. There were no more calls from the compliance Department. Percy clearly saw me as some kind of hoodlum in an Yves St. Laurent shirt.

I was surprised that Percy never filed any kind of complaint about me threatening him. He probably figured that with me only a few doors away, it simply wasn't worth the risk.

Sometimes it really is better to be feared than loved…especially on Wall Street.

CHAPTER 19

YOU'RE NOT JOHNNY

I've read a **lot of books about coincidence** and the meaning of it all. And while I have seen much coincidence in and around my life, nothing compares to what happened to me while I was trying to be someone else.

By the early 1990's, while I was in the midst of splitting up with Debbie, we were getting along so poorly that I couldn't stand being in the same house, let alone sleeping in the same bedroom.

In order to avoid going home, some days after work I would hang out by the bar at Brown Thompson, drinking perfect margaritas or Long Island Iced Teas mixed with tequila. After five or six or seven drinks, I'd eventually find my way home and go into the spare downstairs bedroom that we called the Music Room. Most nights, I'd play sad songs on my acoustic guitar until I got so tired that the alcohol haze helped me fall asleep on the sleeper sofa.

Other days, I'd come home on time and put on my running clothes and sneakers. We lived on a large cul-de-sac which was about a tenth of a mile around. I would start running around and around using some mental cue to keep track of the laps.

My favorite was to think of the first thirty issues of the *Fantastic Four* comics. With each lap, I'd think of what that each corresponding issue was about. The first lap was about the Fantastic Four and the Mole Man, the second lap was about the Fantastic Four and the Skrull, the third was the Miracle Man, the fourth was the Sub-Mariner, and so on.

After about thirty laps, I'd take a shower in the bathroom off of the Music Room, and hide out downstairs until Debbie went to asleep, when I would go upstairs to lie on the couch and watch TV.

But some nights…some nights, I'd wait until about 10 PM, and then I'd take my favorite electric guitar, a white Fender Stratocaster with a "Steal Your Face" Grateful dead sticker on the front, and I'd go down to a biker bar in Bristol, Connecticut called the Common Ground to play in the weekly open jams that they held two nights a week.

Usually, there were a few dozen musicians who would show up to play. Many people knew each other from different bands that they played in. There were a lot of regulars, but no one who I knew, at least at the beginning.

I liked going down to jam night because it gave me a chance to forget about Debbie and Wall Street, and all of the agony that I perceived in my life. I would have a few drinks, get on the stage with a bunch of strangers, and play loud rock and roll music until closing.

Most of the musicians were nice hard working blue collar people who came down to play and forget the stresses of their own lives, which I'm sure were way more challenging than my leaving-the-bitch blues.

Given that that Wall Street firms frown on their managers doing things in public that might expose the firm to undesirable public attention, my playing in a biker bar, toasted on tequila shots, was not something that I particularly wanted anyone to know about.

So I decided to adopt a name that I had made up one afternoon when I was hanging out with Raymond.

We were joking about what we would call our first Wall Street oriented rock and roll band. We both wanted all the band members to stuff the front of their pants with socks. The band would be called the Dick Socks. . Since I was the singer, I needed a good stage name. We were both fans of the Elliot Wave market theory, so we came up with the name Johnny Wave.

When I went down to the biker bar in Bristol to drink tequila and play rock and roll, I was Johnny Wave.

For about a month, I played with a loosely knit group of six or seven guys. The best drummer in the house was a guy named Frank. I enjoyed playing with Frank because he hit the drums very hard, and I could hear him above the din of the electric guitars. I also had fun playing with a young kid named Gus who played a nasty shred metal style of guitar, filled with excessive effects, which fit in well with my drunken classic rock style of playing, or at least I thought so at the time.

I didn't talk much. I showed up just to play. I found it a little disarming when people said stuff like "Hi, Johnny," or "How's it going, Johnny?" or anything where I had to remember that I was Johnny, not Donny.

One weekend, I was sitting in the living room of my best friend George, who always preferred the stage name of "Guitar George." (George was always better at playing the guitar than coming up with anything original.)

We had played in bands together on and off for years. I always thought that we sounded great together, but alas, George wanted me to play like the Boston Philharmonic, with every song being perfect and exactly the same as the last time, and in the same amounts of minutes and seconds.

I just could not do that. I wanted to be Bruce Springsteen meets Jerry Garcia meets Motown. We were always in such different places musically that it was merciful to both of us when we finally stopped playing together, and just hung out as friends.

One weekend, I was telling George about relieving my angst by going down to play at the bar in Bristol. When I mentioned that I was using another name, he said, "Playing under a phony name is just going to get you in trouble."

It was an innocuous comment, which I just ignored at the time. I attributed it to the fact that he was bothered by the fact I didn't ever invite him to come play, not that he ever would have considered it worth his while to drag his ass down to a bar as far as Bristol to play for free.

There was so much going on in my life at the time that I found great relief in playing, My only hesitation was that I knew driving back home late at night, loaded on tequila was not a good idea. If I got stopped at two in the morning with a car full of guitars and equipment, I was likely going to get busted, and DUI's were not particularly tolerated on Wall Street.

I tried to be careful about drinking too much, but it's tough when you're playing and singing with a lot of people who are drinking. Sometimes, it was easy to get carried away.

One night, I had been sitting at a table for hours, having had way too many tequila shots, before I finally found my way to the stage with Frank and Gus, and this very tall burly guy with a huge handlebar mustache who played bass and didn't talk much. He looked like an Olaf or a Sven, but I think he was called Big Jim.

We went on to the stage. I felt a little woozy. I was waiting for the drummer to stop sucking on his beer, when this guy in a leopard skin body suit and beat up brown boots walks up onto the stage with a tambourine, drum sticks, and one of those wood fish percussion things in his hands.

I said something like "Hi, who are you?"

He said, "My name is Chico. What you gonna play, man?"

Chico had long greasy looking black curly hair that hung down randomly down around him. He had a "soul patch" on his chin, and a cross tattoo on the side of his neck facing me. I had no idea where he came from, but I noticed that he had a few friends in the audience, with at least two of them being hot looking Latina women.

I was a little dizzy, but I just had to see what this cat had in his bag of tricks.

"How about some straight ahead rock and roll? Let's start with *Devil With The Blue Dress*, and just go from there?"

"What are you playing man, my mother's fucking music? You want me to play my mother's fucking music? What's wrong with you man?"

I knew that I was very drunk, but I could see that Chico was even more gone, and could easily become an aggressive jerkoff. So, I walked over to the drummer and told him to not stop playing until I gave him the twirling finger wrap-it-up hand signal.

"Yeah," I said to Chico, "Your Mama liked the music when I played it for her last night."

Before Chico could move, I yelled "One, two, three four," and everybody on stage started playing.

After Chico came on stage, two other guitar players also jumped on stage and quickly plugged their guitars into a huge old house amp. It was loud; very, very loud. The lights were hot. My head was spinning, but somehow I was remembering the words.

Everybody in the audience started having so much fun that they were moving the tables from the center of the floor so there was room to dance. Chico was pumping away on his percussion instruments. Everybody did a solo, and then everybody did another solo, and then another solo after that.

Chico was getting flushed. I could see him breathing hard, but he kept banging away. Actually, he wasn't bad at all. I don't know how long it all went on for.

I remember seeing a big biker dude holding a chair and dancing with it. I remember a girl dancing barefoot on top of a table. I remember seeing rainbows in the overhead lights. Finally, I remember Chico in his disgustingly soaked and sweated up body outfit, looking around for someone to wrap it up.

But I waited until it looked like he was going to drop and collapse on the stage.

Then it was over.

My eyeballs were vibrating in my head. My ears were ringing when Chico came over and put his sweaty tattooed arm around my neck.

"So Chico, how was your Momma's music?" I said.

"Good, man, real good." He laughed.

I had another shot of tequila with Frank the drummer, and was endlessly thankful that I made it home safely that night.

A few days later, I was in my office when the phone rang. It was the receptionist.

"Don, there is a broker-of-the-day call on the line, and the broker of the day is out. No one else is answering. Will you take the call?"

"Um, sure, "I said. "Send it over."

It was someone who needed to sell 47 shares of some lesser-known stock that he had received when he left his last company.

I was really busy and stressed that day, but if this guy needed to get rid of a few hundred dollars of stock, I was going to at try to help him. I told him that he needed to either send in or deliver the physical stock certificates, and I would have my assistant, Cathy, set up the new account and help him through all of the paperwork.

He told me that he had called a few brokerage firms in the telephone book, and I was the only one who he could find who wanted to help him. I told him that I was happy to help, and gave him Cathy's direct phone number.

The only thing that I personally had to do to effect the transaction was to sign two forms and write one ticket, which I would do after Cathy had the client fill out all of the new account paperwork and sign the stock certificate.

It should have been one of those antiseptic little good deeds that that is here and gone like a dandelion puff in the wind; sign the papers, push the button, send the client a check; over and out.

Two days later, I was talking to someone on the phone with my door closed, when I heard someone knocking. There was a narrow window in the middle of the door, but the shape outside looked unfamiliar. I excused myself from the telephone call.

I went to the door and opened it, and standing on the other side was Frank, the drummer from the bar in Bristol. He looked astounded. I thought that this could not possibly be happening. He said, "You're not Johnny!"

"Frank?" I said, gasping for air.

"You're not Johnny," he said, almost accusingly. You're Don Goodman, and you're a stockbroker."

What could I say? So I said, "Frank…I am Johnny, but..but..I'm also me…Don Goodman."

"You're not Johnny," he said again, this time with real emotion in his voice.

I was worried that someone was going come by and see this strange scene outside the Assistant Manager's office. I moved to get Frank inside my office. "Frank, come in, sit down, let me explain."
He came in and sat down. I closed the door behind him.

So I told him about not wanting anyone at the office to know that I was rock and rolling drunk at a biker bar every week. I told him how much fun I had playing every week, and how it relieved the stress of all that was going on in my life. I asked him not to mention it when we played at the bar. He seemed cool with it. I had Cathy take care of the stock certificate, and we later sent him his check.

It was strange how Frank had found our firm in the telephone book, only after being ignored by several other firms that he called. Then, with 25 other brokers in my office, he ended up with me because no one else was available.

There were also several lines of defense before someone could just walk into my office. First, there was the receptionist at the main desk. Then, there was my sales assistant, who sat right outside my door; but neither of them was anywhere to be found. When Frank asked the first person he saw which way was Don Goodman's office, they directed him to my office door.

And to this day, I can still hear Frank saying, "You're not Johnny."

CHAPTER 20

GIMME SHELTER

Despite my professional success, despite having finally bought the trophy house in Simsbury, Connecticut, one of the premier bedroom towns in Connecticut, and despite my passion and devotion to my two young children, Ethan and Elissa, it was obvious that my relationship with Debbie had crumbled into a cesspool of misery that pervaded my every waking moment.

I felt smothered by a perpetual haze of depression.

Debbie and I couldn't spend five minutes in a room together without getting into an argument. I thought that Debbie was suffering from hormonal issues because she would go over the deep end over just about anything. She would begin yelling and spewing profanities in lengthy combinations that would have made an angry sailor recoil in horror.

When I suggested to Debbie that she should go see a physician about her violent mood swings, she told me that I was an asshole. When I offered to go to joint counseling with her, she told me not to bother, and that I should just get the fuck out of the house.

There is truly a thin line between love and hate, and Debbie and I had long since crossed that line. The rose of love had not only died, but it had been crushed underfoot.

The end of our marriage took an agonizingly long time.

Month after month, I would do anything after work, rather than engage Debbie in any kind of conversation or activity.

After our kids went to asleep, I would hide out in the extra room downstairs, and play sad songs about lost love on my acoustic guitar. Some of the tear jerker songs that I played to myself regularly were *Neither One Of Us Wants To Be The First To Say Goodbye,* and *You Don't Bring Me Flowers.*

I had the songbook for Springsteen's *Darkness On The Edge Of Town* album, and there was an endless amount of pain and agony to be mined in his songs of that period.

Near the very end of our marriage, I became too depressed to even play rock music in the biker bar that I had come to frequent. It was hard to talk to people, let alone sing and be animated in front of strangers.

One of the most unexpected things that came out of my self-imposed isolation in a corner of the big house in Simsbury was when I began to paint. Throughout my entire life, I had never even doodled.

It began one afternoon when I was hiding out in the garage. I found a few scraps of wood, and some of Ethan's old poster paints. There was some masking tape lying around, so I taped a geometric pattern onto one of the small flat pieces of board, and began painting it in bright colors, accented by small bursts of florescent spray paint.

I quickly discovered that playing with the colors and shapes relaxed me, and distracted me from the sordid environment on the other side of the door that led into the house. As long as I stayed in the garage, I felt safe from Debbie's verbal onslaughts.

I began spending more and more time painting in the garage, until I finally ran out of paint, as well as pieces of wood to paint on.

The next evening, on my way home from work, I stopped at the art supplies store that I passed every day. The store owner was a friendly bespectacled man with a graying pony tail named Scott.

When Scott asked me what I was looking for, I simply said "paint," knowing hardly anything about actual artist's paints. Scott was very patient, and explained the difference between acrylic paints and oil based paints. He strongly suggested that I work with acrylic paints because I didn't want to wait days, or even hours, for my works to dry. I told him that all of my "work" to date had been on pieces of wood, so he suggested that I try canvas.

I remember thinking, "Canvas! What a concept."

Scott showed me some stretched Russian linen canvas that he had a clearance sale on. I'd never felt anything like that kind of material; it had a rippled, shimmery feel to it, I bought several large canvases.

All of my earliest paintings were nonverbal expressions of my sadness, anger and frustration. The few people-type figures that I painted had boxy robot shapes, and were positioned so that they appeared to be overwhelmed by the dark red and dark blue colors that surrounded them. Other paintings were waves of abstract color, paintings without form; attempts at emotional release with no design or structure to convey the message. I'd never taken an art lesson in my life; for me, painting was like therapy. I continued to paint until soon I had finished about two dozen paintings.

Debbie didn't like the paintings at all. She thought that they were a waste of money.

My Italian Uncle Johnny, who no one would have confused with an art critic, looked at some photos of my work, and said assuredly that "a monkey could do that." Maybe he was right, but painting kept me calm. I didn't cry when I painted, while I usually cried when I sat alone in the music room.

I'm sure that Debbie never believed that I would leave; for a long time I didn't either. But as anyone who has been through those kinds of emotional throes knows, eventually the pain mounts and builds, and continues to increase exponentially, until, finally, you need to do something to stop it.

Suddenly, ending a relationship that I had based my life upon became a necessity in order for me to survive and to continue onwards. Eventually, the day came when relief from the pain became the priority, and I was compelled to do something to make the pain stop.

As impossible as it seemed, and as nauseating as it felt, I began checking out places to live.

I started with dumpy little transient hotels and rooming houses looking for temporary dwellings where I could add on to my self-torment; places where I could sit in squalor and feel even sorrier for myself than I already did.

I checked out a dilapidated transient hotel located on Main Street in East Hartford. As I walked through the lobby I noticed a number of old, dirty looking people standing along the walls of the hallway. They all looked like they came from the movie, *Night of The Living Dead*.

The gnarled old man who ran the hotel led me into a small dark green room that had a cot- type bed against one wall, an old lamp on a small folding table, and a TV that may have worked but was missing a few dials.

For just a moment, I pictured myself on the cot, playing my acoustic guitar, watching the cockroaches crawl on the walls, and counting the mice scurrying past on the floor. I hadn't picked a dumpy hotel to economize; it was more to torture myself for the sin of leaving our children. I wanted to put myself in deep dark corner to hide from my shame and failure.

Ironically, I knew that Debbie would have a problem with me spending money on a dirt cheap room if there was even a possibility of me coming back. Debbie had a real issue about spending money on just about anything. Though we were once both very poor, once we weren't poor anymore, she became far worse in terms of her penny pinching ways.

A few months before, I asked her several times to buy Velveeta cheese, one of my favorite foods, when she went shopping. She didn't buy it because it wasn't on sale.

When I pointed out that I really wanted the cheese, and I didn't care if a two dollar item was on sale, she still refused to buy it. We had several arguments about the Velveeta cheese.

After one shopping trip, when she came home without the cheese again, she claimed that the supermarket had run out of Velveeta cheese, in all sizes. I knew that she was lying, and I told her so. I couldn't understand how she could be so cheap, miserable and antagonistic.

The next time she went shopping, I wrote in big letters on her shopping list, "Please get the Velveeta cheese. Please."

She came home without the cheese again, and said that the store still didn't have any.

This time I was pissed, and started calling her names. Then, I got in my car and drove over to the supermarket to buy the damn cheese.

The dairy case had an entire section of Velveeta cheese in all different sizes. I bought the biggest, most expensive hunk of Velveeta cheese that they had. I took my seven dollar chunk of cheese home to display in front of Debbie, and said, "I guess the store just got in a big shipment of Velveeta cheese, *bitch*."

The previous Thanksgiving, I had offered to cook a traditional Thanksgiving dinner, with all the fixin's for the four of us. However, Debbie insisted that it was a waste of time and money, so she went and bought frozen generic lasagna from the discount food store.

Not even brand-name lasagna, but one with the white generic packaging, and the small black print indicating that it was frozen lasagna. It tasted like crap. No one wanted to eat it except for Debbie.

Debbie's cheapness had even damaged our previous vacations, most recently on our trip to Disneyworld, where she booked a tiny, dark first floor room in a small hotel on the strip, many miles away from the theme park.

The tiny bargain room had two single beds wedged in between the dressers on one side, and a small window on the other side that looked out onto the parking lot. Even Ethan and Elissa were cramped in their shared single bed. I preferred to sleep on the small hard side chair, and use my narrow part of the bed with Debbie to put my feet up on.

It was a lousy little room, with no Mickey Mouse or Magic Kingdom, or anything happy anywhere to be found.

A few weeks before we split up, Debbie and I tried a last ditch attempt at a vacation together with the kids.

Debbie told me about a beach on the Rhode Island shore called Misquamicut. I had heard of it, and was willing to go to any nice beach, particularly one that was only an hour or two away. I told Debbie that I would be happy to go; all that I wanted was for her to make sure that we had a nice place to stay, right on the beach.

I emphasized "right on the beach," because Debbie had a habit of going for the cheapest place that money could buy. Debbie didn't tell me much about the place we were staying at in Misquamicut.

I had been abundantly clear when I told her that this was my vacation too, and I wanted to stay in a nice place. I wanted to see the ocean from my room.

All she told me that she had gotten a really good deal on this place. I didn't like the sound of that. I asked her if it was on the ocean. She said it was near the ocean. I liked the sound of that even less.

I asked her for the name of the motel.

She said that we weren't staying in a motel; we were staying in a house.

I had a very bad feeling.

At that moment, there was a sense of hopelessness and resignation that went through me. If I pursued the question of location with Debbie, it would surely start another huge fight, with screaming, shouting, cursing, endless doors being slammed, and children crying. I couldn't bear it. I decided to give the place a chance. Hopefully, it wouldn't be too bad.

The main road into Misquamicut ends at Atlantic Avenue which borders the ocean. As we drove down Atlantic Avenue, I could hear the waves breaking on the shore on the other side of the motels which all faced the ocean.

Debbie had a map with directions, and she told me to just keep driving until we had driven past all of the motels. Then she told me to make a right turn, and we started driving even further away from the shore for at least four blocks.

She was looking at the numbers of the small private houses in the neighborhood, until finally she pointed to an older white house with a driveway bordered by small painted rocks.

"This is it" she said, not making any eye contact with me.

"You've got to be kidding me" I said in an exasperated tone, just as the owners of the house appeared to be coming out to greet us.

The elderly couple who owned the house was nice enough. They led us down the driveway to the rear part of the house, and then opened a side door that led into the garage. The grey steel door looked just like the one that led into our garage at home.

They had divided the garage in two, with one half, the rental room, separated from the remainder of the garage by a large plastic accordion wall that spanned the length of the room. The divider did not quite touch the floor, so the light from the garage side that was still being used for cars was quite apparent in the room.

There was a sliding glass door on the back part of the room. The couple's garbage cans were stored in a corner of the dark enclosed little patio on the other side of the glass. Past the garbage cans, was a mass of tall weeds which obscured any further views past the couple's small back yard.

There was a ratty looking brown fold out couch, with a matching ratty looking fold out loveseat for the kids to sleep in. The TV was big, old, with a rabbit ears antenna, and barely any reception. There was a dead cockroach under the coffee table that was near the couch.

I could not believe the place that she'd picked. We had plenty of money. By anyone's standard, I was making a great living, and I wanted to spend some of it on me – on us.

But something in Debbie just wouldn't let her.

I was so enraged that I refused to talk to her for the rest of the afternoon and evening, preferring to sit in a plastic chair and staring out past the garbage cans. A few hours later Debbie took the kids out for some junk food, and when they got back, I told them all that I was not going to stay in someone's garage for my vacation.

In the morning, I was going to go and rent the nicest room I could find in Misquamicut that was right on the beach. I told Ethan and Elissa that they could stay at whichever place they wanted to,

That night, there was a cricket on our side of the garage, and it kept chirping in the room. At about ten in the evening, the elderly couple who owned the house decided to go out in their car, which was on the other side of the divider. It sounded like the car was in our room when they started it up. Some of the exhaust fumes began seeping into our room.

The smell was disgusting. I sat patiently and silently in the chair all night, just waiting for the morning. Early the next morning, I left the "room" to drive around and scout out the places which were right on the beach. I quickly discovered the Sandy Shore Motel, which was not a block away from the ocean, or around the corner from the ocean, but directly on the sandy beach which led down to the surf.

The rental office opened at about 8 am.

About five minutes later, I walked in, met Tim, the owner, and rented an ocean-front apartment for the week. After I showed Ethan and Elissa the new accommodations, they decided to come along, with Debbie grudgingly bringing up the rear.

The Misquamicut experience provided the foundation for the realization that I didn't have to live under the penny pinching, misanthropic, joyless regimen that Debbie's outlook overlaid on our lives. I was going to break free, and live a better life without her than I could with her,

Standing in the dark, depressing room of the transient hotel in East Hartford, the moment had finally arrived when I resolved to not live the way I was living anymore.

I was not going to exile myself into squalor and self-inflicted pain. I was not going to live in a basement, or in a transient motel. I was going to find someplace nice to live, where there was no darkness, where there was no Debbie.

I felt that I deserved more. I wanted something better than the lousy dysfunctional relationship that I had with Debbie. All three of us deserved better. I decided to forget about living with the zombies. The self-tormenting approach wasn't what I wanted at all. What I wanted was to show my children a new and better way of living.

I stopped seeing "leaving" as a way to punish myself for "abandoning" my children, the way my father had abandoned me as an infant. I began seeing it as liberating my children.

In order to do that, I needed to be able to compete in terms of the lifestyle that I wanted to show my children.

It was still summer, so I knew that I needed a place with a pool to encourage Ethan and Elissa to come and stay with me. I wanted a place that had a lot of kids around. I realized that I couldn't be the only estranged parent in such an affluently mobile area. I looked around for a while, and soon found Avon Place, a condo/apartment complex in Avon, the next town over.

Avon Place had spacious two bedroom apartments, a beautiful tiled outdoor swimming pool, a tennis court, indoor exercise room, recreation room with a huge screen TV, professional pool table, and a large playground area with swings and things to climb on.

The rental office told me that they had a top floor unit available at the beginning of August. It was one of their biggest units, which did not become available very often. They suggested that I come down and leave a deposit if I was interested in the unit. The stark reality of having to leave home was upon me.

The next afternoon, I went downstairs to Frank's, the Italian restaurant on the ground floor of my office building. Instead of lunch, I had at least a half dozen mixed tequila drinks, before leaving work early that day to head towards the Avon Place rental office.

It didn't seem real. It couldn't possibly be happening. I was driving into the apartment complex and couldn't stop crying. Part of the complex was a large drive around a circle, and I kept going around and around until I was able to compose myself. I had an appointment to sign the lease. I finally pulled up to the office, wiped my face, put on my sunglasses, and walked into the office.

For the previous Christmas, I had bought Debbie a calendar filled with different pictures of Ethan and Elissa for each month of the calendar... The calendar was hanging in our kitchen.

For the month of July, there was a picture of me kneeling on the sand beach at Sanibel Island, holding Ethan and Elissa on either side of me. I took a pen and wrote on a few of the final days of the month, "going," and on the last day of the month, I wrote the word "gone."

The next morning, I told Debbie that I had found a place to go, but I still wanted to try to make it work. She didn't seem to care.

In fact, the next day, she wrote on the calendar, "get out already."

So I left.

CHAPTER 21

OH, MAMA, COULD THIS REALLY BE THE END?

By the time the first of the month came, I was already an emotional and physical wreck.

During lunch, I would sit at the bar at Franks' restaurant and drink cocktail after cocktail. I stared blankly at the TV screen, trying not to let Al the bartender see my eyes well up with tears every time that I thought about actually moving out of my house, and away from my kids.

For weeks, I had been drinking a lot more than eating. I could feel the booze wearing me down in a way that it never had before. I felt unsteady, as if I might just break down, fall off the bar stool, and collapse in a heap on the floor. One afternoon, I had ordered some soup for lunch, and found it hard to eat because my hands were shaking so badly that it was difficult to bring the soup spoon to my mouth without looking like I was having a seizure.

Fortunately, it was a relatively peaceful time in the office. There were no stock market crises. Everything was going well in terms of client accounts.

Charles, the Branch Manager, was at peak form, so I had no significant issues that I had to deal with from the supervisory perspective.

All of this allowed me to come into my office, close the door, and deal with my personal agony in the seclusion of my little corner office refuge. Often, I turned around in my chair so I faced the tall window overlooking the street, and watched the people walking by.

I wondered, with my maudlin perspective, if any of them were going through anything similar in their lives. That would usually make me pause, and realize how lucky I had actually been in life, and how my lot in life was certainly nothing to be self-pitying about compared to most of the people who were walking by.

However, I wondered why a universe which had been so kind and merciful to me so far in my life had chosen to smite me down, kick me like a dog, and leave me twisting in pain with a hopeless and overwhelming sense of loss.

I began to think that perhaps it was because of things that I hadn't done.

Maybe, I was so wrapped up in my own self-indulgent agony that I was losing sight of the agony that others were going through. For the first time, I began to feel that I was out of tune with the cosmic music of the universe, and I needed to get myself back in harmony with the greater forces around me.

A few days before the beginning of the month, I had read my horoscope in the local alternative newspaper. It said that I was holding onto the edge of a cliff and struggling to hold on with my bare fingertips, afraid of falling a long way down. The horoscope said that I should let go of the edge of the cliff, and I would find that the fall was only about a foot down, and no big deal at all.

When the first of the month came, I felt like I was falling off the roof of a building all day long.

At lunchtime, I went to Frank's and started drinking cocktails, and stayed there until about three o' clock when I left to go pick up the keys to the apartment.

I knew that my eyes and cheeks were red when I went to pick up the set of keys.

I kept my sunglasses on, and tried to talk very little because I kept finding myself choking up when I tried to speak. The rental lady offered to walk me up to the unit, but I told her that I'd be able to find my way alone.

I was going to live in apartment #313. I wasn't sure if it was a bad number because it had a 13 in it, or a good number because the digits added up to 7. It was a fleeting thought. When I walked in, I was struck by the large emptiness of the space.

The walls were all bright white. The carpeting was a nice light ivory color, and was so new that there were still tufts of new carpet fuzz in different parts of the carpeted rooms. As I did a walk through, I could hear myself taking short breaths, trying not to whimper out loud.

Then I sat down on the carpeting in the middle of the living room, facing the large curtain less windows, and started crying out loud, with nothing to wipe away the gushing tears and runny nose but the sleeve of my dark blue suit.

All I took that night from Debbie's house was our old set of eight oversized "hippie pillows," an acoustic guitar, and a small pile of clothes. Debbie seemed indifferent when I showed up to pick up the stuff; however, as I was putting the stuff in the car, she came out and handed me a coffee mug, a small dented pot to boil water in, and an old Teflon frying pan that was full of scratch marks.

It was evening, but Ethan and Elissa were still awake. I tried to make the whole visit as quickly as I could. I told the kids that I was going to stay at a new place until their mom and I could stop fighting for a while. I tried to make it seem like I would be back soon.

I really did believe that I would be back soon, maybe within days, or hours even; certainly not weeks or months, and certainly not forever.

During my first few days in the apartment, it seemed like very little had changed, except for the fact that I went home to the new apartment to sleep on the oversized pillows.

Each day after work, I would go over to Debbie's house to hang around with the Ethan and Elissa, and would do whatever activities we would have done normally. It was a bizarre arrangement. Change would come slowly and painfully.

I brought a few of my paintings over to the new place to bring some color to the stark white walls, but didn't hang them up because I didn't want to make nail holes in the freshly painted walls. If I moved out quickly, I didn't want to be charged with having the whole place repainted again because I had to hang up all of my artwork. I left the paintings on the floor at the foot of the wall where I imagined that I would hang them, if I was going to be staying.

After a few days, I brought Ethan and Elissa over to spend their first night. They each had two of the big hippie pillows to sleep on, and I had the remaining four pillows. I still didn't have any other furniture or even a TV in the apartment. It was like camping, but way worse because we had so much less equipment.

There wasn't anything to do in the apartment yet. Both of them hated the place. That made me even more depressed.

The next day at work, I was numb in my office.

Bringing them over to the apartment had made me realize the empty existence that I had pushed myself into. It was hard to sit still at my desk. I couldn't focus at all on markets, or numbers or stock prices.

It was all a blur, so at about 11:00, I went downstairs to Frank's and started drinking tequila and diet cokes at the empty bar until a little past noon when the lunch crowd stated coming in.

I decided to take a walk down Main Street so that I didn't have to talk to anyone.

It was an extremely hot sunny day. I was sweating profusely as I walked down the street in my wool suit. I walked by the front door of Brown Thompson, but did not go inside.

Instead, I continued walking down to the end of the street, and then turned around and started walking the other way. I didn't know where I was going; I was walking aimlessly down the street, feeling like a ghost with a head clouded by tequila.

The sun was very strong and hot, beating down on me. I felt the perspiration dripping down the nape of my neck, making the collar on my white shirt wet and sweaty. I wanted to be alone to think, but it was so very hot outside, and I was starting to feel lightheaded.

I was alone on a street full of people.

There was a tall gothic looking church across the street from Brown Thompson. It wasn't much different from many of the other old churches that are located across downtown Hartford.

At one time, the city of Hartford had a large residential population that filled all of its churches, but as a result of poorly planned development, office buildings had supplanted all of the residential housing, leaving many of the churches with small to nearly non-existent congregations. I didn't know anything about the differences between the different churches, but the one across the street from Brown Thompson had a unique sign on it that impressed me every time that I walked by.

The sign said that the doors were always open, and invited people to come in for rest and prayer.

I had never seen a church or a temple that left their doors open for anyone to walk in. It seemed to me to be something that all types of houses of worship should be doing all of the time. After all, when someone needs reflection, rest, prayer, or just a momentary sanctuary of some kind, there should be a place to go, that will take you in and give you comfort through their unconditional acceptance, and flexible hours.

Except for a few weddings, I had never been in a church. The large wooden front doors of the church were across the street from me. I wondered if the doors were really open. I needed some place to go for rest, and maybe even prayer.

When I opened the door, I entered in to an unfamiliar dark coolness. The sun had stopped beating down on me. I walked through a second door into the main hall, filled with rows of pews, and stained glass windows all around. It was a relatively large church, and there were three or four other people there in a room that looked like it could seat five hundred. I found a long empty bench and sat down, dabbing at my sweaty face and neck with some old napkins from Frank's that I still had in my pocket.

Since I had never practiced any religion, I didn't have much to offer in terms of prayers. Instead, I just sat there and felt bad for myself. The cool air in the hall made me feel relieved, and the darkness seemed to comfort me in the anonymity of the mostly empty hall.

Then, I happened to look up at one of the sections of stained glass that was not mounted into one of the windows, but was part of a larger biblical scene that extended from the windows to across the upper walls of the hall. At the bottom of that section of the scene, formed in sections of stained glass, was the name "Goodman."

It struck me as one of the oddest things that I could have seen inside of a church. I had never heard of any biblical character with that name. I had no idea what the scene was supposed to be about, but there it was, big as life. There weren't any other names anywhere, just mine.

I was speechless, sitting there in the semi darkness, with the cool air wafting around me. Having never believed in anything religious at any time in my life, it was definitely caught my attention. Maybe the universe was telling me that there was hope.

When I finally left the church, I went over to Brown Thompson to have a few more drinks, and to reflect on my odd experience.

By the time I left the bar, I decided to go home rather than return to the office to stare blankly at the computer screen. It was still a very hot day, a good opportunity to go swimming at the pool by the apartment complex.

By the time that I got to the pool, I was pretty loaded. I remember jumping into the pool, barely being able to climb out, and then passing out on an undersized towel that I had left on the grass that bordered the pool.

Hours later, I woke up in the dark, my face half on the towel, half on the grass. I was totally disoriented. It already night time, and I had no idea what time it was. There was absolutely no one around; just me in the darkness, struggling to sit up, and wipe off the grass and dirt with a little wet towel.

The night air was cold, and I started to shiver. Eventually, I got myself to stand up and head through the darkness towards the front lights of the building that my apartment was in.

I walked in to the apartment without furniture, without pictures on the walls. It certainly didn't seem like I was going back home anytime soon. I figured that it probably was time to buy some furniture like a bed, a TV, dishes, food, and things like that.

First, I was going to take a shower, and then go out to get something to eat at one of the local bars in Avon.

CHAPTER 22

HERE COMES THE SUN

That very same night was the first time that I walked into Tickets, a sports bar in Avon. I walked up to the bar and ordered a Cuervo Gold tequila mixed with diet coke.

The bartender was a guy named E.T., as in the "Extra-Terrestrial." I mentioned to him that I had just sort of "moved into the neighborhood." We had a short discussion about something New York Yankees related, and then I finished my drink and left. I didn't return back to the bar for over a month.

When I finally went back to Tickets a month or so later, the same guy was behind the bar. When I walked up to sit on a stool, he looked at me and said, "Tequila and diet Coke, right?"

I asked him how he happened to remember my drink. E.T replied that he never remembered names, but he always remembered drinks, and my drink was one that was not easy to forget. I laughed, and then mentioned that the way that I actually liked the drink was to add a little swirl of vodka on top of the tequila and diet Coke. He smiled, and then reached for the bottle of Smirnoff vodka to add the topping to my drink.

Suddenly, I knew that I had found another home away from home.

Over the past month, I finally began to buy some furniture and supporting equipment for the Avon Place apartment.

The biggest emotional commitment was the water bed. There is something about a filled king size water bed, with a bookcase headboard and drawers for clothes under the bed that implies a sense of not going anywhere for a while. The water bed was quickly followed by a TV, a VCR player, a couch and a loveseat.

Eventually, I broke down and made two massive shopping runs through Wal-Mart for things like dishes, glasses, utensils, pot and pans. While I was at Wal-Mart, I bought two ready to assemble clothes dressers for the bedrooms, and a computer desk for the kids' room. This was quickly followed by the purchase of my very first computer, pre-loaded with different kinds of kids' oriented software, which I hoped would keep Ethan and Elissa interested when they came over to visit.

However, just furniture and dishes do not make a home.

At my apartment, Ethan and Elissa were isolated from their world, their friends, and their real rooms. During the early weeks and months at Avon Place, I was always trying to come up with activities and fun things for us to do, but it was an uphill struggle. Just as I was hurt and upset by the situation, it was obvious that they both were as well.

The three of us began playing a game and hide and seek that used the entire apartment building, with the elevator as home base. Sometimes, we would go and try to shoot pool on the professional size pool table; that was always worth a few laughs. There wasn't that much to the playground other than two swings, a set of parallel bars, and a metal structure to climb on, but we gave all of the equipment a few tries.

There was a program on the new computer called "*KidsScape*"; both of them like playing that, so I went and bought more kids type programs. Soon, I had two dozen games that we couldn't quite figure out how to play.

For meals, I tried cooking or putting together a few theme oriented meals, like Hawaiian Friday or Italian Sunday.

For entertainment, I bought copies of all of the original science fiction and horror movies that I had grown up on. We watched the original *Dracula* with Bela Lugosi, and the original *Frankenstein* with Boris Karloff. They weren't particularly enamored with the black and white movies, but did seem to enjoy the sci-fi fantasy movies like *The Seventh Voyage of Sinbad,*" *The Time Machine*, and *Mysterious Island*.

Not long after we had split up, Debbie started threatening to withhold my visitation rights, and said that she would fight for full custody of our children. She said that she wanted everything that we owned, and that I was a piece of shit that she was happy to be done with.

During those first few months, never once did Debbie make any overture towards reconciliation. Instead, she became nastier by the day. Never once did she ever say that she loved me or she missed me, and that's what hurt worst of all.

After twenty years, all she wanted was everything that we had, most of which I, who she liked to refer to as "the nothing," had earned during the years of our marriage.

In order to assure my access to Ethan and Elissa, I soon agreed to a 90/10 split in her favor for all of our assets. I understood my adversary, and decided that the wisest course of action was to buy the peace. It was the best money that I have ever spent.

Soon, I began to sometimes feel myself emerging from my emotional funk. Other times, I felt myself sinking into the morass of my own self-pity, like a rock sinking in a swamp.

However, it was never lost on me that I wasn't wallowing in poverty, hungry, or battling vermin anymore. I was in a very attractive apartment condo unit with a balcony overlooking the woods, and I still had enough money to fund a very comfortable lifestyle for me and my children.

For the past year or two, I had been looking for some sort of charitable cause or nonprofit organization where I could help out.

My first thought was a soup kitchen; so I called a few that I had heard about, and they didn't seem to need any help. I called a battered women's shelter, and they told me that they usually didn't use men as volunteer help because most of their clients had been abused by men.

After I split up with Debbie, I didn't know exactly what I was looking for, but I knew that I wanted to find something that would help me turn around my personal karmic tide.

I needed something that would help to put me in tune with the positive flow of the universe, rather than remain in my pit of spiritual pain. It seemed to me that if I focused on selflessly helping others, that perhaps the fates would be kinder to me.

I saw an article about a nonprofit organization in Hartford that helped bring food and fresh produce to the poor in the inner city. I gave them a call and told them that I'd be interested in volunteering if they had something for me to do. That was the beginning of my short stint with the Hartford Food System.

The Executive Director, Mitch, had me attempt to place posters in the windows of local businesses, which I did with great success; although I felt kind of silly walking around downtown Hartford in a three piece suit, trying to hawk poorly made signs from the organization to compete with the merchandise window displays of the local businesses.

It took very little time for me to realize that this particular non-profit might not be the nexus of my calling. The parting came relatively quickly after

I was invited to attend one of their Board of Directors' meetings. The main discussion of that meeting centered on trying to keep big supermarkets out of the city in favor of having more Mom and Pop type stores in the city.

I tried to offer the classic free market argument that it didn't matter in the least if the stores were big, or if the stores were small. What mattered most was to support whatever stores could bring the best goods, the best food, at the lowest prices to their respective communities.

Everyone else at the meeting echoed the mantra that big was bad, and small was better, with absolutely no consideration to what the end users in the surrounding neighborhoods wanted. The value sets of everyone at the meeting seemed fixed, immutable, and naïve.

I'd grown up in a neighborhood full of Spanish bodegas, which are the ghetto inner city equivalent of small mom and pop grocery stores. There was a small supermarket a few blocks away, and there were two bodegas within a half block of where I lived. When my mom sent me out to the store to buy something, it wasn't one or the other.

Each store served their different purposes for the people in the neighborhood. Some items were more easily purchased at one of the little stores around the corner, while larger shopping trips required taking a walk to the only supermarket in the neighborhood, which was three blocks away.

I didn't understand why the nonprofit organization was against Stop and Shop, or Big Y, or ShopRite, or any of the big stores. I loved the big supermarkets. To me, a major shopping trip was what not being poor all is about. The idea of going into a Big Y and buying everything on the shelves, filling up two grocery carts with groceries, fruits and meats was a wonderful thing.

One of the organization's main issues seemed nonsensical to me. When I tried to have an economic discussion about the issue with the Executive

Director, he looked at me blankly. It didn't matter what I said, it was clear that he was not prepared to listen to anything that contradicted one of the main precepts of his philosophy.

My involvement with the organization only lasted for a few months before I found two new causes that I believed in, and could involve myself in.

The first was joining the Board of Directors for a Hartford non-profit that look care of abused inner city kids.

Given my finance background, the small Board of Directors immediately named me as Treasurer, thus beginning my education in learning how non-profits work, and how to make them work better. The organization's name was Y-US, Youth United for Success.

When I joined, the organization, they took care of about a dozen children, had a staff of two people, and was about to be cut off from all state and city funding due to a number of unsatisfactory audits.

I discovered my second calling when I made a return trip to the church one day during the autumn.

I was still having a hard time coping with my new lot in life. One afternoon, I needed another dose of rest and reflection. However, this time, on my way out of the church, I happened to notice a poster for the Thanksgiving dinner which was being held by the soup kitchen next door. Working in a soup kitchen seemed like a hands on way to help the poor. I understood that some people had no food.

As a little boy, there were several times when my mother didn't have any money to buy food. I remember how scared it made me to open the refrigerator and see empty shelves with no milk or juice or food on them.

A few times, I took all of the condiments from the refrigerator door, and put them on the shelves to make the refrigerator look full, but I knew that it really wasn't full.

One of my favorite tear jerker stories from my impoverished childhood was when I was walking in the street one day, at about seven years old, and saw a one dollar bill on the street. I picked it up, and knowing that we had no food at home, I went to the Spanish bodega.

I bought a quart of milk, a loaf of bread, a dozen eggs, and a tub of butter. Proudly, I carried the big brown grocery bag back home, and up to my Mom's apartment.

When she unpacked the bag, and saw the groceries, my mother was amazed. She asked where I had gotten the money. I told her that I had found the dollar in the street, and knew that we didn't have any food, so I went and bought some.

I remember my mom smiling and telling me what a good little boy I was. Then she opened the refrigerator, and said, "But, Donny, we already had eggs."

After about three months in the Avon Place apartment, I became resigned to the fact that I wasn't going "home" anymore.

At the time, I was reading a book titled, *Wherever You Go, There You Are*. I knew how I had gotten to where I was, and there was nowhere else to go. So, despite having rallied from the depression, I started slipping downwards again.

Except for my activities with the kids, I became a recluse. I spoke to very few friends, except for the Big Man, and by phone to my friend Susan, the same one who I had long ago nicknamed "Q."

Susan had left Connecticut a few years before, and moved to Ohio to get married. Oddly, we spoke on the phone fairly regularly after she left. Whenever she was in town to visit her family, we would go for our traditional tequila, apples and brie lunches at Brown Thompson.

At first, she had liked married life in Ohio, but the wild child in her was still dominant in her personality and by the time that I was living in my Avon apartment, her marriage was crumbling.

There was something in our mutual agony that bonded us in friendship in a way that tequila couldn't. It was safe to tell Q about anything that was happening in my life because she was so far away and couldn't tell anyone. She obviously felt the same.

The Big Man had also just split up with his wife, so two of the people that I had the most interaction with were also emotional messes.

My world of darkness was surrounded by other people's worlds of darkness. All through this, I was waiting and hoping that the dawn would eventually come.

One Thursday afternoon, I was nearly passed out in my office from a long drinking lunch. The previous evening with Ethan and Elissa had been a disaster, with Elissa insisting that I take her back to her mother's house at about ten in the evening.

I had already had two lengthy arguments with Debbie on the phone, both at the apartment and at my office. By midafternoon, I was drained, with my head back, staring at the ceiling, trying not to let tears roll down my face in case anyone came into my office.

Then, the phone rang; it was Susan asking if I'd like some company for the weekend.

My first thought after she asked the question was that there was something kind and merciful in the universe that had looked down upon my earthly misery, and decided to give me a break.

I called the airline and bought her a ticket for the next day.

CHAPTER 23

THE WISDOM OF Q

There has rarely been a more unlikely pair than Q. and me.

After I picked her up at the airport, I brought Q. to my apartment in Avon to leave off her suitcases. For a weekend visit, Q. arrived with a large suitcase and a small suitcase. When I asked her why she brought so much stuff, she replied that the small suitcase held her clothes, and the large white Samsonite suitcase held the important stuff, like her hair dryer, make up, and numerous other implements of feminine adornment.

It struck me as odd that such a naturally gorgeous woman felt she needed all of that equipment to look good. She didn't appear to be either insecure or vain, though once I got to know, I saw both of those qualities in her.

What I knew about Q was that she wanted to be seen as the "party goddess." And of all the women that I have ever known, none was ever more deserving of that title more than Q.

That first night, I took Q. to Tickets for dinner and drinks, and then more drinks, and then still more drinks. The hours started to drift by with us doing shot after shot of tequila. Q. and I had gone drinking together many times, but this was the first time that our partying was not bounded by lunch hours, or me having to go home to my wife. We had no boundaries.

After about ten shots, Q. was getting warmed up, and soon began attracting the attention of just about every single guy in the bar, not to mention a few guys who looked like they wanted to dump the woman that they were with just to take a shot at the loaded hot babe holding court at the bar.

I, for the most part, was just sitting, hanging out at the bar and watching the show.

Periodically, Q. and I would resume our conversation while we drank still more shots of tequila. That night, we both had about fifteen to twenty shots each by the time the bartender announced last call for drinks.

It was one or two in the morning. Q. wanted to go somewhere else, but I explained that every other place would be closed by then. Eventually, I was able to lead her, with both of us staggering, into my car.

Fortunately, my apartment was only a few minutes away, and we made it back to my parking lot without incident. On the drive home, Q. went from singing with the radio to nodding out, in the space of about five minutes. I managed to rouse her enough to pull her out into the fresh air which revived her enough so that we stumbled together into the apartment.

They say that tequila makes people crazy, and they might be right. I remember pulling her clothes off and gasping. Q had a body like a Penthouse pet. Her blue eyes glowed under the moonlight coming through the windows. Thankfully, she had drunk as much tequila as I had. My heart started to beat fast.

In the morning, when I went to the bathroom and looked in the mirror, it looked like I had just come back from a war. I was covered in scratches, bite marks, and black and blues of various sizes and shapes.

In my huge water bed was this naked beautiful girl who looked like an angel in the morning light. All of Q's makeup had rubbed off, and she was wrapped in the bed sheet looking like a dream. I wanted to do something to capture the moment forever, so I went to get my Nikon camera.

My concept was to stir Q. and when she opened her eyes, get a picture of the morning sun reflecting off of the incredible blue color.

I positioned myself over her sleeping body, focused the camera, and began trying to gently stir her from her sleep, so that I could capture the amazing blueness melding into the morning light.

My camera and I were both ready, but when I stirred Q. to open her eyes, the only thing she said was, "Donny, get the fucking camera out of my face, or I'm going to fucking kill you."

I put the camera away. It would have been a great picture.

A few hours later, I was sitting on the couch in the living room after Q. had awakened and taken a shower. She came out of the shower with her brown hair combed back, not a trace of makeup.

One of the first things she said was that she was sorry she snapped at me. If I wanted to take pictures, she just wanted to be ready for them so she could "look good." She asked me to wait until she fixed her face, and then I could take all of the pictures that I wanted.

The way she said what she said was so nice, so unlike Debbie. I could see that there was a side to Susan that I didn't understand at all. Without any makeup, Susan was still one of the prettiest woman I'd had ever met in person, but it was clear to me that she saw herself in a totally different way that I could not immediately understand.

Later that evening, before we were going to go out for dinner, Q. said that if I wanted to take pictures, I should do it after she was all "prepared" for it. A short time later, she came out of the bathroom looking like something out of a wet dream, and sat there patiently while I lamely took a dozen pictures of her blue eyes.

The next night was very much like the previous night. We set in motion a dynamic of two good friends who were very much opposites in everything, wanting to hang together, drink together, screw together, and when the weekend was over, go back to whatever lives we were leading in our own spaces.

Within a few weeks, I knew all of the airline schedules between Ohio and Connecticut.

Q's marriage was getting worse by the day. The fact that she was flying into Connecticut to spend weekends with me wasn't helping matters on her end. One weekend, she flew in, and when I went to give her a hug when she got off the plane, she pushed me away.

She said that she was very bruised because her husband had punched her, and thrown her into the hood of a car.

To me, Q was a beautiful woman who flew in on weekends to party. To Q, I represented her most convenient escape from whatever her married housewife life in Ohio was like. As the weekends rolled by and we spent extended amounts of time together, I finally got to really know Susan as a person, and not just as a party goddess.

Q. may not have been the most academically oriented woman that I have ever met, but she knew more about certain aspects of relationships than anyone I have ever known.

All of her life, Q. had been this beautiful woman who had been hit on by every type of male human being imaginable. She may not have had any idea of what she wanted in a man, but that was only because she had spent her entire life, from the time that she hit puberty, dealing with men of all kinds trying to get into her pants.

Q.'s wild streak had led her from South Windsor, Connecticut where she grew up, to Hollywood, California for a few years of partying all around the West Coast, before returning to South Windsor, all by the time she was 21. One her first real jobs was when she was hired her to be the receptionist at my branch office.

She once told me that some slimy Hollywood types had tried to talk her in to "modeling," but nothing had come of it. With better career guidance she might have made an awesome Playboy playmate or Penthouse Pet, but she wasn't interested in that kind of work.

Prior to getting married, Susan had been involved with a long succession of different biker type guys. Q. just wanted to have a good time in life, and the heck with everything else. She was self-aware, but at the same time in denial about the long term consequences of not wanting to let the party end.

The following weekend, I got to see more of the different faces of Q.

That Friday night, we were going to a nice Italian restaurant for dinner. I was waiting for Q. to finished getting dressed when she walked out of the bedroom in a very conservative plaid woman's business type suit and skirt. Her hair was neatly made into a bun. She was wearing cute little wire rimmed glasses which gave her a very corporate chic look.

She looked like something out of a rock and roll video where you expect the well-dressed corporate looking babe to start dancing wildly to Motley Crue music, while flinging off the glasses, shaking down the long hair, and then stripping down to her black underwear.

As we were heading down the elevator to get to my car, my head was starting to swim in the scent of the Amarige perfume that Q. was wearing. As I looked at her outfit, I wondered if she was wearing black underwear.

We had a very nice dinner, and one of our best conversations. Afterwards, we headed back to Tickets, and started another round of drinking tequila shots until closing, before heading back to the apartment.

The following morning, we began our tradition of starting each day by drinking mimosas, which were a mix of champagne and orange juice, until midafternoon, while watching movies or TV, listening to music, and talking.

It wasn't surprising to either of us that we liked totally different things.

On TV, Q. liked to watch old movies and game shows, and I liked to watch the National Geographic or Discovery channels. As for music, I liked Grateful Dead and Bruce Springsteen, but Q. wanted to listen to Metallica and Megadeath. There was a little common ground, but not much.

One thing that we could agree on, at least for a while, was the very heavy techno music that they played at a dance club bar that we soon began to frequent. The next evening, we planned a late start because we were going to go to a dance club in Hartford called The Loft.

I was waiting for Q. to come out of the bedroom, figuring that she was certainly going to wear something less conservative than she had the night before.

Susan came out of the bedroom wearing black leather pants with a narrow chain belt, black boots with spike heels, and a seriously undersized black leather bustier that she wanted me to zip up in the back. Susan's small tight leather top gave her cleavage that you could have passed out into.

She had put on heavy blue and green eye shadow, and lots of mascara, so her eyes glistened outwards in an animal blue glow. I looked at her and gulped, and then tried lamely to come up with a reason why we should just stay in so I could undress her sooner rather than later.

But after all the time she had spent getting ready, Q. was not to be denied her night on the town. By about 11:00 PM, we finally made it to The Loft, already quite buzzed, and ready to dance and drink until closing.

For a short time back then, The Loft was one of the most decadent public clubs that I'd ever seen. Women would show up in such small outfits that the dance floor looked more like a strip club where everyone participated. The dance floor was very dark with lots of flashing strobe lights, and a sound system that shook the floor under your feet. They played booming repetitive techno dance music that usually had minimalist lyrics and excessive pounding bass.

I'd never heard any of that kind of techno music, so it was all new to me.

I liked it, particularly, when I was really buzzed from all of the tequila.

At the Loft, Q. didn't stick out too much in the crowd, even in her leather sex goddess outfit. The Loft seemed to attract an inordinate amount of super-hot women, as well lots of druggies who did lines of coke in the corners of the club.

That night, Q. and I stayed until closing. During one part of the night, we were huddled in an alcove off to the side of the bar. Q. was standing with her face about a foot away from my face.

I smelled the liquor and the breath mints on her warm breath, mixed with the scent of her perfume drifting off of her sweaty bare shoulders. I felt totally enveloped by the blueness of her eyes. I reached over to kiss her, when she pulled away abruptly, giving her head of hair a little shake that said no.

"Don't be so aggressive tonight," she said in a teasing sort of way, and then paused for a moment before adding, "Let me show you what I want." She pulled me towards her and wrapped me up in one the longest wettest kisses that I can ever remember.

My knees nearly buckled, and I hoped that everyone in the dance club was watching.

Hanging around with Q. on the weekends had given me a whole new perspective on life. All of a sudden, from the depths of despair, I now had a wonderful party fantasy to look forward to on certain weekends.

From Q's perspective, coming to visit me got her out of Dodge, but each time she returned to Ohio, the shit there got deeper and deeper as her husband got angrier and angrier.

In addition, Q. had mentioned to me that there was this other guy in Ohio who she had been seeing pretty regularly. She even showed me a picture of him. He was a big burly guy with a bushy black beard who looked like he should be a lumberjack or a football player.

Q. had said all along that she regarded us as friends, not anything else. One of her most memorable lines was when she told me one afternoon, while we were struggling to find something that we both wanted to watch on TV, that she really liked partying, visiting and screwing me, but we could never be boyfriend and girlfriend because we just didn't have anything in common.

At first it hurt my feelings to hear that. As I thought about it, I began to rationalize it by saying that a gorgeous woman just told me that she likes me as a lover and a friend, with no strings attached. I should probably be honored, and not hurt.

Of course, Q. was right. She had a certain wisdom about things that was the result of a lot of experience and hard time with the different men in her life. She didn't want to get emotionally attached to me, and she wanted to be sure that I didn't get hung up on her. I came to accept that my relationship with Susan was what it was, and it wasn't so bad at all.

One Friday night, after I had picked up Q at the airport, we drove down to Hartford to hang around at Brown Thompson, and see if any of the people that she knew from her time in Hartford would be hanging out after work. We ran into Raymond, the Big Man, but he was heading out the door, so Q. and I settled in at the bar for food and drinks.

There was something going on between Q. and the pretty blonde bartender named Melissa. It was like they knew each other, but didn't want to acknowledge that the other one was there.

I knew Melissa for years, and couldn't imagine what the two of them might have in common, or even how they might know each other. After more than a few drinks, Q. told me that they had both been seeing a guy named Rob at the same time, and, by the time of this conversation, he had apparently dumped both of them, alternately.

It really surprised me when Q. told me that she still fucked that guy Rob on rare occasions, and that she would crawl through broken glass to get into bed with him. She told me that some people just made her teeth itch, and she would fuck this guy any time for any reason. At that moment, I felt like a used piece of toilet paper.

Never once had Susan ever said anything like she would crawl through broken glass to fuck me, or how I made her teeth itch. I figured that I couldn't be all that bad if we had such a good time playing together, but maybe this guy Rob had some god like sexual powers that I could not comprehend. I definitely felt second or third rate, but I tried to console myself by remembering that at least I was in the mix.

Later, during that work week, I happened to stop in to Brown Thompson while Melissa was working at the bar. Melissa was also a beautiful woman, with striking blonde hair, and a body not quite as curvy as Susan's, but not far off either.

I told her what Susan had said about how both of them were seeing the same guy. I asked her what had happened from her perspective, and asked if she was still seeing the guy. Melissa told me that after Rob dumped Susan for her, he subsequently dumped Melissa for yet another girl.

I had no idea of who this guy Rob was, and couldn't quite believe that he had dumped two of the hottest women that I knew in life. Melissa told me that he occasionally stopped in to the bar, and she would point him out to me if I was around. There was something about the way she referred to him that made me believe that she would have also have crawled through broken glass to jump into bed with him one more time.

I started feeling very small and inconsequential compared to the obvious sexual prowess of this guy, Rob.

As it happened, I finally got to see what this man god looked like a few weeks later when Melissa pointed him out at the bar. He was about thirty five years old, maybe 5'7," with dark hair and a sharply receding hairline. He looked like a cross between Woody Allen and Gabe Kaplan during the *Welcome Back Kotter* era. I didn't get it at all.

Without being crass, looking at him, I knew that his dick couldn't be that much bigger than mine. He didn't look like an acrobat or a contortionist. I just didn't get it, but as Q. had said, some people just make your teeth itch, and you don't know why. Apparently, Rob had the magic of making women's teeth itch, and I didn't.

It didn't take long before Q. and her redneck husband split up, and she was splitting time living with one of her girlfriends in Ohio, and her bearded trucker boyfriend. Without anyone to support her, Susan had to take a job cooking and cleaning for a disabled woman in a nearby small town in Ohio. Her evolving personal situation made it difficult for Q to come to visit me.

One Sunday night called me to tell me that she had been arrested and gotten a DUI, and needed four hundred dollars right away; which I sent overnight mail. I didn't see Q. for a month or two after that. We spoke a few times, but she was clearly preoccupied by other things in her life.

In the interim, I had finally emerged from the egg. I no longer sat in my office at work feeling all bummed. Work was fun again, and life away from work was improving rapidly.

About a year after splitting up with Debbie, I was filling the void with my painting, music, and my non-profit work. I began increasing the time that I spent trying to make the world a better place.

As Gandhi had suggested, I tried to "be the change that you want to see in the world."

My participation with the soup kitchen grew into a mission to upgrade the holiday meals from low grade culinary presentations to banquets with multiple courses which included fresh fruits and salads.

There were numerous crises occurring regularly at Y-US, the non-profit that took care of abused kids. Working with the rest of the Board, we created many initiatives which soon put the organization on sound financial footing, and allowed it to begin offering services to even more children.

I believed that the universe looks down kindly on those who selflessly try to help others. The greater the effort put forth, the greater the potential reward in terms of quality of life and personal fulfillment.

By the late fall of 1995, I could not have imagined that the universe was about to kick it up a notch.

It all began with the computer that I bought for Ethan and Elissa. When they weren't around, I was trying to learn how to use it for things like e-mail, word processing, and eventually chatting.

My online provider at the time was Prodigy, and they had a number of proprietary chat rooms that I began to explore. Since the chat rooms were defined by subject matter, the only room that I began to frequent was the "Arts and Writing" room.

There were about a dozen regulars who hung out in the room, mostly women, who would sit there and chat among themselves about all sorts of things, few of which involved writing. Since the people in the room had absolutely no idea who I was, and couldn't see me, I liked to barge in and generally be somewhat obnoxious in my attempts to humor myself.

Occasionally, I would "read" some of my poems to the crowd which always seemed to impress the women. I found out long ago that women really seem to like men that do sensitive things like writing poetry. In college, my poetry writing had always scored me lots of female company. I wasn't expecting any of these online women to jump into their cars to come to Connecticut to visit and screw the poet, but you never know.

Maybe I'd get lucky.

CHAPTER 24

THE COMING OF ANNIE

One of the chat room regulars was a woman who went by the screen-name of Lady Melisande. I thought that I recognized the name "Melisande" as the name of a cat from some Disney film. I figured the woman behind the name must be weird if she was using the name of a cat.

Everyone else called her Lady Mel. She was supposed to be one of the "real" writers who hung out in the chat-room; her first novel had just been published, and her screen name was borrowed from one of her own characters. Although Lady Mel seemed very bright from the few times I chatted with her, I knew – from my own experience – that people sometimes pretend to be things they're not, so I didn't pay much attention to what she said.

Since Lady Mel didn't seem to be any more interested in chatting with me than I was in chatting with her, we pretty much ignored each other. However, after I'd been visiting the room almost every morning for about two months, I received an instant message from one of the other women in the chat room telling me that I should start talking to Lady Mel because she and I sounded alike.

I didn't think that we sounded particularly alike at all. Then another woman said the same thing to me. I was going to mention it to Lady Mel, when one day I received an instant message from Lady Mel herself.

"So-and-so and So-and-so told me that we should talk because we sound alike," she typed.

"And what do you think?" I typed back.

"I'm willing to find out," she wrote.

So we started chatting, regularly in fact. Although I had no idea what she looked like, there really was something incredibly interesting about the way she "sounded" in her chatting.

I learned that her real name was Anne. That struck me as a bit of a coincidence, since Anne was always one of my favorite girl's names. I had even used the name in a number of my poems, as well as the play that I was writing.

Anne – or Annie, as I very soon began to think of her - was about as different from Q as it was possible to be. A writer with four kids, living in Bethlehem, PA, she was in the middle a divorce even more punitive than the break-up I was going through with Debbie.

Annie's ex was a lawyer, who sounded every bit as mean and vengeful as Debbie. Annie and I dubbed them the "Norn King and Queen" and joked about putting them both in a cage to fight over a piece of meat. Annie said it would be a draw, but my money was on Debbie.

After a few weeks of chatting every morning, we traded pictures. I sent her copies of some of my poems, a few of my rock and roll articles that the newspapers had published, and a bunch of photographs of my artwork. Just in case she was hot, I figured that I would overwhelm her.

Annie sent me two photographs and her first novel, just in case I still had any doubts that she was a "real" writer. One photograph showed Annie with her four kids, and the other was a black-and-white artsy photograph. All I could really tell from the photos was that she was really a girl, with dark hair, brown eyes, and a preppy look.

I started reading her novel – or trying to. It was very different from what I was used to reading, and it took me three or four tries to get past the first few pages. The story was intricately plotted, and Annie's writing was dense and convoluted, each sentence packed with meaning. Although by the time I was finished I wasn't sure I liked her book, I could tell Annie wasn't pretending to be a writer.

Since I had an 800 number at work, and chat was still expensive, we started to talk on the phone. I found that I enjoyed talking to her on the phone as much – if not more – than I enjoyed chatting online. Annie had a very sweet feminine voice, and sounded smart and sexy at the same time.

When I learned that Annie's sister was going to the University of Connecticut, not far from Hartford, and that Annie occasionally came up to see her, we talked generally about meeting one day. I told Annie I'd be happy to take her out to dinner when she visited her sister.

Christmas and New Year's was rapidly approaching. Annie had plans to go to the West Coast to see her dad and a deadline for her third novel, which she was finding very difficult to finish given all the stress going on in her life.

One morning, about four weeks before Christmas, Annie told me that she'd had to cancel her trip in order to meet her deadline. She sounded so sad and disappointed, I wanted to do something to cheer her up.

I hadn't heard from Q for a few weeks, so I assumed she was going to be with her burly Ohio boyfriend for New Year's Eve. I decided to call Annie and ask her if she wanted to meet me in New York City on New Year's Eve.

Since Annie lived in Pennsylvania and I lived in Connecticut, it seemed like a good halfway point; in addition, it was my home town, so if we weren't as compatible in person as we were online and on the phone, there were a lot of activities and distractions available.

I called the St Moritz, a fancy hotel overlooking Central Park I'd always wanted to stay in and Debbie would never agree. By coincidence, they happened to have a cancellation. "I'll take it," I told them.

Then I called Annie. "You're not going to write on New Year's Eve," I told her. "Come to New York and meet me there. If you're just a tenth as nice as you seem to be, we'll have a great time."

Annie hesitated, just a little…and accepted my invitation assuming her mom would watch her kids. We decided to meet in front of the St. Moritz, and start with a trip to the Metropolitan Museum to check out a Rembrandt exhibit Annie wanted to see.

Two days before New Year's, Q called to see if I wanted to get together. I was quite surprised to hear from her, and even more surprised I turned her down and told her that I already had a date.

On the afternoon of December 31st, I was walking towards my car, and it hit me that I was about to drive all the way down to New York City to meet someone I had never met. Even worse, I had blown off someone with whom I knew would have had a good time, to rendezvous with a total stranger,

I remembered I didn't even like Rembrandt. I began picturing walking past dozens of boring dark paintings instead of sharing shots of tequila with my blue eyed party goddess.

I stopped at the car door, thinking that I could just go back up to the condo and call Annie with some excuse why I couldn't make it.

Then I realized that she was probably already on the road from Pennsylvania.

I briefly considered just not going, and if she didn't talk to me anymore, I figured it would be no big deal. She was just a stranger, after all, someone I'd never met.

New York City seemed like a long way away.

I turned away from the car, and started to walk toward the doors of my condo building. Then I thought about what a rude nasty thing it would be to not even show up. I was embarrassed that I had even considered it.

Whatever happened, it was only one day in my life. So I got in the car, and headed down to New York City to meet Annie.

I was sitting in front of the St. Moritz hotel in my black leather jacket and my sunglasses, trying to look cool without looking like either a tourist or a hood when Annie drove up in her blue minivan that she called her mommy-mobile.

Annie seemed nervous about driving into New York City. As a former taxi driver, I gave her an exact route, with lane changes, that would land her right in front of the St. Moritz with hardly any left turns.

When she pulled up, I recognized her right away. After I was sure that she'd noticed me looking cool, I walked over to her driver's side door, and signaled for the doorman to come and take her car. I reached over to kiss her cheek thorough the open window, and was a little taken aback when she seemed to slightly recoil away from me.

I thought that this might not be a good sign, so I backed off, and helped to hand off her van to the doorman.

Unlike Q, the only luggage Annie brought was a small knapsack, which seemed incredibly light when I brought it over to the Concierge desk to hold for us until our room was ready. At first glance, I wasn't sure what to think. She was very different from almost all of the women I was used to.

Besides the fact she wasn't wearing any makeup at all, her body was hidden under layers of clothing. Beneath denim overalls and tan work boots, Annie had on at least a sweatshirt, a flannel shirt, and what looked to be at least another layer or two under that. There was no chance she was going to be cold if we walked around the city.

I liked her down-to-earth look; Annie immediately struck me as someone who seemed comfortable enough with herself to let me see the real person without a suitcase full of beauty products in between us. I noticed she had big brown eyes, dark hair, and the sexiest nose that reminded me of a Playboy pin-up in my college apartment.

Annie was a lot different from Q in a lot of ways: not only was she the mother of four, she'd grown up in a beach town at the South Jersey shore and her taste in music included Irish folk – something I knew nothing about. She was well educated: she'd graduated from an expensive prep school and been to boarding school in England. And she had a degree from Johns Hopkins in something that involved knowledge of Latin, Anglo Saxon and a lot of dead poets.

I suggested a drink; Annie suggested coffee, so we went over to the coffee shop in the hotel and started talking. All of the nice flow that we had online and on the phone seemed kind of flat in person. I realized that kissing her hello had made Annie uncomfortable, but it was too late now.

I suggested that we head to the museum to see the Rembrandt exhibit.

The focus of the exhibit was on Rembrandt's students and so most of the paintings were by his students, not Rembrandt. I didn't like Rembrandt in general, and his students weren't very interesting at all. The whole exhibit was drab and boring. It was crowded, hot and noisy.

I was surrounded by the dark paintings that I had envisioned. We paused in the doorway, hesitating on the threshold. I'd started to think that the date was not going well.

Suddenly Annie tugged on my arm. "Okay," she said. "We can leave."

"We can?" I was shocked. Had she been reading my mind? Heard what I was thinking? Maybe I'd said something without realizing it.

"Sure," she answered. "I saw what I came to see."

"You did?" I was still too surprised to find we were on the same page.

"Yes," she said. "Looking at the paintings, it's like reading a publishable manuscript – you know one when you see one because something reaches out and grabs you by the throat, and maybe you don't know what it is, but you know it when you read it."

I must've looked confused, because she started to point around the room. "That's the Rembrandt, that's the Rembrandt, that's the Rembrandt. And that's one over there. The rest are garbage." And with that she tugged on my hand on again. "Come on, let's go see the Impressionists."

We both liked the Impressionists. As we walked around, I took her hand. She didn't pull away. I noticed she had nice hands – her nails were neatly filed without any polish at all. "I can't have long nails," she shrugged when I commented on it. "And any color polish just chips…I type too much."

At around the same time, we both noticed how hot and stuffy the museum was. I was starting to find the person I had come to enjoy talking to so much online and on the phone. I hailed a cab, and we headed down to the West Village area to a bar called Chumley's, that I especially wanted Annie to see.

Chumley's dated back to the prohibition era when it was originally an illicit speakeasy. There was never any sign indicating where the tavern was; instead, you had to know to either walk down an alley, or to open a nondescript wood door to enter the bar. Over the decades, the bar had been a gathering spot for many writers, and the walls were lined with the book jackets of the many writers who had also been customers.

I first discovered Chumley's back in college when I used to go to various locations around New York City to read my poetry in public. Two of my favorite places to read in the New York City area were at the St. Marks Poetry Project, and at Chumley's.

When Annie and I got there, I mentioned that the interior looked exactly like it did when I had read there years before. I had a few opportunities to visit Chumley's over the years since college, and nothing ever seemed to change in the place; that was part of its charm.

Annie liked Chumley's. The food was good for bar food. The service was friendly. Somewhere between the museum and Chumley's, Annie and I rediscovered that flow we'd found online and over the phone, and I realized we were talking about something like nine things at once.

I also started to realize just how pretty Annie's big brown eyes were behind her little glasses.

At some point, Annie got up to use the ladies room, and when she did, for no reason, I grabbed her hand, pulled her back and gave her gentle little kiss on the lips. This time she didn't recoil at all.

On the taxi ride uptown, the little kiss exploded into much more serious kissing in the back seat. We were almost at our next destination, when Annie noticed that she had left her glasses on the table at Chumley's. We were already uptown, and she was visibly upset. I told the taxi driver to turn around and head back towards Chumley's.

Annie went into the bar, and came out a few minutes later, smiling, with her glasses in hand. I'd become a knight in shining armor. She kissed me some more on the taxi ride back uptown.

My date with a stranger was turning out to be a lot of fun. I had found someone who was the girl version of me: down-to-earth, comfortable with themselves, really smart, with a healthy liking and appreciation for genuine carnal lust.

Annie and I had so much fun on New Year's Eve that we made plans to see each other in Connecticut the following weekend before we said goodbye on New Year's Day.

If my ride to New York City had been full of doubt, my drive home was full of flashbacks of the incredible time we'd had together. In terms of time and money, it was probably one of the most expensive first dates I'd ever been on; I was thinking it could be worth it.

The second day of January I was in my office, still tingling, imagining the fun we would have when Annie arrived the following night. When the receptionist phoned from the front desk to tell me I had a delivery, I wasn't expecting anything special, until I walked out to see the huge bouquet of flowers Annie sent me.

No one had ever sent me anything even remotely like it.

A few months later, Annie told me her lawyer had advised her to leave Pennsylvania and find a home in a state where her ex wasn't licensed to practice law. She was moving to Connecticut. The first few months of our relationship had made me feel that I'd found a soulmate. This seemed to confirm it.

Between Annie and Q, it had been quite a few months, but finally, my depression had pretty much gone away. Things were going well across the board, when a new unexpected source of angst would rear its ugly head, this time at work.

The branch manager suffered a massive heart attack. Suddenly it was me who was in charge of the lunatic asylum; supervising twenty five temperamental brokers with huge egos, and a supporting cast of dozens. Endless forms to sign, telephone calls to answer, and problems to solve.

It looked like I was going to be very busy for quite a while.

CHAPTER 25

Taking communion

One morning, I walked into my office, and on my desk was a very small pile of accounts that had just been assigned to me because yet another broker had bit the dust. I could barely remember the lost neophyte broker, who was now gone like so many others before them; so many others.

He or she was just another face that briefly roamed the halls and offices before ever understanding why they were there in the first place. Many aspiring brokers came thinking that a Mercedes and a yacht was just a telephone call away.

They left, in most cases, before ever learning the keys to survival in the financial jungle. The faces of all of the brokers that I have known is like a room full of ghosts; vague memories, snippets of conversation, the remembrance of a moment when their presence in the office could still be seen and heard.

Everyone watches movies about Wall Street and thinks that every stockbroker/financial advisor is Gordon Gecko.

It is the people who come into the business with that illusion that usually fail the soonest.
Many others are simply overwhelmed.

Within a year or two, most people are blown away by the massive amount of material that has to be learned, the massive amount of information that needs to be assimilated on a daily basis, as well as the endless stream of regulations, testing and restrictions that must be complied with.

Add to that, the ceaseless challenge of building, maintaining, and growing a list of client accounts in a world filled with do-not-call lists, and with dozens or hundreds of brokers competing with you for the same potential clients, it was clear why many new broker/financial advisors had a lifespan shorter than goldfish.

With all of the people coming and going all the time, the only lasting evidence that a failed broker was ever there are the client accounts left behind.

I was assigned three accounts. Two of them had no assets in them. The other account had about $1,600 in a money market account. From the account records, it looked like the account had been passed from one broker to another over the years; after all, who wants a $1,600 account?

I put the account records near the phone so I could call the client later and introduce myself. I noticed that the account was owned by an Ed and Julia Foster who lived in South Windsor.

About a half an hour later, I got a telephone call. It was the voice of an old grumbly man on the phone. It was beyond a "gravelly voice." This was more like the sound of someone gargling and chewing the gravel at the same time.

"This is Foster in South Windsor. What are you bastards trying to do to me?" he grumbled.

I saw the name on the account sheet lying near the phone.

"Ed Foster? Hello sir, it looks like I was just given your account records…. um…how are you this morning?" When confronted by an angry client, try to be friendly and find out what's bothering them. After all, nice really does matter.

"The girl on the phone told me you were handling my account…and now I find you're charging me thirty five dollars! For what?" he asked angrily.

"Um, Mr. Foster, I'm not personally charging you anything for anything. " I said with a touch of humor in my voice, but I wasn't sure if he understood my humor.

I was able to access Mr. Foster's account records up on my screen, and looked at the account activity, and there it was. The thirty five dollars was the fee for having the account with the firm, and was an annual charge. The firm had deducted the fee from his account the previous month. Mr. Foster was pissed because fee had eaten up all of the interest that he had earned that year on the sixteen hundred dollar account balance.

"What kind of outfit do you have there? Where do you get off trying to charge me this kind of money for…for nothing….for absolutely nothing! If you bastards think you can get away with this, you got another thing coming!"

Mr. Foster was getting himself really excited. I wanted to calm him down. I'd never wanted someone to stroke out over a thirty five dollar fee. Life is too short.

"Mr. Foster, relax…" I offered, "Let me take care of this fee stuff for you. Let me see if I can…fix it. I think I can." I assured him.

Mr. Foster stopped screaming.

"Mr. Foster," I continued, "You see, I know some people who know some people who are close to some of the people in the back office. I can get the matter taken care of…if you catch my meaning."

I think I was trying to sound a little like Sheldon Leonard in some of those funny gangster roles that he played. I was hoping that Mr. Foster was getting the joke, so he didn't think that I was connected to the mob or something.

"Seriously though, Mr. Foster," I said," I will get the charge reversed for you, and your account will be credited the thirty five dollars in a day or two."

"Well, you know…" he paused, "I'd sure appreciate that." He sounded more like a grandfather, and less like a Grinch.

I told Mr. Foster to give me a call if I could be of any further help at any time, and left it at that.

I was able to write off the thirty five dollar fee against my top line production revenue in a way that, after all was said and done, it would cost me about eight dollars to absorb the account fee and make a grumpy old man happy; not too bad; my good deed for the day.

Time flew by, and all of a sudden, it was almost a year later when my sales assistant dropped off at my desk a long computer printout showing the various client account fees to be billed for the coming year. It was about two pages long, and there near the bottom of the first page, I noticed Ed Foster's name on it. Another thirty five dollars was going to be charged to his account the following month. I didn't want to be yelled at again, so I gave him a call.

"Hello, Mr. Foster. How have you been sir? This is Don Goodman from Prudential Securities. We had spoken briefly last year when I was assigned your account."

He grumbled acknowledgement, and I explained why I was calling.

I told him that if he wanted to maintain the $1,600 account at the firm, that it was fine with me, but I wanted to help him avoid the fee so he wouldn't get upset and call to yell at me.

I told him that if I sent him the $1,600, and he held it for about a week, the account appear as empty, without assets, when the computer scanned the accounts for the fee billing. Then, he wouldn't be charged the thirty five dollars, and then he could send the $1,600 back into the account.

"It'll cost you the price of a stamp and a few days interest, but it will save you the $35," I said, relatively confident that my idea would work, and the computer would be fooled into not billing him.

"You bothered to call to tell me that?" he asked in a way that I wasn't sure if he was annoyed or not annoyed.

"Well, I get upset when people yell at me. I'm very sensitive," I said in a way hoping to gain some sympathy.

"That's a mighty nice thing you did." He sounded like he was crunching rocks between his teeth. "Send me the check, and that's what we'll do."

I figured that it was more than likely that he would just deposit the check into his local bank account and that would be the end of it. If no assets were returned to the account, I would just have the account closed and deleted from the system. No assets, no account, no fees, no problem.

A few days later, the receptionist called me to let me know that there were two clients in the office to see me.

I wasn't expecting anyone, so I asked who they were.

"Mr. and Mrs. Foster, from South Windsor," she answered.

I wondered if he had come personally to deliver the check back into the account, or if he was angry about something else. My sales assistant brought them both into my office. They were both elderly, at least in their eighties.

Mrs. Foster was a little old lady, with white hair and an old fashioned flowered dress. Her name was Julia, but I heard Ed refer to her as "Jewel" as he guided her into one of the office chairs. Then he shook my hand and sat down. I thought that his pet name for Julia was so sweet.

"That was a very nice thing you did back there. What do you think of this?" He said with a quieter grumble in his tone. Then he handed me an account statement from another firm, Smith Barney.

The account had over $1,800,000 in it; the portfolio was a random mix of different kinds of corporate bonds, some preferred stocks, and a few Connecticut municipal bonds.

I was familiar with all of the securities in the portfolio. It wasn't a bad portfolio, but it wasn't the way I would have put the portfolio together.

I looked it over a few minutes, assessing the mix. I knew there was no way that Ed Foster had selected any of these securities.

"There is some good stuff here, and there is some stuff that I don't particularly care for in the portfolio. But Mr. Foster," I began.

"Call me Ed," he interjected.

"Well, Ed, it depends on a number of factors as to determine which way to direct the portfolio. I guess I need to ask you some questions."

We spoke for about a half an hour. It was clear that he had way more assets that just the Smith Barney account. He also owned 12 houses, that he rented; 2 farms, one of which he lived on; 2 commercial buildings, and about 400 acres of land in and around South Windsor.

He and Julia never had any children. They didn't even speak of any close relatives. They were married for over sixty years, and lived on their farm the entire time.

It sounded like Ed spent his days working around the property, and tending to the affairs of his other holdings. Ed was in his mid-eighties, but still seemed to get around pretty well.

After a while, it came out what Ed really wanted from me.

"I don't want to pay any more damn taxes on this money," he said referring to the Smith Barney account. "Not one red cent! I am sick and tired of paying those bastards. Not one more red cent!"

I like it when people know what they want, particularly when it is something that is perfectly appropriate for the portfolio.

I pointed out that he already owned several tax free Connecticut bonds, and that he didn't have to pay any taxes at all on the income generated by the bonds. He could simply start converting the rest of the portfolio into similar bonds, and all of the income would be totally tax free.

He seemed to understand everything that I was talking about.

"And I want everything insured," he paused, "I'll show those bastards. I'm not paying those thieves another dime. Not one red cent!"

It was easy to make Ed and Julia happy. Over the next few weeks, I began transforming the portfolio into a mighty, insured, totally tax free money making machine. Ed wanted the bonds that paid the most income, so we bought long maturities.

Thus began a wonderful relationship with Ed and Julia for many years.

Ed eventually transferred another million dollar account to me, and we reconfigured it to become a part of his tax free money machine. Occasionally, he would send chunks of other money, presumably from his rentals. Even as he moved into his nineties, he was still an astute businessman. I used to tell him that I wouldn't want to play poker against him. He was sharp until the end.

One day, I called, and he was beside himself. Julia had a heart attack, and was in the hospital. Ed could barely talk; he sounded like he was going to cry. I didn't know what to say. I felt so indescribably bad and sad for him, but there was nothing I could do except to send my best wishes and try to encourage him to be strong for Julia. The tears were welling up in my eyes.

That was the last time I spoke to Ed.

About a week later, I called Ed's house, and a younger sounding man answered the phone, and identified himself as a great nephew. He was the one who found his Uncle Ed dead on the floor dead in the kitchen when he had come to check up on him a few days before, after Julia went into the hospital. Ed had a heart attack, undoubtedly because he was so upset and concerned about his beloved Jewel.

Julia was sent to an acute rehab facility. She was very frail.

The nephew seemed to know who I was because Ed had mentioned me a few times. He had also recently seen my name on Ed and Julia's account statements. He had no idea that his aunt and uncle had so much money in their account.

He told me that the funeral was in two days, and asked me if I would be a pallbearer. It appeared that with hardly any relatives, and virtually no personal friends, they were having trouble coming up with enough people to carry the casket. I had never done anything like that before, but I was honored and said yes.

Fortunately, I have not been to many funerals. This one wasn't too dissimilar to one's that I'd seen, although, there was way more incense burned. The priest waved the lantern full of the burning incense around so much that the streams of incense smoke filled the church, until it seemed overwhelming.

They put me in the first row at the church with the other pallbearers. I was directly in the path of the waves of incense smoke.

Then the priest came over to us in the front row with a box full of the wafers that I had seen priests feed to people in the movies.

I know very little about any sort of religious ceremonies in any type of house of worship. My relative theological ignorance encompasses all faiths and denominations. However I'd seen the wafers in the past, and I actually wondered what they tasted like. I didn't think that they would be a good as an Oreo cookie, but I doubted that they would be anything too offensive. After all, they were just wafers.

The priest walked over to the first person on the aisle, who subserviently opened his mouth, and the priest put the wafer in it. He seemed to be able to chew and eat it quickly, and with no problem. I was confident that it was OK for me to eat one, though in the back of my mind I wondered if I might be doing something wrong or disrespectful, since I was not a true believer of any kind.

But it was too late; the priest came and stood in front of me. I opened my mouth, remembering not to stick my tongue out like I was taking a hit of acid in college.

He put the wafer in my mouth. I ate it. It tasted like a mix of paper, Styrofoam and a stale saltine cracker mixed together. I gave it a few chews and swallowed it down. It wasn't worth the wait.

I looked forward to asking Annie about it, since she had been a Sunday school teacher, her stepfather was an ex-priest, and she was my first source for any sort of theological information.

After the church ceremony, the small crowd moved on to the burial. Some attendants took care of transporting Julia in a wheelchair from the church to the cemetery. Julia looked very small and weak, covered in a blanket, with an aura of sadness enveloping her.

When I got home, Annie asked me about the funeral. I told her about eating the wafer, and I had some questions.

"You took communion?!" she said with a startled tone in her voice.

I had heard the phrase taking communion," but didn't really understand what it meant.

"I didn't take anything, I just ate the wafer." I responded.

"That's what taking communion is," she said instructively.

Annie proceeded to explain in great detail what "taking communion" was all about. I understood it when she was telling me, but I don't remember much about it anymore.

Hopefully, I won't be eating any more wafers any time soon.

CHAPTER 26

Heavy is the Head

One of the reasons that I decided to leave Prudential Securities was for the money, which I needed to replace some of the money that I had given to Debbie. It was the price paid to keep the peace, and assure my access to my children.

It probably would have been far less expensive to have hired lawyers and fought for both money and custody of the kids. However, I had such pervasive sense of loss, and felt such deep pain from the separation, that any more confrontation and fighting were unacceptable. So, I gave her the money, and hoped that the opportunity would come to recoup some of my lost assets.

Having spent my entire career at one firm, I really had no idea what it was like in the outside world of other Wall Street firms. Not only had I been sheltered in the womb of Prudential Securities, but I sat in the corner office almost immune to criticism since I helped manage the office, and was the one in charge, at least some of the time.

I had grown up in the branch, and everyone knew me as both a broker and an Assistant Manager. I was one of the top producers in the office, even while handling my share of the managerial duties during the course of the business day. I was like the Derek Jeter of the Hartford branch.

When Charles had a heart attack, , I had to spend way more time helping to manage the team and handling the office affairs, while simultaneously trying to maintain my business, and deal with the breakup of my marriage.

There was much chaos in my life for many months. I was working too hard, trying to be too many places at one time, and trying to do too many things.

By the time the firm found a new Branch Manager, a guy named Phil who had been the Branch Manager at Advest, a well-known regional firm in town, it was clear that I needed a change. It was time for me to leave home, and go explore the rest of the world of Wall Street.

Prudential Securities was a very nice and comfortable place to be. The firm reminded me of the Minnesota Twins, a strong smaller market team, but certainly not the New York Yankees. I was already a star on the Twins, and I wanted to go play Wall Street for the equivalent of the Yankees. If I could make it there, I could make it anywhere.

It is said that you can never know how good your wife is in bed, unless you've slept with other woman. Prudential Securities had been my wife for 16 years, and I wanted to try something new.

I made two telephone calls. The first was to the manager of Smith Barney in Hartford, someone who I had never met, but had heard a lot about, a gentleman named Jerry M. who sported the nickname the "Radish Man."

The second call was to Roland, the assistant manager at Merrill Lynch in Hartford, who had a short stint of as my branch manager at Prudential Securities. Considering that I had only contacted two people about my wanting to move to another firm, the strangest things began to happen.

Strange people from other firms started calling, wanting to meet in strange places to discuss different types of offers. I hadn't planned on being a "free agent," and courted by other teams in the league. I was disarmed by the fact that everyone seemed to know that I was moving on.

One of the first unexpected calls that I received was from Advest, the regional firm that the Phil, the Branch Manager, had been recruited from. They wanted to know if I was interested in taking over the downtown Hartford branch that Phil had just left as branch manager. I was surprised by the suggestion because the Hartford branch was the flagship branch of the firm.

I had never indicated any interest to manage a branch, at any time, to anyone. The only reason that I was Assistant Manager in the first place was because Michael had asked me to do it as "payback" for him hiring me.

Advest had a recruiting guy named Howie who made the initial contact with me. I thanked him for his interest, but told him that I wasn't interested in the job, but thanks anyway.

I had heard through the grapevine that the Hartford Advest office had been decimated by many of their brokers moving to other firms. By the time Phil had to leave," half of the broker offices in the Hartford branch were empty.

I had also heard some rumors about the Phil's alleged "unsavory" behavior, and some potential legal issues. I began to wonder exactly why Phil had left Advest, and why Prudential would have overlooked those kinds of overhanging compliance issues.

All of a sudden, I began to feel very uncomfortable, not only with the timing of the Advest job offer, but also to any potential exposure that I might have working with the Phil, right where I was.

I didn't want to manage, but I also didn't want to stay put where I was, just in case the Phil was a little on the dark and shady side. It certainly seemed like it was time for me to pack my cleats and go find another team to play on.

Ironically about a year after I left, the Phil did in fact get nailed for alleged money laundering, or something similarly cheesy. I'd also heard some talk about several Brazilian strippers being involved, but I don't know what actually happened because I wasn't there at the time, fortunately.

After Advest called, the floodgates seemed to open. All of the major firms in town began contacting me, wanting to know if they could talk to me about either working for their firms, or if I'd be interested in managing their local offices.

I had no idea how word had gotten all around town, but I knew that I had to resolve this one way or the other before Prudential found out. My own firm might try to lock me out, or do something adversarial, which is the procedure when an established broker leaves one firm to go to another.

I wanted to play for the Yankees, and the Yankees seemed to be Merrill Lynch, but Smith Barney seemed a lot less onerous, and more like the Los Angeles Dodgers. The Dodgers used to be from Brooklyn, where I grew up, so I reasoned that Smith Barney would be okay to play for.

Going to Smith Barney would be like going to the West Coast to play ball in the sun. Going to Merrill would be like moving back to New York City to conquer the great worlds of finance, and play ball under the big lights.

That was the sort of sports-meets-life reasoning that I was using at the time.

I was going to have lunch with Jerry M, the "Radish Man," and manager of the Hartford Smith Barney office. Jerry supposedly got his name because he lived on a small farm in a town outside of Hartford and grew radishes. He would occasionally bring bags of them into his branch office to give away to the employees. Jerry was very well liked in the broker community; the people who worked in his branch said that he was a real "broker's manager." Even people who had left his office said that he was a nice guy to work for.

Since nice really does matter, that made a big difference to me.

In the meantime, Advest decided that they didn't want to take no for an answer. Howie the recruiter called again asking if I would meet with the President of the company and a few department heads. I politely said no, but that didn't even seem to faze him; he was quite insistent. I figured, what the hell, let's go see what they have to say.

My first meeting at Advest was very pleasant. All of the people I met were very bright, pleasant people who genuinely seemed interested in finding the right person for the manager's job. The offices were bright and modern, with new but not overly ostentatious furniture. They had a more modern computer system than we had at Prudential Securities; I was impressed that their computer screens were flashing green and red stock quotes on the screen, indicating if the stock prices were going up or down.

The empty Branch Manager's office was large and enclosed in glass, overlooking a large board room filled with broker desks. There were more ornate private offices on the periphery of the room. I looked at the Branch Manager's space a few times, and couldn't see myself sitting there. I tried to visualize it, but didn't feel any enthusiasm to be there.

The President of Advest, and Howie the Recruiter, had a very nice New York style deli lunch brought into the Conference Room, where we all had a homey friendly meal of corned beef and pastrami sandwiches, half sour pickles, potato salad, cookies, and, black cherry sodas.. Even the CEO named Burton came to join us.

Burton was a little overdressed in his dark pinstriped three piece suit, with a gold pocket watch sticking out of his vest pocket. He wore one of those magnetic copper bracelets that are supposed to promote health. It was an odd thing for an older man to be wearing. I wondered if he had health problems.

After lunch, the President of the firm, named Bruce, brought me into his office to talk.

Bruce laid out a very attractive offer involving money, stock, stock options and a significant cut of the office revenues if I would take the job. He told me how I would be a wonderful fit, and how everyone was looking forward to working with me.

It was all very nice, but it wasn't at all what I wanted, so I respectfully declined, outlining my selfish reasons which revolved around the fact that I simply didn't want to have to work that hard. I wanted to be a ball player, not a manager.

I thanked Bruce for his time, and headed off to meet the Radish Man the next day, with Roland from Merrill Lynch the day after.

Jerry, the Radish Man, was everything that he was cracked up to be, in the most positive way. He was large garrulous happy man who seemed to enjoy everything about our business. He told me about his farm and his family. He asked me about my life, my kids, and my hobbies. We shared an interest in working to help the poor and homeless in Hartford through service to non-profits in the community.

There were a number of brokers who I knew that worked in his downtown branch office; Jerry told me how all of their businesses had improved since moving over to his branch. Most people on the outside of the industry do not realize how important a supportive branch manager is to the brokers in the branch.

Jerry seemed like the kind of guy who wanted to help his brokers succeed, and that counted just about as much as being nice.

Near the end of lunch, the Radish Man laid out his offer; I had no problems with it, and it sure looked like I was going to be playing in the sun for the Dodgers. However, I had lunch with Roland the next day, so I told Jerry that I'd be back with him in a day or two.

I was interested in hearing what Merrill had to say, but I was already picturing myself in Dodger Blue.

When I got home that evening, Annie was standing in the kitchen with an envelope in her hand. "You just received a telegram," she said, her fingers exploring the envelope as if to test its reality.

"A telegram? I didn't even know that they still sent telegrams." I reached out for the yellow and black colored envelope.

I opened it. It was a real Western Union telegraph. It was from Advest, asking me if I would come in to meet with their CEO, Burton, to discuss the Branch Manager's position.

"Jeez," I said to Annie. "Those guys are persistent. They just send me a freaking telegram. Annie, you have got be impressed by people that send you a Western Union telegram." I ruminated for a moment, and then began my meditation out loud as Annie stood listening.

She poured some half and half into her hazelnut coffee.

"Maybe I should go talk to this guy again. Maybe….Annie…..maybe… I should rule. Maybe it is my destiny to go forward and build a great and mighty branch office where wise and powerful brokers with go forward to battle the forces of darkness in the financial markets, so that their clients may prosper and live happily on," I continued.

Annie sipped her coffee and listened while I rambled on. I talked about the brokers that I knew in town who would join me at the Round Table that I would soon have installed in the Conference Room at Advest.

I talked of the grand Christmas parties that I would host, and the blinding array of charitable causes that we would sponsor. I spoke of growing the revenues of the branch, and growing the business so as to become the dominant and pre-eminent investment firm in town.

It would take an incredible amount of effort; it would be an incredible amount of work; but, I could see the visions appearing before me. I could feel the power swelling up within my being. I took a deep breath, thinking big thoughts, imagining the possibilities.

I looked to Annie for affirmation. Debbie had never encouraged me to do anything. I wanted encouragement; but I also wanted to know what Annie really thought.

Annie looked at me, and said, "Heavy lies the head that wears the crown."

I thought about what Annie meant by that for a while. I realized that she meant I had to ask myself what it was that I wanted from life.

Sure, I wanted to rule, but I knew I'd be profoundly unhappy once the novelty wore off, and I had to deal with the reality of sixty hour weeks, traveling, recruiting, meetings and reports, all while wanting to maintain my personal life.

The idea of leaving Prudential was to simplify my life, and not clutter it up with a thousand more tasks and commitments.

So with Dodger blue skies in my eyes, I went to meet Roland from Merrill the next day for lunch in the back corner of a secluded bar in downtown Hartford.

Roland proceeded to tell me how "different" Merrill was from not only Prudential, but from all other firms.

Merrill was far more "structured," and they had their own way of "handling client accounts," ostensibly to develop "deeper relationships" with the clients. It certainly sounded a little Orwellian.

Roland was usually a pretty loose kind of guy with a big smile, a good sense of humor, perfect hair, and classic Wall Street suspenders, but something about his description of the firm seemed like it was coming off of a teleprompter or cue cards.

Roland said candidly that if someone did not start their career at Merrill, that they are always viewed as sort of a "step child" of the firm; however, those who are able to "adjust" usually find it a financially rewarding place to work.

Merrill Lynch certainly sounded like a different kind of place to work, maybe too different. I just wanted to go somewhere I could bring my clients to practice my trade, and go happily ever after into the investment sunset. Boot camp was not what I had in mind. Still, there was something intriguing, something that challenged me to go into the darkness and conquer it.

I had been intrigued by the Merrill "mystique' from the beginning of my career. Merrill always seemed to lead all of the other firms in just about everything, from technology to investment banking. Their brokers there were always quoted to have had the highest production in the industry. I knew that I was doing well at my firm, but it seemed like the bar was raised higher at Merrill. For some reason, the people over there did more business that their counterparts at other firms.

I couldn't imagine why that would be so, particularly since Merrill had a reputation for being a repressive bureaucracy that told their broker/advisors what to put in clients' portfolios. Merrill felt that they knew what was right for the clients, and the brokers didn't.

In Hartford, the Merrill office had not recruited any significant producers from other firms in years. Anyone looking to change firms usually shunned Merrill like poison ivy.

However, I knew several people who had come over to our firm from Merrill; none of them seemed to have been tortured or beaten.

The only evidence that they had come from a place where they may have been abused was that they were all very quiet and seemingly timid for many months, as they slowly became acclimated to their new office environment.

I didn't realize at the time that they were demonstrating the same sort of behavior that a terrified or abused little puppy might show after being released from a cage.

It is clear now that many of the brokers who left Merrill were suffering some sort of post-Merrill traumatic stress that took some time for them to overcome once they had freed themselves from the binds of oppression. Unfortunately, I didn't realize that then.

I became friendly with one of the brokers who came over from Merrill, a Chinese guy named Kei Lam. He usually wore a black or dark blue suit with a white shirt and a tie. Kei was portly, not tall, with thick dark rimmed glasses.

Kei always had a reserved tone in his voice when he spoke. He spoke more like a teacher than as a broker. Many of Kei's clients seemed to be Chinese. It had never occurred to me what an untapped market the Chinese community in and around the Hartford area was. Kei was the only Chinese broker that I knew in Hartford, so I figured that he had the whole market to himself. No wonder he was so successful in the business. Kei was the voice of Wall Street, as well as the local American capitalistic connection to the Chinese investing community. What a great marketing concept.

A few times, I asked Kei about being a broker at Merrill, and why he had left the firm. It strikes me now that he was carefully evasive. I couldn't solicit a straight answer from him. It wasn't like he didn't know; it was more like he didn't want to remember.

Maybe, something had suppressed his memory like in *Men in Black* where they use the flash apparatus to erase the memories of the people who have seen the aliens. Kei would only say things like "It was different then," or other cryptic comments which made his time at Merrill seem like a world far away and long ago.

Roland laid out the Merrill offer. It was about the same as the Smith Barney offer, with the addition of a fixed salary for the first six months to give the broker time to properly "transition" to the Merrill experience.

It certainly appeared that Merrill was trying to be supportive of their recruits. Maybe, Merrill's bad reputation was overstated, I thought; maybe this would be a challenge that I would enjoy. It was an interesting prospect, but I knew I was probably going to take the sunnier easier road that led to Smith Barney.

After receiving the telegram, I agreed to meet with Burton, the CEO of Advest, one last time. I had already told both Bruce the President and Howie the Recruiter that I definitely did not want the job. I even told them that it was between Merrill and Smith Barney; they were all undeterred.

Two days later, I was, sitting with Burton in his huge top floor office filled with antique furniture and magnificently framed paintings. We sat in a small seating area in a corner of the office. The furniture was very impressive. I had never seen a CEO's office; it was fancy all over. Burton had the kind of big leather chairs that you see in movies or expensive catalogs, the kind with the metal rivets running along the sides. We were separated by a very pretty, small polished wood table.

Burton seemed to think that my lack of interest in the job was some sort of negotiating tactic, so he wanted to offer me more, much more. Not only could I manage the Hartford office, but I would also be in charge of all of the satellite offices in the nearby towns. He was willing to increase the cash offer, the amount of stock, and my percentage of the action from the branches.

As he spoke, I kept hearing Annie say, "Heavy lies the head that wears the crown."

I slowly explained to Burton that I didn't want to work that hard, and while I was flattered, the answer was no, definitely no. I unambiguously told him that he would have to look elsewhere for his person. I wanted to spend more time with my kids and my girlfriend.

It was more important to me to be able to coach all of my son's little league games and practices than it was for me to make more money. At that point in my life, I told Burton, I wanted to be a Wall Street ballplayer and a practitioner, not a manager.

It took about another half an hour of Burton's polite arm twisting before I could bring the conversation to a close, and head out the door, thanking Burton and all of his people for their time and consideration. I even gave him some names of people who he might contact.

Now it was time to give the Radish Man the big news.

The next day, I met with Jerry the Radish Man for lunch at Scarlett O'Hara's, a particularly dumpy little bar on Pratt Street in downtown Hartford. Scarlett's was one of my favorite places to go for lunch because it was highly unlikely that you would run into any other Wall Streeters there. It seemed like an appropriate place to do the deal.

We were in the middle of lunch when Jerry suggested that we go over to the branch office to meet Alex, who was the new Branch Manager in Hartford. I did a double take, and then another one, before asking him what he meant by the "new Branch Manager?"

After all, the Radish Man was the Branch Manager that I wanted to sign up with. I didn't even know Alex. Who the hell was Alex? What made this guy think that I wanted to work for someone who I had never even met?

It was clear to me that I had just been pimped; sold and transferred like a piece of meat.

Jerry would have gotten a huge bonus for recruiting me, probably about thirty thousand dollars, so he was going to sign me, seal me, and deliver me, before he left town to go manage a smaller branch out of town. I was pissed.

Jerry said that I could certainly go and work in his new branch, but I didn't want to work out of town. I couldn't believe how he had tried to play me. I was offended.

I had been double crossed by the Radish Man.

This revelation immediately squelched the Smith Barney deal. I made some harsh comments to the Radish Man, and then walked out of the bar, leaving him sitting there. I guess it was time to go play ball with the Yankees.

I obviously wasn't thinking clearly at the time.

CHAPTER 27

BEDBUGS

If there ever **were a real life omen** of biblical proportions, it came a few weeks after I had signed with Merrill, and the weekend before I was to go to Merrill's "campus" in Princeton, New Jersey for a week of training and re-programming.

The employment contract signing with Merrill had gone extremely smoothly. The Branch Manager, Cynthia, immediately put together a team of six experienced Merrill support people to handle all of the paperwork, letters, announcements, and transfer documents that would be necessary to move over all of my hundreds of client accounts. Even after sixteen years in the business, I'd never seen organization like that.

Cynthia rented a suite in the Goodwin Hotel, the premier hotel in Hartford. There were tables lined up in a big room, with snacks, bottled waters and juices, and an array of boxes filled with blank forms.

When clients began returning the signed transfer forms, there were people who looked at the forms, separated the forms, followed up on any missing forms. There was a dedicated Fed-Ex basket to send and receive overnight items that were being sent out.

ROCK & ROLL STOCKBROKER

I had actually known and spent time talking to Cynthia before I knew that she was the manager of the Merrill office. She and I both spent excessive amounts of time after the markets closed in the same bar at Max's Downtown, an upscale restaurant that was on the ground floor of our building complex.

Cynthia was one of the happy hour regulars, a largish woman with bleached blonde hair and very neatly tailored women's business suits. Cynthia drank a lot, smoked a lot, and had a loud open mouthed laugh that you could hear across the bar. She usually sat at the bar surrounded by a small circle of people from the Merrill office.

Usually there were one or two very young looking brokers with heavily moussed hair, suspenders, and shiny shoes trying to gain her attention. Cynthia clearly enjoyed the young bucks currying for her favor. Sometimes she sat with a dour looking older lady, who wore very plain clothes and had badly colored dark hair, and who always seemed to have an annoyed look on her face; that was her assistant Elsie, who I would later nickname "The Toad."

Something about Cynthia reminded me of the coffee mugs that say "She Who Must Be Obeyed."

I had no problem taking orders from the team manager of the Yankees. I assumed that having gained such a lofty position, she would rule with wisdom and experience, and would possess information which would enable her brokers to achieve all-star levels of performance. The fact that she liked to drink and smoke a lot seemed indicative of someone who liked to work hard and then party hard; both of which I embraced enthusiastically.

My first week at Merrill was filled with paperwork, contacting clients, and learning basic office procedures, like how to get quotes and enter orders. To my surprise, not only weren't the computer systems state of the art, but it was technology that most firms had abandoned years before. The small monitor had a black background with tiny white letters and numbers; compared to what I was used to, it seemed like something from the dark ages.

In order to access all of the basic client account functions, the computer still used cryptic commands that were like vestiges of some old cyber code. There was something about the darkness on the face of the computer screen that made me feel adrift in the blackness of outer space.

Within a few days, I'd look at the screen, and feel like "Major Tom" in David Bowie's song *Space Oddity*. I could hear Bowie's echo filled voice singing as I stared into the black screen.

The office furniture was old and beat up. My desk had dings and bruises all along the edges and drawers. The greenish carpeting that covered the office floor was worn, with areas that were alternately faded and soiled.

Merrill's office space was far larger than Prudential's. All of the private offices were built around the perimeter of the building, with a huge "bullpen" area in the middle where all of the lower level brokers and sales assistants sat.

The lighting in the office was far more florescent looking towards the center of the large room due to of the lack of natural sunlight, which was blocked by the private offices on the perimeters. The people who sat towards the center of the room had an unhealthy looking pallor because of the overhead florescent lighting.

Looking across the expanse of the office, it had the feeling of a ship filled with the dead.

It didn't help to raise my spirits rise when the person who I had to deal with the most frequently was Elsie, The Toad. Never before had I ever encountered a more unpleasant bitch of a woman in a Wall Street office than The Toad.

There was nothing positive about the woman.

The Toad never smiled. She always grimaced or scowled, and made everything she did seem like she was doing you a favor. The Toad acted like she wouldn't have bothered assisting you if she wasn't being forced to. She didn't like it when you needed to ask her a question about anything, and would tell you to go ask someone else. She had a fat face with pasty looking jowls, unflattering cheap black glasses with imitation rhinestones on the corners of the frames.

Her face looked distinctly toad like, with a touch of warty goblin. Every time I tried to be pleasant and charming, it was clear that she wasn't having any of it, and would become more curt and nasty in tone. The Toad was Cynthia's primary go to person. It didn't take long before I was seeing the shades of darkness unfurling before me.

Fortunately, I was going to be out of the office for a week to go to Merrill Lynch's Princeton campus for training and indoctrination.

However, before I was to leave on the following Monday morning, I decided to take Annie down to Misquamicut Beach for a long weekend at what had become my favorite motel there – the Sandy Shore, the same one I'd discovered as a result of that last trip with Debbie.

Since the Sandy Shore was open year round, Annie and I would sometimes go in the off season, when the streets were empty, and the beach was quietly deserted; a perfect time for long meditative walks near the shore.

The weekend before I had to leave for Princeton, I took Annie to the shore to reflect upon the curling waves, and the seagulls gliding against the brightening spring sky. The motel was nearly empty. We booked one of the corner oceanfront rooms so we could have the cross breezes off the ocean flow over us as we slept.

We arrived late in the afternoon, and met Tim for drinks at a little Italian restaurant that the Misquamicut locals went to. Then, Annie and I headed to our room to relax and watch some TV, as the sea breezes blew across our corner motel room; until, finally, we went to sleep, planning for a long walk on the beach in the morning.

It was about two in the morning when I began to squirm in the motel bed. I was itching uncomfortably, and had a hot flushed feeling. There was something about how I felt that struck up deep dark repressed memories that I had tried to forget over the years.

I had felt this bad feeling before; it was like some horrible creature had reemerged from the darkness of my childhood experience in the ghetto of Brooklyn.

I'd fought this foul beast before. I knew immediately what I was feeling, and the startling nauseating realization woke me up, and sent me jumping out of bed, quickly turning on the light. I looked down at the sheets, and quickly prodded Annie to sudden consciousness.

"Annie, quick…..get out of bed…get out of bed now!" I cried.

Annie woke up, startled, with a look like I was going to tell her that I had a bad dream.

But this was real…horribly, terribly, and disgustingly real.

"Annie…get out of bed…there are bedbugs!"

"Bedbugs? There's no such thing as bedbugs…that's just a nursery rhyme," she said with all the assurance of someone who'd gone to prep school.

"Oh, no, Annie, they're real and that's one right there."

I pointed down to a reddish brown bug on the bed that looked like an ugly darkly colored ladybug, but smaller. All around the sheet, mostly on my side, there were numerous little specks of blood. I had been bitten dozens of times. They'd found me, after all the years.

"Are you sure?" She obviously still didn't believe it, or maybe didn't want to believe it, but I remembered those bugs very well.

Annie knew that I had grown up in a tenement in the Brownsville section of Brooklyn, the heart of the New York City ghetto. My building was an old, unmaintained six family apartment building built above three stores, two of which were abandoned and boarded up. The third store was a Puerto Rican restaurant where my mother sometimes sent me down to eat yellow rice and beans when she had no food in the refrigerator.

Not only did the building have armies of cockroaches, herds of rats and mice, and big black water bugs, but our apartment also had bedbugs, lots of them. By the time I was six years old, I knew what the bedbugs were. They lived in my room, and they tried to eat me at night. I knew the horrible disgusting feeling of their bites, when they sucked out my blood, and left stains on the sheets.

As a little kid, I tried to scrounge up loose change from the bottom of the closets, or from the nickels and pennies that my mother would give me from her tips that she made as a barmaid.

When I had enough change, I walked a few blocks to the hardware store and bought whatever sized can of Black Flag insect killer that I could afford.

Then, I would go back to my mom's apartment to pull the sheets off my mattress, and spray the clusters of bedbugs that gathered in the corners and folds of the mattress.

I had done battle with the creatures before. I knew them, and they had found me again.

Annie stared intently as I walked over to the corner of the mattress, ready to pull off the corner of the fitted sheet. I asked her if she was ready, she nodded, and I pulled off the sheet exposing about 20 bedbugs clustered around the corner of the mattress.

There was clearly a growing nest of little black dots on the mattress' cloth material which were bedbug eggs. Annie's brown eyes opened even bigger with a look of horror. I hoped she wouldn't pass out.

"We need to collect our stuff. Put everything in something plastic, and make sure that it's tightly wrapped up. Let's get out of here."

Annie seemed wobbly, but in less than five minutes, we checked each other, and then inspected our clothes for bedbugs. Quickly, we were packed up and out of there, leaving the room key in the drop slot as we headed home in the middle of the night.

As we drove home in the darkness of 2:30 am, I could feel the bites all over my body starting to itch and swell. I felt feverish.

This was not how my send off to Merrill boot camp was supposed to be. It seemed like an omen, like the locusts in biblical Egypt, or maybe even worse. I had been attacked by the bloodsucking insects yet again. It reminded me of the bad things that lurk and lie in waiting for the moment that you let your guard down.

There were no lights on the road most of the way home. I was trying to focus on the dark road ahead of me. The drive was a long two hours of painful discomfort.

I had been bedbug food.

The next morning, the phone at home rang at about 7:30; it was Tim. He had found our room keys when he came into his office in the motel, and couldn't understand why we had left so suddenly, particularly since we had planned to stay for two nights.

When I told him what had happened, he couldn't believe it. Tim said that he had never even seen a bedbug in his life. He asked me how I knew that they were indeed bedbugs, so I recounted the story of my growing up in the ghetto, and assured him that they were definitely bedbugs.

Tim was obviously stunned, and said that he would go over to the room to check it out, and would call me back shortly. During that time, Tim's wife Jill immediately went out and bought some books or magazines to identify the creatures.

When Tim called me back; he was mortified, apologetic and genuinely upset. Tim subsequently ended up stripping the room of all furniture, and calling in professional exterminators to handle the problem. Ultimately, he ended up closing off an entire wing of the motel to allow the exterminators to totally eliminate any signs of the bugs. He told me that they had to drill holes in the walls to make sure that they killed anything that was living between the sheetrock.

It seemed like a plague that had been sent as punishment, but it was really a warning, a sign of things to come.

My weekend getaway with Annie was totally blown, and I spent Sunday dabbing my clusters of bedbug bites with hot washcloths, alcohol and calamine lotion. When I was a little boy, the bites had never even fazed me; it was no worse than being bitten by a mosquito, but as an adult, there was something about the bug bites that was making me sick to my stomach.

The next day, I had to drive down to New Jersey, and by the morning, I was feeling much worse. I started to wish that I had just stayed in the comfort of my warm little corner office at Prudential; but it was way too late for that.

I had not chosen wisely, and I was being punished for my transgressions.

CHAPTER 28
THE EVIL WITHIN

The dozens of **bedbug bites bothered me** during the entire trip down to the Merrill "campus" in Princeton, New Jersey. Perhaps if I had been feeling better, I would have enjoyed my week there much more than I did. Instead, I began to feel worse each day that I was there.

The campus facility itself was impressive. It encompassed a hotel, several restaurants, lecture halls, a banquet facility, a very elegant bar stocked with exotic liquors and cigars, and even a medical office.

There was another large wing of the campus that housed various trading and administrative areas of the firm. The entire complex of buildings was surrounded by various trails and walking paths, accented by numerous fountains and attractively landscaped sitting areas. There was a health center and gym area, but I never got around to checking it out.

My room was very well appointed, certainly the equivalent of any nice hotel room. By the time that I arrived, I was getting feverish. I was surprised that the bug bites were making me feel so bad, but I was determined to shake it off, and get on with making the best of my week there to learn everything that I needed to know about being a successful part of the Merrill Lynch machine.

As soon as I arrived, I wanted to take a nap, but there was no time. One of the first activities was a reception in the banquet area. I wasn't hungry at all, but there was an amazing spread of food.

An entire large table was full of different kinds of shellfish and seafood. The salad area looked like a farmers market, and for the entrees, they had everything possible, from ham to roast beef to Cornish hens, pastas, veggie dishes, and, endless hors d'oeuvres, I wandered around, tentatively looking at all of the offerings, sampling small amounts of a few, before gravitating towards raw clams and oysters.

I don't know what possessed me to want to try raw oysters when I had never eaten them before. I put a few small clams and oysters in my plate with a little cocktail sauce on the side, and headed towards a table.

Someone at the table was starting to say something to me as I went to swallow one of the clams, when there was that unmistakable taste of a spoiled clam in my mouth. I grabbed for the cloth napkin with my other hand, and put it to my mouth. I didn't want to spit the foul clam into the napkin in front of all of the people at the table, so I closed my eyes and quickly swallowed it. I immediately began to feel even sicker that I had felt before.

I wanted to go back to my room when one of the hosts began to speak. I didn't want to be rude by bolting out of the room at that moment, so I sat down and tried not to puke as the speaker began the introductory comments.

After I finally went back to my room, I became sick to my stomach several times, and spent time in the bathroom trying to expel whatever was making me feel so awful.

If the bedbug bites weren't annoying enough, I was allergic to something that I had eaten because I was breaking in hives all over my body. My head ached. I could have used some Benadryl, but I was feeling too nauseous to go out and find some.

I hunkered under my blanket, feeling like death was coming for me, and struggled through until morning.

I was part of a group of about fifty brokers that Merrill had hired away from various firms. Once a month, the recruits from all around the country would be brought to Princeton for their indoctrination and training before joining the Merrill army.

The whole process was very organized and orchestrated to assure that all of the newbies understood the Merrill ways of doing business, as opposed to how they had done things before.

The next morning, everyone was gathered in the lecture hall, and the one of the first speakers was the head of Merrill's retail operations, Rodney Smith.

Smith looked like a powerful guy. His black pointy shoes had a mirror shine that I could see from up in the fifteenth row. His suit looked like it cost more than my car. He began by talking about some multimillion dollar deals that he had recently brought into the firm to show that he was still a player, and not just a manager.

He seemed very classy and professional, but there was a Mephisthophelean quality about him that I couldn't put my finger on. He reminded me of a *Twilight Zone* episode where a regular looking man morphs into Satan, sprouting horns on his head, cloven hooves and a tail.

Over the next two days, there was a procession of speakers from the different managed money product areas.

It was clear that Merrill saw their sales force as asset gatherers, and not portfolio managers. Each speaker made their pitch as to why the brokers should give their clients' money to their particular asset management program. There didn't seem to be much room in the Merrill way for brokers who wanted to manage their clients' portfolios by themselves.

I had always personally managed my clients' assets. It was what I liked best about the business. I felt that I did it as well, if not better than most money managers. Since I had to be accountable to the clients, I wanted to be the one to make the investment decisions. If anyone was going to mess it up, it was going to be me.

I wasn't going to take the blame for the lousy performance of some nameless portfolio manager who did not know or care about my individual client; but I cared, so I preferred to do it myself.

The product areas that I was most interested in got very short shrift in the presentation line. Merrill obviously felt that everyone already knew about the traditional investment vehicles like municipal bonds, blue chip equities, and options, so the firm wanted to focus on the things that made them different.

In short order, it was clear that Merrill really did do things totally differently that other firms, and my way of doing business was what they were trying to weed out, and not to assimilate within.

By the end of the day, my physical condition was deteriorating rapidly. My breathing was becoming labored. I felt a wheezing in my lungs when I breathed too deeply. The rash was spreading and intensifying, even as the bedbug bites were swelling up in between the hives. I had a fever, and all of the Advil in the world wasn't making me feel any better.

I wanted to go home, but I was only halfway through the week.

The following day could only be described as slow torture as I sat there writhing from the rash and the bites, with intermittent chills. My throat was swelling and closing up as the hours went by. I had to miss a few presentations to lie down in my room. I hoped that they weren't taking attendance. I envisioned them sending storm troopers to my room to drag me back to the lecture hall.

That night, I was going to call 911 to take me to the hospital. I could barely breathe. There were hives and welts all over my body. I was burning up and shaking like a leaf at the same time.

I called Annie to tell her how lousy I felt, but didn't want to worry her. I resolved to try to hang in until the morning when I could go to the medical center in the complex.

By the time, I made it to the infirmary, I felt miserable, and looked ten times worse.

When I went in to see the doctor, I was further mortified when the doctor was a young woman who looked like Jessica Biel. I stared vacantly into her soft blue eyes as she asked me to take my shirt off.

By that point, I looked like a survivor of a nuclear attack, covered in welts, hives, rashes and bites.

I told the pretty doctor about the bedbugs and the bad seafood. I was very embarrassed when I took off my shirt and exposed the eruptions and red bumps on my skin. I asked her if I could come back when I was all better to show her how much better I looked when I wasn't so gross looking.

She smiled and said that would be fine, and then she gave me a small envelope filled with antibiotics. The pretty lady doctor was the highlight of a so far awful experience. I swallowed a few of the pills, and by the next day, I was looking and feeling somewhat better.

When the final day of training and indoctrination had ended, I headed back home not realizing that my experience with the campus would soon seem like a holiday compared to actually trying to work in the Merrill system.

My first lesson in the reality of the Merrill gulag occurred within a week of my returning from training. I had decided to buy about a half dozen clients the stock of CBS, the television network company. The day after I entered my trades, I received a call from the head Compliance Officer in the branch named Rodger.

When I was first hired, I had a brief conversation with Rodger, and he certainly wasn't anything like any compliance person that I had ever known before.

Rodger was a skinny little man, with a sneaky looking thin mustache, who overdressed for the job to a noticeable extent. Rodger always wore well-tailored three piece suits which made him look way more like a successful affected broker, than as part of the support staff.

It was clear, that Rodger didn't see himself as part of the support staff, he saw himself as the tyrannical overseer and enforcer of the ways and dictums of Merrill Lynch.

There was no right way or wrong way; there was only the Merrill way. Rodger could see or understand nothing that conflicted with his Master's directives. He and I would have at it for the next several years, with both of us disliking each other from the outset.

The outset began when I told him that I bought the CBS stock because I liked the company, thought it was cheaply valued, and would go up in price. Rodger immediately pointed out that I couldn't buy CBS stock because Merrill did not have a buy recommendation on the stock. I couldn't imagine why that would even matter.

All of my career, I always bought any quality stock that I wanted to for my clients. I knew that any stock that had a lot of analysts covering it usually had a wide range of opinions about the stock. Often, there were similar numbers of buy and sell recommendations on the same stocks at the same time. Everyone had different opinions about certain stocks; that what it takes to make a market, buyers and sellers.

Rodger told me that CBS had a D338 opinion from Merrill's research so I could not buy the stock. My exact response was, "What the fuck is a D338, and why should I give a shit about what Merrill's research thinks about a stock?"

Rodger was aghast. He looked at me like I was some insolent refugee that was sitting in his office. He began to describe how Merrill's rating system worked, with the first letter signifying the quality of the company, the first number representing the short term opinion, the second number representing the long term opinion, and the third number representing something else which I wasn't really listening to because I couldn't believe that he took this rating crap so seriously.

I asked him if he had several TV's in his home. He said yes. I asked him if he had CBS on all of the TV's in his house. He said yes. I asked him if he watched shows that were on CBS. He said yes. Then I told him that my clients also had TV's that had CBS, as did everyone else, and I didn't give a rat's ass if Merrill liked the stock. I'd buy all of it that I wanted to, whenever I wanted to.

If Rodger would have had a gun, he probably would have shot me. It would be fair to say that any chance of Rodger and I becoming buddies was pretty well destroyed at that moment.

In an effort to try to inject reason into the conversation, I tried to point out that using Merrill's research as a tool for directing the purchases and sales of securities was a clear and blatant conflict of interest. Further, as Compliance Officer, he had a responsibility to recognize and address this obvious conflict of interest with his superiors, because not only was this policy wrong, it was clearly unethical, and probably a violation of some securities laws and directives.

Rodger didn't agree with me or any part of my argument, It was clear that my perspective was so far from his belief set that he simply couldn't assimilate it any way whatsoever. Further, I had clearly affronted him by suggesting that he did not understand what his professional responsibilities were, as well as questioning the quality of his job performance.

I was about to call him an asshole, or something even more graphic, when I thought better of it, and just decided to end the conversation. However, I had just gained a valuable perspective on the Merrill headset that I would see replayed constantly over the next few years.

One of the biggest problems within Merrill Lynch was a systemic level of unintentional corruption and conflict of interest which was not a result of anyone wanting to do wrong. Rather, it was a result of all of the lifetime brokers and managers at Merrill Lynch not knowing that there was any other way to do things other than the Merrill way.

No one was trying to be evil; it was that they did not even know that what they were doing was inherently corrupt and wrong.

There were no bad guys, there were only people trained to do their jobs, not understanding that their ways of thinking and practicing had been distorted and twisted by the evil within.

Rodger and I went at it repeatedly. After a while, my insolence resulted in Rodger looking for things to hassle me about. One of my nastiest conversations occurred a few years into my sentence when I bought two thousand shares of General Instruments' stock for myself in my own account.

Merrill had a lousy rating on the stock, which was all the more reason to buy it, since I had observed that Merrill's research was usually about as wrong as it could be. Anytime I bought any Merrill research buys for my clients, something bad seemed to happen within days to cause losses in my clients' accounts.

Over the years, I'd periodically bought General Instruments stock as a trading vehicle, and it looked cheap, so it was worth a shot.

I bought my stock in the morning, and to my total surprise, that afternoon Merrill changed their research rating from a negative one to a positive one. Within a half an hour of their change of opinion, the stock jumped up in price over four dollars a share, so I immediately cashed out, taking a profit of over eight thousand dollars in a few hours.

After having repeatedly lost money on everything that I tried to do the Merrill way, it looked like Mother Merrill had thrown me a peace offering. Unfortunately, Rodger didn't see it that way at all.

That very afternoon, Rodger called me into his office to interrogate me about the trade.

He asked me how it was that I just happened to buy the stock hours before the research department upgraded their opinion. I told him that it was obviously a total coincidence. After all, how could I have possibly known what Merrill's research was going to do? He seemed unconvinced, which seemed too stupid for words to me. I was getting a little annoyed.

Rodger pointed out that I had made a profit of over eight thousand dollars in my own account in a few hours, and asked if I called that pure coincidence as well. I replied that what I called it was "my money," and if he had any further problems with the trade, he needed to take it up with someone else because I was tired of his bullshit. I was going to tell him to go fuck himself, but restrained myself.

Each time that I fought with Rodger, he would go complain to Cynthia, who would then come into my office to hassle me, and threaten to reassign a number of my client accounts.

It certainly didn't help matters that I was constantly defying Cynthia by refusing to participate in whatever offerings the firm was underwriting. I wouldn't accept someone telling me to buy securities for my clients just because Merrill Lynch needed to place the shares of whatever offering they were helping to bring to market.

Cynthia had an evolving and ever changing list of "critical objectives" that she wanted the brokers to meet. I thought that they were all bullshit, and ignored just about all of them.

Soon, Cynthia rescinded my parking privileges in the building. Then, she changed my sales assistant from one of the best in the office, to one of the newest and most inexperienced sales assistants.

She even came into my office one day to tell me that she wanted me to lower the height of one of my paintings on the wall. I responded that it seemed to be all right just as it was. She said that if I didn't lower it, she would have it removed from the office. I wanted to call her a cunt, but I didn't think she knew what one was, let alone had one.

CHAPTER 29

GOODBYE OLD FRIEND

My captivity at Merrill Lynch was made profoundly more difficult by the financial market events taking place during that time period.

It began with the dizzying inflation and then the violent collapse of the Internet Bubble, and subsequent implosion of the NASDAQ market, which disintegrated the stock prices of vast swaths of the technology area, causing massive losses for most market participants,

And that was followed by the knockout punch of the horror of 9/11, and the protracted stock market panic which soon followed.

If all of that wasn't bad enough, I ended up losing one of my best and oldest friends even as I sought to help guide him through the dark market storms which enveloped Wall Street.

Over the decades, I have had dozens of friends, relatives and acquaintances ask me to handle their accounts, and manage their financial assets. I am always honored and flattered, as well as acutely aware of the risks in handling the accounts of people who you know personally.

Usually, it's a layup. Since I know what I'm doing, the competence quickly shows, and the account becomes just another account that I handle without any emotional angst or personal involvement.

Most of my friends never call me at home about their portfolio matters, and my relatives generally just want me to handle it and bother them as little as possible.

But sometimes, it doesn't work out like that. Sometimes, things can go terribly wrong.

I first met Dean when we were freshmen at Brooklyn College. He was a white kid from the East New York ghetto in Brooklyn, and I was the white kid from the Brownville ghetto in Brooklyn. We had a lot in common in terms of life experiences. Personality wise, we were quite different.

I was the mellow hippie stoner, and he was the hyper, loud excitable guy who was prone to taking excessive quantities of Quaaludes for no particular reason. That was ok with me because it calmed Dean down enough that we could hang around together and have a good time.

Dean was born to be a salesman. He started in college by working for a friend who had a truck. They would take large quantities of assorted close out goods down to the Wall Street area of Manhattan, and sell individual items at high markups to the masses during the busy lunchtime hour in the city.

He soon moved on to selling electronics and appliances for a well-known chain store. He made a salary and commissions. Dean was so good at selling, that by the time we finished college, he was a store manager first, and then quickly became a regional sales manager.

While I was still driving a taxi, and walking the streets of Manhattan selling my mops and Fuller brushes, Dean was making real grown up money, and had an office on one of the upper floors of the Empire State Building.

Dean had discovered the financial markets early in life because I remember him telling me in the late 1970's and early 1980's that he had been speculating in the silver futures market, and had lost a bunch of money. That was coincident with the gold and silver bubble of that period.

It was clear early on that Dean had a propensity for being drawn into hot speculative markets which would follow him through the years.

After I started in the investment industry in 1981, I saw Dean pretty regularly when he passed through Hartford for meetings with buyers for several of the large department stores that were in town. From that time on, whenever we spoke about the markets, he would always tell me about the latest hot stock tip that he was buying into, and ask me what I thought of them.

Any time that I checked into his stocks, they were always story stocks of the moment, usually without any substance behind them. Often, they were stocks being promoted by boiler room operations, hot potato schemes where the last one in was left holding not only the bag, but a lot of worthless stock as well.

Even during the powerful bull market of the 80's, Dean refused to believe in the rally all of the way up, and finally began investing on margin as the market was topping out in 1987.

During the crash of 1987, he sold out on the day of the big plunge.

When I told him that I had bought stock for clients on that day, he remembered that remark over the coming years. Finally, when he became tired of losing money doing things his way, he asked me to handle his accounts around 1998, just as the internet bubble was beginning to grow rapidly.

Fortunately he had taken some of my advice over the years, and had set up custodial accounts for his two sons, and invested the money in some quality mutual funds.

However, aside from his kids' accounts, all that he owned at the time that I took him on as a client was a load of cash, a few IRA accounts, and several hundred thousand shares of an obscure penny stock that he had continued to buy intermittently to average down, as it dropped for several dollars to less than a cent a share.

We established three new accounts, two IRA's and a personal joint account with his wife. Dean agreed to let me handle the accounts the way I wanted to, with his participation but not his interference.

I set up the three accounts in an classic mix of mutual funds which was moderately aggressive, but still balanced between volatile growth oriented funds and more conservative value oriented funds, with a small taste of one of the global technology funds which were surrogates for participation in the internet explosion which was taking place.

It looked good on paper, and started to work right away.

After a few months, all of the accounts were very positive. As with any mix of mutual funds, some had done better than others. That is always the case since not everything rises at the same rate at the same time.

However, the logic of this reality did not seem to reach Dean on any level. He began calling me at the office to ask why we were holding funds that had returned eight percent when we had others that had returned eighteen percent. He began pestering me to change the mix of funds, which I had to continually debate him about.

And as the stock markets continued to rise, with NASDAQ in a ferocious parabolic rise, Dean began calling me more and more often at home and at work. Almost every evening, he would call me at home to point out that his internet fund was going up way faster that everything else, and he didn't know why we weren't moving more money into the sector.

At one point, before the internet bubble reached a crescendo in March of 2000, Dean was calling both my office and my home on a regular basis. On one hand, he wanted to argue that we should change the portfolios, but on the other hand, he would regularly acquiesce to my suggestion that we just leave things alone. It wasn't until near the tip of the bubble bursting that I had him make a change.

One evening Dean called me to tell me in a mocking and insulting way that if he wanted his money" in the bank," he would have put it there. He wasn't happy with the way I was handling the portfolio.

According to Dean, I treated his portfolio like I was "investing for an old lady."

I pointed out that his portfolios were up and positive, with returns in the high teens. He responded by telling me that he had taken his kids' accounts and moved them out of the mix of mutual funds that they had been invested in, and he moved all of their money into a global technology internet fund.

He pointed out that in two months, their money had grown from about sixty thousand dollars to over a hundred thousand dollars.

Those final weeks before the internet bubble burst in early 2000 were bizarre by any standards.

I had blue haired ladies from Florida calling me to ask if they should be selling their insured eight percent tax free bonds in order to buy Yahoo. I had at least a dozen clients insist that I buy them a nameless internet fund that started with an "M"; I refused most of them. All anyone talked about on the financial stations were internet stocks.

People were going crazy.

Most of Merrill Lynch's top stock picks were internet stocks. A blind person could see the end was near; I hoped that the madness would soon come to an end.

But, it is never that easy.

Experience had shown me is that greed is far more dangerous than fear.

Fear makes people pull back, withdraw, hunker down. Fear makes people protective of what they have, and concerned about losing what they have left. Fear makes people withdraw from the market, and to reassess their stand.

Fear makes people stop to breathe for a moment.

Greed on the other hand makes people go fucking nuts.

The idea that someone else is making more money seems to drive some people crazy. When markets get hot, everyone is interested. If something, almost anything, is rising in price dramatically, it draws money to it like moths to a flame, with similar results, a fiery painful death.

Greed makes people's hearts beat faster, and puts them into an irrational frenzy. If speed kills, greed annihilates both the flesh and the spirit.

It certainly didn't help that Merrill's promotion of the internet stocks was relentless.

Their vaunted research became nothing but a whore to their investment banking relationships. Classic blue chip stocks were all saddled with underperform ratings, thus "discouraging" their sales force from buying them. The internet stocks had the highest ratings because of their potential, but not their reality.

If blue haired ladies from Florida were getting swept up by the irrational exuberance of the internet stocks, what chance did someone like Dean have against the siren call of the wild stock market?

But I had seen this market madness before; I had seen it in many ways over the years, disguised differently each time. As T.S. Eliot wrote, "I have known the eyes already – known them all."

It was with the hysteria and shouts of the coming of a new world that I had Dean sell his global technology internet fund, after, of course, a lengthy argument during a lunch at Brown Thompson.

Dean's face had a look of anger mixed with frustration, because I was somehow preventing him from making money. I'd seen this greed driven mania before, but never quite this bad.

However, our internet fund money tree had yielded much fruit, and I was determined to have Dean harvest that fruit.

Over the next few weeks, Dean called me regularly to tell me about how well his kids' accounts were doing. I encouraged him to sell out all or most of their holdings, but he refused. Instead, he indicated that he was probably going to move out his accounts so that he could invest them the way he wanted to.

He felt that I was causing him to miss a big opportunity; he knew that he could do better without me.

Then the bottom dropped out.

When the internet bubble finally burst in March of 2000, it didn't just deflate, it exploded, and then the pieces that were left evaporated violently like dry ice in water.

Once the decline began, it was brutal, with the NASDAQ falling nearly ten percent in the first six days. Then the broad stock market joined in the decline which continued, with some brief pauses, for nearly two years.

As badly as NASDAQ fell, it was nothing compared to the almost total destruction of nearly everything that was internet related. The global technology funds began their decline by dropping fifty percent in a hurry, and then continued to melt down for endless months. Many individual internet stock issues declined over ninety percent, with some just disappearing altogether.

Dean's accounts with me were falling in value, but nothing compared to what was happening to him away from the accounts that I managed.

He had recently mentioned to me that he had taken a large part of his joint savings accounts and bank CD's and invested them into the global technology internet fund in which he'd invested his children's money.

By this time, he had started his own small company where he acted as a representative for different manufacturers around the world. Some of the money that he was diverting to the global tech fund was operating capital for his business, not to mention the general operating account which funded his flashy lifestyle, complete with Mercedes, tennis clubs, and personal trainers.

When the decline started to accelerate, Dean's headset began to change dramatically. I wasn't surprised. His kids' account had declined by seventy to eighty percent within a few months. They would eventually decline by over ninety percent before Dean sold out their positions.

Dean's business operating capital began shrinking rapidly, and combined with a sudden absence of new business because of the suddenly unstable world economy, he began having cash flow problems. This led him to call me more and more frequently to get my input on the market decline, as he watched the funds that he had thought were too conservative also decline in value.

All of a sudden, Dean began complaining that I had him positioned too aggressively. He didn't understand why we owned anything, and didn't just cash out of everything.

Fortunately, there were some intermittent stock market rallies that allowed his portfolios with me to begin to bounce back. Nonetheless, every time the market had a sharp decline for a day or two, he would be calling me several times a day at my office to get updates on the market action.

His personal and kids' accounts were being decimated, but I was confident that if I could keep Dean calm over the coming months, we would be able to maneuver our way back to profitability.

Unfortunately, the markets did not cooperate for very long, and each market rally was met by yet another market decline accompanied by anguish filled telephone calls from Dean several nights a week when I got home.

I might have been able to eventually get Dean to break on through to the other side, to emerge a stronger and wiser investor when the ultimate nightmare occurred, 9/11.

There is no way to adequately describe the panic and hysteria in Dean's voice each and every time that we spoke after that horrific event. However, the lessons of many years of experience had shown me the proper course of action.

With each wave of selling, I contacted clients to continue to aggressively buy any and all quality stocks that were being irrationally marked down in price. All of my clients who had been with me throughout the years, and the past market apocalypses, knew the drill.

I met little resistance, except from Dean. He was frozen with fear.

A few days after the 9/11 attack, the market dropped sharply yet again. That evening, I spent nearly two hours on the phone with an emotional anguished friend, trying to not let him do anything that would exacerbate the situation and cause irreparable damage to his portfolio.

I repeatedly explained that if he couldn't find the strength to be proactive and aggressive, that he should at least do nothing. He owned excellent funds, and I pointed out that if he did nothing at all, his portfolio would totally recover as the market conditions calmed and returned to normal.

That night in particular, there was no calming him. He was acting like such a scared, whining little bitch that I told him to stick his hands down his pants to see if he still had a set of balls. But even the inner city shock treatment had no effect.

I continued to give Dean market therapy whenever we spoke for months on end. I knew that one day soon, the market would begin to rebound, and then this would all seem like a bad memory, as it always does.

Unfortunately, this time the inevitable took a little longer to occur. The stock market did not finally bottom until the fall of 2002. . By that time, I had already repositioned some of Dean's assets in high quality undervalued stocks that I knew would outpace the market on the way up.

However, there was nothing that I could do about the immense financial damage that Dean had done to his children's accounts, as well as his personal/business assets that had also been blown away by his greed and fear.

One afternoon, I was returning one of Dean's calls, and reached his wife on the phone.

Dean's wife Lori , who I had known since the evening that they first met, seemed more than a little annoyed with me, and told me that Dean had told her how I lost them a huge amount of money, not to mention destroying their children's college accounts.

Dean had basically blamed me for everything.

Since she had heard him talking to me all of the time, she "knew" that I must have been giving him bad advice.

She told me that Dean was in the process of transferring his accounts, and that basically, I should go away.

I was hurt, insulted, and felt abandoned by an old friend. However, I have to admit that understood it perfectly.

Dean couldn't bear to lose face in front of his wife, and I was the perfect fall guy. In the big picture, a beautiful woman who would comfort him at night was way more important than me. I understood it, but it still makes me feel awful.

I sent Dean and Lori Christmas cards for a few years, and never once heard back

For several years, I tracked the portfolio that I left Dean with, and by the time the stock market hit a new all-time high a few years later, the portfolio had soared way past the general market's performance.

As I kept telling Dean, all he had to do was to do nothing, and it would all be fine. It was too bad the way it all worked out; the experience was one of the great bummers in my career.

Goodbye, old friend.

CHAPTER 30

CALL-IN CENTERS AND SCHINDLER'S LIST

While I was at Merrill Lynch, the firm pushed two significant repressive initiatives.

The first was the development of their call-in centers, where they segregated the smaller client accounts from the more affluent ones.

The second was the establishment of client account minimums that were required in order for a broker/advisor to be paid any compensation for handling the account.

The purpose of both of these initiatives was clear from the start. Merrill wanted their broker/advisors to send all of their existing small clients to the call-in center, where their accounts would be serviced by customer service representatives, and not the brokers of record.

For the brokers, this meant giving up accounts with clients and relationships that had existed for many years. If the account was too small, it had to go. It didn't even matter if the account had potential to become larger. It was a numbers game. The people behind the portfolios meant nothing to Merrill Lynch, neither did the wishes of the broker.

If a broker chose to keep the client, the account was handled with no compensation for most products; however the liability remained if something went wrong. Once the clients were sent to the call in center, they would be guided into investing in products that provided the firm with an ongoing stream of revenue from annuitized products, with a very small residual payment going to the broker.

This policy was particularly onerous to me because I had a very large number of client accounts, and many of them were smaller investors. I always found that small investors often know people with lots of money. My view was to treat every client equally, and give all clients the best effort possible, regardless of account size. I'd often seen how from a small account springs the giant account of a friend or relative.

I had a real problem with sending any of my clients to the call in center.

I thought that the policy sucked, and consistently rebelled against it.

At one point, Cynthia, the branch manager, insisted that every broker in the office go through their accounts, and hand in at least a certain minimum amount of their accounts to be reassigned to the call in center. It didn't matter if you had a personal relationship with these accounts, or how long you had done business with them. They had to go.

Every broker had "suggested" amounts of client accounts that had to be sacrificed and put on the railroad cars to be sent downwards to the bargain basement ovens of Merrill Lynch.

Sadly, it was not like the "suggested amount" at a museum or a fundraiser; it was more like paying off a bully to leave you alone.

I received several memos detailing the required of amounts of client accounts to be ritually sacrificed, and the related procedures to assure the transport of client assets to the Netherworld.

I chose to ignore the memos, all of them.

I tried to raise the group consciousness by talking to fellow brokers, and suggesting that resistance was possible.

Merrill Lynch was nightmarishly surreal in how the body politic had so totally submitted to the will of their masters. Deviant thinking was regarded as inconceivable and unacceptable.

Suggesting to other brokers that established client relationships need not be forsaken and cast off on the basis of an arbitrary metric such as account size was simply greeted with comments of disbelief, and immediate withdrawal from the conversation.

"After all," I would say to brokers who gave me their ear for at least a moment, things like, "Does not the mighty great oak grow but from a tiny acorn? Don't poor people have rich relatives? Shouldn't we stick with the clients who have stuck with us over the years?"

Absolutely no one had any interest in fighting off the hungry jaws of the call in center. It reminded me of the way people passively marched into the rooms to be executed in *Logan's Run*, or the way the humans served their Morlock masters in *The Time Machine*. The spirit of individuality had long since been extinguished. Merrill Lynch had created their own *Matrix*.

I knew that at some point a red light would go off on someone's computer and a report would be generated that would have my name on it. I was not naïve. I knew that Big Brother was not only watching, but was also evaluating the level of punishment to be inflicted as a result of the disobedience.

I knew that they were coming, I just didn't know when.

As a diversion, I sent about a half dozen accounts that were long dormant and contained absolutely no assets down to the belly of the beast. I found a few more that had some residual small balances in the hundreds of dollars that were simply being ignored by their owners, who probably just had never bothered cleaning out the accounts when they stopped doing business with the firm years ago.

A few more weeks went by. I received more memos. It was coming, closer and closer. One Monday morning, Cynthia, the Branch Manager, came into my office with the look of an executioner, thin red lips and a nice manicure.

"I told you that I wanted you to "participate" in the firm's drive to build up the call-in center," she hissed. "You are the only one who is stopping us from having "full participation."

She walked closer to my desk, almost touching the front of it with her body. She was not a small woman. She had hair like a blonde helmet and a pasty pallor. I was hoping she wouldn't reach for the stapler or the letter opener, because this seemed really important to her.

Her master had obviously told her that "full participation" was necessary, and anyone not cooperating should be…dealt with.

"I want twenty- five of your accounts on my desk by the end of the day. If I do not have twenty five "appropriate" accounts, I will take fifty of them on my own…and they won't be the smaller accounts. Do you understand, Don?" She gave me a disgusted sneer out of the side of her lips, turned around and walked out.

This was like *Schindler's List* in reverse. I was reminded me of it as I slowly picked through the account records. There were several retired people who had small income producing accounts with me that they used to supplement their social security or pensions.

There were a few younger couples who were still in the rearing children and early asset building phase of their lives. Many of these accounts were referrals from existing clients who had been with me for years, and had subsequently grown into larger clients from the same sort of humble account beginnings.

Finally, there were several custodial accounts that had assets that had been put aside for children by their parents or grandparents and in two cases by their great grandparents.

I thought of inscribing the account records with tattoo like identification numbers before leaving them on Cynthia's desk, but abandoned that thought as being tasteless and offensive, although probably appropriate in a twisted sort of way.

The next day, Cynthia reassigned three of my larger municipal bond clients to other brokers in the office. The punishment had clearly begun.

I knew that it was time to plan my escape from Merrill Lynch, before it was too late.

CHAPTER 31

Escape From Merrill Lynch

"The supreme art of war is to subdue the enemy without fighting"

(Sun Tzu)

I've seen Alcatraz, and I've read about Devil's Island. Both have become known through the years because of their reputations as cruel institutions which tormented as well as imprisoned those unfortunate enough to be sentenced there. Escape from either was thought to be nearly impossible.

While Alcatraz was still operational, the prisoners had to brave the icy shark infested waters and raging currents off of the coast of San Francisco in order to attempt an escape. Several reportedly tried, but there is no evidence that anyone survived.

Devil's Island was a disease infested prison run by the French from the mid nineteenth century to the mid twentieth century. Of the 80,000 prisoners sent there, most were never heard from again. The only means of escape was by boat, or through dense jungle. One famous escape attempt was immortalized in the movie *Papillion*, but this escape also is not backed up by historical fact. Indeed, most of the prisoners on Devil's

Island succumbed to the harsh conditions, and died before completing their sentences.

And then there was Merrill Lynch.

There was no doubt in my mind that getting away from Merrill Lynch with my client base even reasonably intact was going to be challenging, and was fraught with the greatest professional danger that I had ever encountered.

Merrill had a reputation for going through great lengths to punish brokers who were foolish enough to try to leave the firm. Merrill typically used injunctions, court orders, intimidation, and the threats of innumerable types of legal and financial actions to prevent the offending ex-employee from taking any clients with them when they left the firm.

Merrill saw all of the clients of the firm as their property. Even if the broker had brought the clients with them from another firm, once they were at Merrill, they belonged to Merrill.

However, my Merrill experiment had gone terribly wrong, and I knew that I had to escape before it was too late.

Prior to joining Merrill, my production had gone up for sixteen straight years. During my five years at Merrill, my production dropped for five straight years, with the decline initiated and exacerbated by the surreal requirements put upon me by my alien masters.

I just wanted to buy stocks and bonds for my clients. I was happy to have the resources available to help them fulfill all of their investment objectives, but not all broker/client relationships had to result in blood brotherhood or permanent bonding; sometimes, a client just needed you to invest a certain pool of their money and then leave them alone.

Merrill's approach was to burrow into their clients like a cancer feeding on their bone marrow, to try to create a financial and logistical connection which bound the clients to the firm in the same way that the creature in the *Alien* movies used the bodies of its victims to feed its alien spawn.

But I would not succumb. I would not place Merrill's crappy, newly created closed end funds into my clients' accounts. I would not force all of my clients to fill out extensive financial profiles, so that Merrill could have their mindless product droids solicit them for every possible cross-selling opportunity. I would not abandon my small loyal clients to the call in center because they were not worthy. Most of all, I would not stop doing the things that my clients actually needed me to do for them.

Merrill began putting limitations on what kind of securities the "financial consultants" could buy for clients and still be compensated. If a client account was too small, they basically were deemed too unworthy to buy stocks like IBM or GE or AT&T. They were deemed to be too small to be worthy of individual transactions, like buying tax free bonds or CD's, which met their specific needs. If the client would not agree to all that Merrill demanded, they would be sent away like poor relations looking for a handout.

My rebellious anti-Vietnam War, anti-establishment attitudes of my early adult years had never even remotely surfaced in my Wall Street experiences. But at Merrill, all I wanted to do was start a revolution.

However, a revolution only works when you can get others to join in the fight. At Merrill, there were no others.

All of the people who had spent their careers there had absolutely no idea what I objected to. A few others who were more reflective and aware of the situation simply expressed their acceptance of what they knew could not be changed.

There was no hope. There could be no revolution. Enlightenment was out of the question. All that was left was the possibility of escape, the possibility of redemption, the possibility of going back to how it had been, before it had all gone wrong.

My five year contract had expired just a month or two before, and I was looking for a way out before I didn't have any business left.

Over the previous year, I had literally dozens of accounts taken away to be sent down to the "call-in center." I had numerous large accounts reassigned to other brokers in the office for not "cooperating" in helping the firm achieve their strategic objectives by placing Merrill underwritings, and new offerings in my clients' accounts.

I was not eligible for reassigned accounts because I did not complete the assigned amount of financial plans for my customers, thus failing to meet my "critical objectives," despite the fact that there was no reason to do financial plans for those people other than for Merrill to collect another set of fees, and steer the clients towards their "managed money" platforms.

I had gone to Merrill Lynch to play for the Yankees, but I now realized that not only weren't they the Yankees, but they were the furthest thing possible from a ball club; they were far more far like the Gestapo.

I had wanted to play ball with the best club around, but instead I felt like I was a victim in a Nazi camp.

There was no joy in Mudville.

But getting out of Dodge wasn't quite as easy as tapping my ruby slippers together and saying that I wanted to go home. I didn't have a home to go to anymore.

With my client base and production somewhat depleted, I certainly wasn't the hottest commodity in town in terms of looking to move to another firm.

Being a retail stockbroker is like being a baseball player; if your batting average falls five years in a row, no team wants to waste a spot in the lineup by signing you. I wanted out, but I needed someone to want me back.

I contacted the mother ship, Prudential Securities, but the captain had changed several times, and I was already an old memory in the branch. The new Branch Manager had barely heard of me ever having been there. Many of the people that I had known there before were already gone.

Prudential Securities' manager at the time was named Barry Andrews., a man devoid of any aspect of a pleasant personality.

After I called him on the phone to invite him to lunch, he spent most of our hour together talking about the flaps in his eyes that he had as a result of Lasik surgery. I disliked him from the word go, and never even bothered to tell him that I would have been willing to come back for free, with no signing bonus, no special bonuses, nothing at all.

I sent a short note to my former suitors at Advest, under the premise that I needed some sort of back up opportunity in case I couldn't find my way into a better situation; but having been repeatedly spurned by me, they got even with me by not even responding to my note.

Fortunately, fate soon decided to intervene when I was approached by an acquaintance that had recently joined Smith Barney as the assistant manager. Greg was part of their management training program. One of his primary directives was to try to recruit experienced brokers from other firms to help build up his West Simsbury branch. He needed a body to recruit, and asked me if I'd be interested in moving over to Smith Barney in West Simsbury.

This was the same West Simsbury branch that Jerry the Radish Man had moved to, and the place where I had refused to go. However, at that point, a small satellite branch in West Simsbury sounded like Hawaii to me, and I was ready to travel; the sooner the better.

As a result of my depleted status, I was offered a contract with modest incentives. However, Smith Barney was willing to pay a small bonus for me to come, probably figuring that I'd have to spend most of it on a legal battle with Merrill Lynch. They didn't know that at the time I would have paid them a bonus to take me in.

Jerry the Radish Man had been fired as manager of the West Simsbury branch of Smith Barney about a year before. The new branch manager at Smith Barney, an ex-branch auditor named Ken, warned me that Merrill would try to take forceful action to prevent my clients from transferring with me, and I should be prepared for a fight.

Ken indicated that Smith Barney would not be there to help me battle the evil legions and dark horses of Merrill, and it would be my problem to deal with any restraining orders or court actions that they threw at me.

We discussed a start date the following week, thus giving me time to gather enough client information so that we could coordinate a mass mailing of transfer documents to my clients immediately after I handed in my resignation to Merrill Lynch.

The rules of engagement are such that a broker cannot solicit clients to move to a new firm until he has resigned from the old firm. By early the next week, we had the hundreds of envelopes and Fed-Ex packages ready to roll; take off would occur as soon as the resignation was tendered.

Now, my problem was how to deal with Merrill. I had a plan, a concept, and an inspired idea that could have come right out of the movies. I needed to scam

Merrill into not taking any action against me until I could escape under the cover of darkness, without my clients being assaulted by Merrill's legions of doom.

I consulted Sun Tzu's *The Art of War* for inspiration, noting the applicable quotes such as:

- "The supreme art of war is to subdue the enemy without fighting."
- "Let your plans be dark and impenetrable as night, and when you move, fall like a thunderbolt."
- "Be extremely subtle, even to the point of formlessness. Be extremely mysterious, even to the point of soundlessness. Thereby, you can be the director of the opponent's fate."
- "If you are far from the enemy, make him believe you are near."
- "What is of supreme importance in war is to attack the enemy's strategy."
- "The art of war is the art of deceit."

With all of this in mind, I composed a letter of resignation to Cynthia, the branch manager at Merrill Lynch.

Usually, a letter of resignation is the trigger which unleashes Merrill's hounds from Hell upon the departing broker.

This letter was designed to freeze them in their tracks, confusing the enemy, and creating enough of a smokescreen that I could whisk my clients out of the poisoned claws of the Merrill monster, to take them to safety where we could again live and invest in peace.

My letter was far more than just a letter of resignation; it was a letter about America!

It was a letter about how Charles Merrill had founded Merrill Lynch with the dream of "bringing Wall Street to Main Street."

I wrote about Charles Merrill's concept that all people should have access to the financial markets of our great country, and everyone should be able to participate in our great financial system by buying the stocks of our great American companies.

I wrote about how Charles Merrill would have wanted small investors to be able to buy stocks like General Electric or Disney, or Johnson and Johnson, and how the present Merrill system was designed to deprive the small investors of that opportunity.

I wrote about how the smallest of investors were sent away to a call in center because the firm did not feel they warranted the attention of a full service broker.

I asked how Charles Merrill would have felt about that.

I wrote about how I had come to Merrill to make more products and services available to my clients, but instead found an environment which herded investors into pens separated by account size, and fed whatever it was that fattened the firm, and not the clients' accounts.

I spoke about right and wrong, and discussed the systemic conflicts of interest that were prevalent in their management and compliance functions. I mentioned the need for these issues to be brought to the attention of the regulatory authorities, and that I hoped to be able to raise these issues in my forthcoming correspondence with the various regulatory agencies.

Most of all, I talked about fair dealing with clients and putting their interests first; how the success of our clients should be our priority, and how it wasn't that way at Merrill Lynch.

I somberly pointed out that Charles Merrill would be turning over in his grave if he could see what his firm had become.

Some of the parts of the letter were so pretty and inspiring that I seriously considered sending a soundtrack along with it; something like Neil Diamond singing *America* with a full orchestra.

If Charles Merrill could have read my letter, he would have cried.

Most importantly, at the bottom of the letter, I clearly indicated that I had sent copies of the letter to the CEO, the President, and the Chief Compliance Officer of Merrill Lynch.

Cynthia read the letter in front of me with a stunned look.

I made sure to mention that I also had sent personal cover letters to all three of the senior executives, with the copy of the letter that I had given her, and was anxious to hear back from them.

I thanked Cynthia for the opportunity to have come to Merrill, and expressed regret that things didn't work out, but I needed to go to a place that cared about its clients in a way that would have made Charles Merrill proud.

I told Cynthia that she had a responsibility to make the world a better place by making Merrill Lynch a better place, and if she ever wanted to go for a drink and talk about some of my ideas, I would look forward to it.

I might have laid it on a little thick, but I knew the Merrill mindset. I understood the enemy's strategy, and I needed to buy some time so I could get all of my clients' accounts transferred, before Merrill made their move.

I also knew there was no way Cynthia was going to do anything against me until she heard back from her superiors after they received my letters.

I reasoned that there was no way that she was going to reach out and contact any of them about the matter; she would wait to receive instructions from above. Typically, one of the senior executives would have dished off the matter to a regional manager, who then would have contacted Cynthia and told her to send the hit squad after me.

I'm sure that Cynthia thought that she would get a quick response from her superiors, and since it takes a few weeks to get a large scale amount of client transfers in process, she obviously figured that she had plenty of time before unleashing the dogs of war upon me.

What she didn't know, was that I never sent copies of the letter to anyone else.

Not to her bosses, or the regulatory agencies, or anyone at all.

While she waited for the inevitable response, she was unable to act.

Sun Tzu would have been proud; I had subdued her without a battle.

The other tactic that I had utilized in the letter was to clearly infer that I would be involving the regulatory agencies. That would have immediately forced any of the senior or regional managers above Cynthia to forward the letter to the Legal and Compliance areas of Merrill for review and evaluation before anyone took any action.

Cynthia would have expected that the response that she was waiting for could have been delayed by this additional process. However, since no regulators or internal compliance officers ever received the letter in the first place, it was likely to be a very long wait indeed before anyone sent forth any instructions, to Cynthia or anyone else.

As guided by Sun Tzu, I had made my plans "subtle" but "impenetrable." While the enemy believed that I "was near," I was really getting further away, as quickly as I could. My "deception" had Cynthia frozen in a lattice of waiting for something to occur, when there was nothing that could occur. My departure embodied "soundlessness" as it eliminated any sound or direction that Jane might hear for guidance and direction.

Two weeks later, most of my clients' transfer forms had been received over at Smith Barney, and most of their accounts were already well into the electronic transfer process.

I still hadn't heard a peep out of Merrill Lynch.

During that week, I received a call from a lawyer in the Law Department at Smith Barney asking me about the status of my litigation with Merrill Lynch. I told the gentleman on the phone that there had been no litigation or contact of any kind from Merrill, and told him that I really didn't expect any, in the near future at least. When he asked me why I felt that it was unlikely that Merrill would pursue me, I told him about my strategy, and forwarded, at his request, a copy of my letter.

The next morning, he called me back to tell me that he had read the letter, and couldn't believe that I thought that I could get away with chumping Merrill Lynch, while acknowledging that I obviously had.

I pointed out to the lawyer that if Merrill had not come after me up until then, there was little chance that there would be any follow up on their part. If Cynthia had not received any direction from above, she would have gotten herself into deep shit by bringing up the issue after several weeks had passed.

Technically, she was probably compelled to report the matter upon receipt of my letter, but since she likely hadn't, all it would have done was to have shown that she had not followed the proper procedures. It appeared that she had been conned.

The lawyer was surprised that my tactic had worked. I was, too.

I was also thankful. I had escaped.

CHAPTER 32

The Second Time Around

Having been spared **by the Market Gods,** I arrived anxiously at the small satellite Smith Barney office in the neighboring town of West Simsbury. The branch was in a small office center surrounded by trees, numerous flower beds, and some picnic tables scattered around the perimeter of the complex. There was ample free parking, and near the main roads so that a trip back to Hartford took very little time.

I felt really stupid that I had not gone there the first time around with the Radish Man.

On a Saturday morning, when no one was around, I brought all of my personal stuff from my former Merrill office to my new Smith Barney office.

Greg and the Branch Manager Ken had come to open the office and help me carry my stuff inside. The empty office area had a totally different vibe than at Merrill. My plants looked at home from the moment I put them on the file cabinets that ran under the windows.

The plants hadn't been doing well at Merrill; they obviously knew something.

In the hallway, there was a large office picture that showed all of the brokers and Operations Department people together at some outdoor function, with everyone smiling and looking like they were having a good time. At Merrill, smiling reportedly was forbidden if you had not met your "critical objectives."

One of the people in the picture was a lady named Nellie who I had worked with years before at Prudential. I had even gotten to know Nellie's daughter Tess who interned in our office one summer, and happened to be interested in poetry, so we had a lot to talk about.

I liked Nellie. She was a few years older than me, and always said that she liked men who were "bad boys." I was pleased when they assigned her to be my sales assistant; it made me comfortable from the outset.

I soon found that the people in the picture were smiling for a good reason; the branch was a genuinely pleasant and nice place to work. The Branch manager's assistant was a very pretty statuesque woman named Danielle who was sweet, pleasant and always willing to be helpful. If Cynthia had the evil Toad as an assistant, Branch Manager Ken had Glenda the Good Witch.

Another striking comparison between the two firms was that the Compliance Manager for Smith Barney was a nice woman named Lynne, as opposed to Merrill's neo-Nazi Rodger.

Lynne was a cheerful administrator who saw her job function as helping to facilitate the sales process, and to work with brokers to avoid problems that resulted from sometimes contradictory policies.

Lynne understood that sometime rules do not always promote what is best for the clients, and that the well-being of the clients of the firm was the real priority.

The rules and general directives at Smith Barney were far more of the typical traditional guidelines that I had come to expect from my years at Prudential Securities. Most of the brokers in the office handled their clients in an "old school" manner, with all of the normal buying and selling of securities like IBM, GE, and AT&T. It was a world that I understood once again.

Over the next few years, my business recovered and rebounded to a new level far above where it had been when I originally left Prudential Securities.

The office also had a bunch of quaint customs like baking contests, cooking contests, and even picnic outings at the local minor league baseball park. I still have my two First Place ribbons from the baking contests.

Just about everyone in the office was very friendly. I even became chummy with one of the senior brokers in the office named Henry. It seemed that we had many similar experiences in the business over the years, so we had an endless procession of stories to exchange.

The Smith Barney office was populated mostly by older, more seasoned brokers. There were a few obligatory trainees, but they lived in the far end of the office, and kept to themselves.

One of the biggest changes in the industry in general over the years was the relative lack of attention and nurturing given to new people entering the business.

While Michael felt that his success was tied into the success of the new brokers that he would hire and develop, the hiring of trainees had become a statistical requirement, where every Branch Manager had a quota of trainees that they were required to hire as part of meeting their "critical objectives."

While the failure rate of new people entering the business was always absurdly high, in this newer era, with no nurturing or guidance, it became even more difficult for a trainee to find their way through the educational and regulatory maze of requirements.

Even prospecting for new clients had changed enough through the years so that the constraints on calling prospective clients became so profound that the only way a new broker trainee could survive and grow was almost by the sheer chance of finding enough "acceptable" clients.

Fortuitously, the market happened to bottom in 2002, just about when I went to Smith Barney. It was as if a horrible sickening dark dream was finally ending.

As all of the transferred accounts were being established, the market began steadily rising, so that all of my client accounts began showing significant gains from day one.

With the freedom to once again buy and sell whatever seemed to be appropriate, my clients' account values began to rise and rise until, within a year or two, all of the damage of the internet bubble, 9/11, and the parasitic policies of Merrill had become a sad memory.

Within a year or two, most client account values were hitting all-time highs.

Branch Manager Ken, for the most part, was a pleasant hands-off manager who just wanted to run the branch, and grow it by hiring experienced people to build their businesses in peace.

Ken was an ex-branch auditor who used to work for Prudential Securities. He decided to go into Branch management as an avenue to rise in the larger corporate ranks. He clearly saw himself rising from a Branch Manager to a Regional Manager, and then beyond.

His method was clearly to build a strong branch with growing revenues, and then, hopefully, move on to one of the really large and prestigious branch offices, which would provide a pathway to greater glories. He was ambitious, but in a nice way. He understood that if he kept everything running smoothly, and everyone happy, good things would surely come his way.

For about three years, everything was hunky dory in my broker world. I enjoyed both the atmosphere and the people in the branch. The aforementioned Danielle and Lynne both embraced my work with the Hartford soup kitchens, and became large contributors to the holiday meals efforts by donating carloads of food and goods to the cause.

We even had a Secret Santa tradition in the office where the people in the office all bought relatively nice gifts for the other participants.

One of the brokers in the branch happened to be my old office-mate, Elliot, the commodity trader who I knew from Bache, who had God as his client.

I drew Elliot's name in the Secret Santa drawing, so I made him a "basket of commodities"; an actual basket with a roll of pennies to represent copper, a box of cotton balls for cotton, a few dimes for silver, a piece of wood for lumber, some wheat germ for wheat, and so on. The basket was the hit of the Secret Santa celebration.

At the reception desk was a remarkably sweet woman named Missy, who was very efficient as a telephone operator, and charming to clients who came to the office. On Missy's front credenza was a large pretty bowl filled with candy. It was the common office candy bowl, and everyone pitched in to keep it filled with goodies.

And so it was with the candy, baking contests and the smiling people for many months, until one day, I saw this skinny looking neatly dressed guy stopping in the branch to talk to Branch Manager Ken, and tour the branch.

As I was walking through the office, Ken happened to stop me to introduce the guy as Max Berne from the management trainee program.

There was something disturbing about Max from the start. He seemed stiff, nervous and very uptight. He was about my height, and as I shook his hand, I noticed that his blue grey eyes and strange facial expression reminded me of the bulging eyes look on Marty Feldman's face in the movie *Young Frankenstein*.

It soon became clear that Branch Manager Ken had achieved his goals, and was being rewarded with a much larger and far more profitable branch down in southern Connecticut. Max was going to take over the West Simsbury branch as his first real managerial assignment.

CHAPTER 33

Homeward Bound

I remember being **a little concerned** that upper management was letting an inexperienced rookie pilot our little branch full of seasoned market sailors. However, I rationalized that we had a smooth sailing ship, so that the new manager would just sit at the wheel and let the wind continue to carry the branch forward. .

Unfortunately, it soon became clear that someone had let a dangerous person on board.

During the first few weeks, Max invited each of the brokers in the office to go out with him to lunch so he could get to know everyone, one at a time. When my turn came, I suggested that we go to my favorite nearby bar, The Corner Pug, which had good drinks and daily specials of well-made comfort foods.

As I recall, Max had a salad and a club soda, and I had meat loaf and several vodka and diet Cokes. It was clear that we had different views of appropriate Wall Street lunches.

Max told me that he had been an instructor in the firm's learning center where he helped to teach and train new potential brokers. He had decided to try the sales and production side, so he spent a short time as a broker before going into the management training program. Max obviously had very limited experience actually being a practitioner in the field.

I told him about my twenty years of experience going back to 1981, and how I was Series 8 licensed, and had helped to manage a branch for many years. I offered to be of any assistance that I could while he was getting his feet wet in the branch.

Max had an odd demeanor look to begin with, but I could tell that there was something about what I had said that had disturbed him.

He asked if I was planning to go back and manage again, and I said it was unlikely, unless I could find branch as nice as our West Simsbury branch. He didn't seem to like that either.

It occurred to me that maybe he felt threatened and insecure by my license to manage, but since it was a remote possibility that I would ever put myself in the managerial rat race again, I just decided to ignore his reaction.

In the office, Max was very intense and serious all of the time. I could hear by the way he spoke to his assistant Danielle that the days of smooth sailing were behind us. More significantly, the office atmosphere which he began to develop was one of a junior high school math teacher dealing with his unruly class.

Max sat in front of his computer for hours, taking notes, and reading reports.

Occasionally, he would call brokers in his office to discuss items showing up on different reports. There were a lot of reports generated at the branch lever regarding just about everything. A manager who did not know what was important and relevant could drive themselves insane trying to deal with every item on every report.

It didn't take much to get Max to cross that threshold, and become Psycho Max.

My first run-in with Psycho Max came when he called me in to ask me about several of my clients which had been on the active account list, which shows high levels of activity in trading oriented accounts. However, the accounts that he asked me about were not at all active. Each of the accounts had only a handful of transactions for the entire year.

I pointed Max to another screen on the computer system to show him that the accounts had experienced only rather subdued activity, but after glancing at the screen, he simply picked up the hard copy list on his desk and said that if they were on the list, he would require a full explanation of all of the activity in all of the accounts.

I reiterated that there was nothing there to report on or explain. He became irritated and argumentative. I told him that he should stop being so dependent on his dumb lists, and start looking at the client accounts, their structure, and most important, their investment results. He kept referring to his dumb list. I could see that we were going to have a problem.

Over the next few months, the scene was repeated over and over with not only me, but numerous others as well. Psycho Max was obviously overwhelmed by his position. He was so insecure and uncertain that he couldn't discern what was relevant, and what was not.

Even more disturbing was the way he would often lock himself in the office when he was on a telephone call. You could see him through the glass walls talking on the phone, looking incredibly agitated and upset, and then the color transformation began.

As Psycho Max became more and more flustered on his telephone calls, his head would begin to change colors.

The top half of his head would turn purple with veins bulging out, and the bottom part of his head and face would turn a bright red. His head looked like an eggplant on top of a tomato. I began to worry that his head might explode, or he would more likely stroke out and die at his desk.

As time went by, his head turned colors more and more often. There were already many grumblings in the office about him having no idea what he was doing. I was worried that Max's problems went far beyond the inability to do the job, and instead indicated a far more serious problem.

My concerns were realized when I saw first-hand exactly how insecure and paranoid he was.

I was sitting in my office working with the door open when he came by and leaned in the door opening and said, "I know that you're trying to get me."

I was looking directly at him when he said it, and I still couldn't believe it. "Trying to get you?" I said incredulously, "are you ok?" I asked.

"I know what you're trying to do," he said, as the color began to build in his face.

"Max, you sound very paranoid. I have no idea what you're talking about. I just want to be left alone and to do my work. You need to go out and have a drink or something."

The next week, he came into my office and closed the door. "You think I'm stupid. You think I'm an idiot," he said.

"I don't think that you are either stupid or an idiot, but I definitely think that you are quite disturbed. Are you on any medication, Max?"

I though at that moment his eggplant/tomato head was going to explode and splatter all over the walls and furniture in my office, but he just walked out and headed back towards his office.

By this point, I was having real concerns about the sanity of Psycho Max.

In my professional career, I had seen brokers who were drunk, stoned on pot, twisted on cocaine, but I had never seen anyone so mentally unstable. It made me concerned about the people in the branch.

What if he just totally snapped? Does he have any weapons?

Did Psycho Max have a gun in his desk? I envisioned him with a rifle, shooting out the glass wall in front of his office, and then going through the branch killing people.

I began to wonder if he was on some kind of medication, and if not, maybe he should be. I hoped that the firm had run a psychological profile on him before hiring him for the Branch Manager's job.

Things reached a crescendo between the two of us when a few weeks later he called me into his office. I don't recall what he was bitching about, but it was so stupid that I was visibly annoyed. I could feel the four letter words rising towards my lips.

The veins on Psycho Max's head were protruding, and his watery blue-grey eyes were bulging out of their sockets when he got up from his desk, and closed the long curtains that ran across the front of his office so that no one could see us. Then, he closed the little curtain that ran across the small window between his and Danielle's office. I had never even noticed that there was a curtain there.

He stood up and moved toward me in the chair, almost threatening to lean over me. We were all alone. "Now, what do you really want to say to me?" he said with menace in his voice.

I was amazed by what was happening. It looked like he wanted to fight me.

I entertained the thought for a moment. It would have been quick. It was tempting, very tempting. But I realized that not only wouldn't it be fair, it would involve messy stuff like police and ambulances; and ultimately, fucking him up wouldn't serve any purpose at all.

"I don't want to say anything to you. You have no idea what you're doing, and Max….you need professional help. This job is not for you."

With that, I got up and walked out of the office, hoping he did not actually have a gun in his desk.

Suddenly, I realized that I was stuck in a branch with an emotional misfit who at any time might come in and start shooting up the place. Either that, or he might break down mentally and decide to kill himself and his family. I could see the headlines.

In either case, I didn't want to stick around to find out.

Maybe it was all of the accumulated good works that I had done through the years, but the Market Gods decided that they weren't going to let me get shot, maimed, or otherwise damaged.

A few days later, Annie and I left for Hawaii, to take a much-needed, two week vacation.

When I was first planning the trip, I asked Annie if she would like to get married on some quiet Hawaiian beach. She said yes.

We didn't tell anyone. I arranged, through the hotel, to have a native Hawaiian officiant name Reverend Koko meet us on the beach early one morning, and perform a short non-denominational ceremony. Part of the "wedding package" included a photographer, and the woman in the hotel who I booked the package with offered to act as our witness.

I didn't think that I'd have to deal with psycho-freak Max until I returned, but I was wrong.

Annie and I had just landed in Chicago when I noticed a curious message from my close friend and long-time client Ricky. I couldn't imagine why he would be calling me on my cellphone. I noticed that he had left the message at about 7:00 in the morning, just as Annie and I were leaving the airport in Connecticut.

Ricky is a doctor, and I called his office from Chicago telling his assistant to tell him that I was returning his call. Usually, it took hours or days to get Ricky to call back about anything portfolio related. I had been handling his portfolios since he got out of medical school and started his accounts. After twenty years, the accounts had built up to millions.

To my astonishment, Ricky was on the phone in seconds, and the first thing he said was,

"Don, are you OK?"

I told him that I was at the airport on my way to Hawaii, and asked him what was wrong. I thought that something might have happened to him or his wife Evelyn; something that required immediate attention.

Instead, he told me a bizarre tale of how Psycho Max had called him at home the previous evening at some late hour, sounding disjointed and unfocused. He told me that he didn't quite understand what the call was all about. He inquired if Max might have been on drugs. He said it sounded like something had happened to me, and after talking to Psycho Max, he was calling to make sure that I was ok.

I listened to this in the airport. I was ok, but, I was getting really angry.

After calming down Ricky, I called my office and got Psycho Max on the phone. I don't remember what I said, but none of it was nice. I used a lot of crude language, and told the jerkoff that when I got back, I was taking his psycho demented ass to the regulatory authorities, and I would write to management to have him psychologically evaluated.

But while my trip to Kauai with Annie might have had a rough start, once we got there, all other life issues faded away into magical energy of the Hawaiian Islands. Annie said that she felt the energy almost as soon as we got off the plane. It was a very long ride, but I knew that she would like the place.

Our third morning on Kauai, we met Reverend Koko down in the lobby of the hotel. He asked if we had picked our spot on the beach. Annie and I had scouted the nearby beach, and found a spot where a stream ran down from the mountains and met the waves from the ocean.

Annie assured me that this was a very spiritual spot.

We walked down the beach with Reverend Koko. Reverend Koko said something about it being a perfect Hawaiian morning, and when you married outside on the beach; you were marrying in front of "everyone."

All of a sudden I had the sense of Annie and I standing there together, holding hands in the center of the universe, with all of the spirits in the heavens watching us.

The native Hawaiian salt ceremony took about five minutes. It was one of the most perfect moments of my life. Just as the ceremony concluded, a large wave came and washed over all of our feet; even as the water from the mountain above came down to meet it.

I started to cry, Annie started to cry, the witness started to cry, and even Reverend Koko started to cry. The photographer was standing in the background, and he probably would have also cried if he wasn't sweating so profusely from carrying all of his equipment a few hundred yards down the beach.

When Annie and I returned two weeks later, Psycho Max was out of the office for a few days, so I didn't have to deal with him when I returned to work. It was just as well because I was still glowing from our trip to Kauai.

About a week after I returned, my office buddy Henry came into my office one morning, shut the door, and sat down in the client chair across the desk from me.

"Are you interested in moving to Wachovia Securities with me?" he said.

It surprised me because Henry was a Smith Barney lifer, and had never worked for another firm in nearly thirty years. He was also the biggest producer by far in the branch.

Something must have really motivated him to consider making such a drastic change. I didn't know exactly what all of his issues with the firm were, but I knew what at least one of them was from personal experience.

Wachovia Securities was the latest incarnation of my original firm Prudential Securities, formerly Prudential Bache, formerly Bache Halsey Stuart Shields; the name of the firm has since changed yet again.

I remembered Homer's *The Odyssey* where the main character Odysseus goes on a journey for ten years before returning home. It had been about ten years since I left the mother ship to go and explore the lands of Merrill

Lynch and Smith Barney. I immediately embraced to idea of finally returning home.

Henry and I met with the complex manager John and the Branch Manager Alex at the Avon, Connecticut branch office. When I originally left Prudential Securities, there was no Avon branch, only the main office in downtown Hartford.

The little Avon branch was adorable. Nestled in a small office building in a quiet part of a gorgeous little New England country town, the firm's management was looking for experienced brokers to come in and man the brand new offices that they had added to the branch.

They really wanted Henry, who was a huge producer, and they offered him a huge bonus with extra incentives if he could bring any other experienced brokers along with him.

I knew that I was being pimped out again, but this time my pimp was going to leave me off in front of my house.

The whole process went very quickly. Within a few weeks Henry and I were set to go. One morning we walked into Psycho Max's office one at a time and resigned. Henry resigned first, and when I handed Psycho Max my papers, he turned a whiter shade of pale.

That afternoon, Henry and I went to our new Avon office to check in. Scott, who I had worked with for many years in Hartford, came to greet me. Scott had become Compliance Manager for the complex.

Cathy, my former Sales Assistant, who was now the Administrative Manager for the complex, came as well. When I walked into the office, they both hugged me. It felt like coming home.

Thomas Wolfe, the author, once wrote, "You can't go home again."

I was hoping that maybe I could.

The End